W9-DCZ-899

CHURCHES
THEIR PLAN *and*
FURNISHING

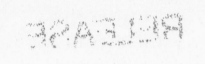

CHURCHES
THEIR PLAN *and*
FURNISHING

BY PETER F. ANSON

Illustrations by the Author

Revised and edited by

The Very Rev. Msgr. Thomas F. Croft-Fraser
CHIEF MASTER OF CEREMONIES OF THE VATICAN BASILICA
(1935–1940)

AND

The Rev. H. A. Reinhold
ST. JOSEPH'S, SUNNYSIDE, WASH.

*"Domine dilexi decorem domus tuae,
et locum habitationis gloriae tuae"*
(Ps. 25:8)

THE BRUCE PUBLISHING COMPANY, MILWAUKEE

Nihil obstat: JOHN A. SCHULIEN, S.T.D., Censor Librorum
Imprimatur: ✠ MOYSES E. KILEY, Archiepiscopus Milwaukiensis
February 18, 1948

NA4820
A 62

TO

THE VERY REVEREND MONSIGNOR THOMAS F. CROFT-FRASER
CHOIR SACRISTAN OF ST. PETER'S, ROME (1929–1931)

CHIEF MASTER OF CEREMONIES
OF THE
VATICAN BASILICA (1935–1940)

LAIRD
OF
INVERALLOCHY, ABERDEENSHIRE

AND

THE REVEREND HANS A. REINHOLD
ONE–TIME ORGANISER OF THE GERMAN APOSTOLAAT DES MEERES
AND PORT CHAPLAIN AT HAMBURG

PASTOR
OF
ST. JOSEPH'S, SUNNYSIDE, WASHINGTON, U.S.A.

IN GRATEFUL MEMORY OF THEIR
LONG FRIENDSHIP

EDITOR'S NOTE

Peter Anson has asked me to Americanize his book, and to add such notes as will make it provocative for the reading public in this country. He insistently told me not to pull any punches, and to be my own self as he knows me from articles and letters.

Peter and I are old friends from the days when he drifted into our rectory at Bremerhaven to our last meeting in Ascot and my visit to his temporary home near Gravesend, where he had time to indulge his passion — looking at ships.

His marine background and love for the sea should not deceive us. As a former Anglican and then Catholic monk of Caldey, and as a Tertiary of St. Francis and addict of quiet little monasteries in small Umbrian towns and on Tuscan hillsides, his architectural training and ecclesiastical background are more than sufficient to equip him to write this book, and to write it well enough to make it not only interesting, but also safe and instructive reading for priests, architects, seminarians, and sacristans.

It competes with any ordinary book on matters rubrical and liturgical by its use of common sense and historical knowledge, instead of piling up mountains of authors, authorities, and mere legal decisions.

The outstanding feature is the fact that Peter Anson represents the liturgical wing of art, architecture, and rubrics. He is thoroughly and refreshingly British, but not to a degree which might make him appear as foreign on our shores. He is imbued with what is good in tradition, and modern with an ingredient of Anglo-Saxon humor.

I had little to add, and less to change, and when I did so, the initials H. A. R. warn the reader of it. In a few places, as Anson's excursion on rood-screens, I registered mild disagreement. In a few places I felt called upon to reinforce the color of the author's statement, which seemed too pale to me, in view of the fact that he had touched on a subject more burning here than in Britain.

This is a practical book. It will help any man who feels that he agrees with the tenets of the liturgical movement, but cannot find a down-to-earth application of its lofty principles. Especially the parish priest and the architect who cannot go to the expensive places that "make the right things well" will welcome this book as a good friend for those who have to make small means do.

H. A. R.

March 1, 1946

FOREWORD

The object of this book is to provide the clergy and laity with a practical guide to the building and remodelling of Catholic churches, and to give a summary of the laws governing their planning and furnishing.

When it was being written nearly four years ago I imagined that in all the war-stricken countries of Europe, once peace had been declared, there would be a revival of church building on a scale that had never occurred for many centuries. Many churches needed to be rebuilt. Others which had been destroyed by enemy action might not be required, for everything pointed to a general decentralization of industry, and a rapid development of small towns and villages where there was no provision for Catholic worship. It was unlikely that there would be much money to spend on building or rebuilding. In most dioceses the ecclesiastical authorities found their resources limited. For this reason it was important to ensure that money was not wasted on superfluous ornament but devoted to essentials. However, subsequent history has proved that I was wrong, at least so far as Great Britain is concerned. Government regulations have put a stop to the building of any new churches, and it is difficult, if not impossible, to obtain licenses to rebuild those which were damaged or destroyed during the war. So the re-vival of ecclesiastical architecture, which seemed likely in 1943, grows more and more distant as I write in the autumn of 1947. The situation is more hopeful in certain countries on the continent of Europe. In France and Belgium the reconstruction of churches is going on apace. Countless books and pamphlets have been published during the past three years, all designed to give practical advice to priests and architects. Those issued under the auspices of the Dominicans in the *Editions du Cerf* are more than enough to prove now that there is an enthusiastic and wide-spread interest in the building and remodelling of churches in France.

During the past forty-five years I must have visited and examined more than one thousand Catholic churches in Great Britain and Ireland, together with an even greater number of non-Catholic churches. I have also travelled extensively in France, Belgium, Holland, Italy, and can claim to have a superficial knowledge of many other countries. Again and again I have realised that a particular church was a "bad" church just because it was inconvenient to worship in. Like so many modern private houses these "Houses of God" looked attractive enough inside and out. They may have been "devotional," but they were certainly not "liturgical," i.e., suitable for *public* worship, no matter how well adapted to stimulate individual piety. The mistakes in planning and furnishing were due in almost every instance to an obvious ignorance of functional requirements, in other words, the purposes of a modern church.

Such mistakes, though found in every part of the world, are due in Great Britain and Ireland to a history of the Catholic body in these islands. For nearly three centuries the public exercise of religion was prohibited by law. Our ancestors had to return to the catacombs. Traditions of public worship were forgotten when only the bare minimum was possible, in danger of fines, imprisonment, banishment, or death. Can it be wondered, then, that Catholic church architecture in England, Scotland, and Ireland leaves much to be desired when we remember that it had to be reborn a little more than a hundred years ago? With regard to the United States and Canada the problem seems to be the lack of any strong national tradition in architecture, at least ecclesiastical architecture. They have inherited many of the worst traditions of Europe.* Such traditions are hard to uproot.

Before an architect can design a

*The word "tradition" in such matters as architectural needs must be used with caution. In practically all countries of Europe tradition, that is, historical style, is as dead as in the United States. Any architect trying to hitch his wagon to Europe's great styles of the past is in no better position than his American colleague who gives building the color of "Colonial" (American Georgian) or American version of Spanish Baroque style. Since the immigrants carried their usages across the ocean in the barren nineteenth century and came from "classes" devoid of higher culture, no wonder that so much of what they built is shoddy, imitative, and gaudy. — H. A. R.

church he must understand the functional nature of the different parts of the building. It matters very little in the long run whether he has "good taste"! For as the late Eric Gill loved to remind us: "unless a workman knows what he is making he cannot make anything. Whether it be a church or only a toothpick, he must know what it is; he must have it in his mind before he begins, before he can even choose his material or lay his hand on a tool."[1]

The trouble with so many churches erected during the past century is that architects have been far more concerned with the superficial "beauty" than with the nature of the building. Their object, so it seems, was to create a building that *looked* what most people believed a church *ought* to look like rather than a building that fulfiled the practical functions of a place of worship. They often managed to erect a building that superficially reproduced the plan and details found in houses of God in past ages, but which were an anachronism in modern times. Such architects did not know *what* they were making. Very often they took no trouble to learn. They wanted to create a "work of art" and ignored the fact that nothing can be a work of art if it does not properly fulfil its end.

Before planning or remodelling a church an architect must study the clear and definite rules which have been drawn up by Canon Law during past centuries, and which have been modified from time to time as occasion has arisen. The main object of this book is to provide such information in a convenient

[1] Numbered notes will be found at the end of the chapters.

and compact form. It says little or nothing about art or "good taste," for the obvious way to plan an ecclesiastical building is that which guides domestic or commercial buildings — a strict regard to structural utility in conformity with civil and ecclesiastical legislation.

The aim of a church architect should be, first and foremost, to create a "house" in which the public worship of the Church can be carried out according to canonical requirements. "The aim is not a 'style,' whether past or present, but the meaning of the *Mysteria* and the true purpose for which this House is to be built. . . . The Church is not a remnant of the 'Middle Ages' or any other, and does not in any way force them upon us. She does not oblige us to erect buildings which create an 'atmosphere' of bygone times, thus making it seem that she belongs to a romantic or sentimental Past and shirks the hard task of Christianising our day and generation. She is an eternally young and a prolific Bride of the Spirit. Architects are these important apostles. They must announce the message of our times."[2]

Nevertheless, it must not be forgotten that, however important it is that architects should announce the message of our times, it is equally important (in the words of Canon Law) that "care should be taken in the building and restoration of churches that the forms handed down from Christian tradition and the rules of sacred art are observed."[3]

In these pages will be found most of the "forms" and "rules" that must be observed in the building and remodelling of churches, together with the careful regulations concerning their furnishing.

Canon Law has also laid down that "with regard to the material and form of sacred furniture, it is necessary to keep to liturgical prescriptions, to ecclesiastical tradition, and to the greatest extent possible to the laws of sacred art."[4] Such is the mind of the Church. If her directions are observed, the result will be a more beautiful and convenient place of worship than if the architect allows his imagination to run riot.

In conclusion, it should be made clear that the liturgical prescriptions given in this book only apply to churches where the Roman rite is followed, i.e., the greater part of Western Europe and in all countries colonised from Western Europe. The Roman rite is used exclusively by the secular clergy and most religious orders in the Latin patriarchate,[*] with the exception of the dioceses of Milan, Toledo, and Braga, and in the surviving groups of Byzantine Catholics in southern Italy, Sicily, or

---

[*] The dignity of being the head of the Universal Church has to a high degree eclipsed the pope's other lawful titles — and rights. We easily forget that he is the bishop of Rome and that his cathedral therefore is not St. Peter's, but the Archbasilica of the Our Saviour in the Lateran. Few Catholics seem to realize that he is also the metropolitan of Latium and the primate of Italy. While these titles do not have an immediate bearing on our condition, the far more important fact that the pope is the patriarch of the West (of the Roman Empire), as there are patriarchs in Alexandria, Antioch, etc., is often, if not forgotten, hardly realized in its importance. On the right understanding of this cardinal distinction hinges the whole question of difference in Canon Law, rite, liturgical language, married or unmarried clergy, etc. While the sad rift between Orient and Occident has now reduced the patriarchates to a shadow of their tremendous significance, they are a helpful means to raise ourselves above the damnable tendency of confusing unity with intolerant uniformity so common among our contemporaries. — *H. A. R.*

Corsica, likewise among the other Uniate bodies in various parts of the English-speaking world. A modified form of the Roman rite is to be found in a few other dioceses of Europe, e.g., Lyons, as well as among the older religious orders — Carthusians, Cistercians, Calced Carmelites, and Dominicans. Each has its own ceremonial traditions and rules which have to be followed even when they differ from those prescribed for the diocese of Rome and all other dioceses bound to the Roman rite as revised and reformed by Pius V in 1570.

I must not omit to acknowledge the help given me by many friends in writing this book, particularly the following: the Rt. Rev. Msgr. William Clapperton, D.D.; the Very Rev. Msgr. T. Croft-Fraser; the late Very Rev. Fr. Fabian Dix, O.P.; the Rev. Joseph Heald; the Rev. Alfred Sandwell; Dom Oswald Sumner, O.S.B.; Dom Bruno Webb, O.S.B.; Dom Benedict Steuart, O.S.B.; Dom Edmund Fatt, O.S.B.; the late Dom Anselm Moore, O.S.B.; Geoffrey Webb; and J. N. Comper. Special thanks are due to the Rev. J. B. O'Connell and the Rev. Ivor Daniel who revised and corrected the original manuscript, likewise the Rev. H. A. Reinhold who was responsible for editing it for the American public.

Much help has been derived from articles in *Liturgical Arts* and *L'Artisan Liturgique.* The editor of *The Church and the People* (Prinknash Abbey) must be thanked for allowing me to include portions of articles which have appeared in his magazine. Finally, I must mention the authors of books often quoted or referred to, particularly Rt. Rev. Harold E. Collins (*The Church Edifice and Its Appointments*); Dom Rinaldo Pilkington (*La Chiesa e il suo arredamento*); Rev. Benedict Williamson (*How to Build a Church*); Nevil Truman (*The Care of Churches*); J. N. Comper (*Further Notes on the English Altar, or Practical Considerations on the Planning of a Modern Church*); Rev. M. S. MacMahon (*Liturgical Catechism*); Rev. Ramund James (*The Origin and Development of Roman Liturgical Vestments*); Rev. E. J. Forse (*Ceremonial Curiosities*); Dom E. Roulin, O.S.B. (*Nos Eglises*); the editors of *Directions for the use of Altar Societies and Architects;* The Incorporated Church Building Society; the Warham Guild; the Alcuin Club; *Cahiers de l'Art Sacré.* Acknowledgements must be made to the editor of *The Universe* for allowing me to use drawings which appeared in this paper.

PETER F. ANSON

Harbour Head,
Macduff, Scotland
Michaelmas, 1947

NOTES

1. Gill, Eric, *Beauty Looks After Herself,* p. 226.
2. Reinhold, H. A., "A Revolution in Church Architecture," article in *Liturgical Arts,* Vol. VI, p. 126.
3. C.J.C. 1164, § 1.
4. C.J.C. 1296, § 3.

BIBLIOGRAPHY

BOOKS

Augustine, P. Charles, O.S.B., *A Commentary on the New Code of Canon Law*, Vol. VI, Administrative Law (St. Louis and London, 1931).

Ayrinhac, Henry A., *Administrative Legislation in the New Code of Canon Law* (New York, 1930).

Bishop, Edmund, *Liturgia Historica* (Oxford, 1918).

Bliley, N. M., *Altars According to the Code of Canon Law* (Washington, D. C.).

Braun, Joseph, S.J., *Der Christliche Altar* (Munich, 1924).

—— *Die Liturgische Gewandung im Occident und Orient* (Freiburg, 1907).

Bridgett, T. E., *History of the Holy Eucharist in Great Britain* (London, 1881).

Cabrol, Fernand, O.S.B., *Dictionnaire d'archéologie chrétienne* (Paris, 1907 ff.).

—— *Liturgical Prayer: its history & spirit* (London, 1922).

Casagrande, *L'Arte a servizio della Chiesa*, Vol. I., *La Casa di Dio* (Turin, 1931).

Catholic Encyclopedia, 16 vols. (London and New York, 1912).

Cavanaugh, W. T., *The Reservation of the Blessed Sacrament* (Washington, D. C., 1927).

Clarke, B. A., *Church Builders of the 19th Century* (London, 1938).

Collins, Msgr. H. E., *The Church Edifice and Its Appointments* (Philadelphia, 1932, new ed., 1940).

Comper, J. N., *Further Thoughts on the English Altar, or Practical Considerations on the Planning of a Modern Church* (Cambridge, 1933).

Cox, J. C., *English Church Fittings, Furniture and Accessories* (London, 1933).

Cram, Ralph Adams, *Church Building*, 3 ed. (New York, 1924).

d'Agnel, G. Arnaud, *L'Art Religieux Moderne* (Grenoble, 1936).

Dearmer, Percy, *The Parson's Handbook*, 6 ed. (Oxford, 1906).

—— *The Ornaments of the Ministers*, new ed. (London, 1920).

Dix, Dom Gregory, *A Detection of Aumbries* (London, 1942).

Duchesne, L., *Origines du Culte Chrétien*, 2 ed. (Paris, 1898).

Duret, D., *Mobilier, Vases, Objets et Vêtements Liturgiques* (Paris, 1932).

Fortescue Adrian and O'Connell, J. B., *The Ceremonies of the Roman Rite Described* (ed. 1940).

Hope, W. H. St. John, *English Altars* (Alcuin Club Collections, London, 1899).

James, Raymund, *Origin and Development of Roman Liturgical Vestments*, 2 ed. (Exeter, 1934).

Lowrie, W., *Christian Art and Archeology* (London, 1901).

Malherbe, *Le Mobilier liturgique* (Luttre, 1927).

Martinucci-Menghini, *Manuale Sacrarum Caeremoniarum*, 4 vols. (Rome, 1911).

McMahon, M. S., *Liturgical Catechism* (Dublin, 1927).

Micklethwaite, J. T., *The Ornaments of the Rubrics* (Alcuin Club, London, 1901).

—— *Occasional Notes on Church Furniture and Arrangement*, new ed. (London, 1908).

Morris, Joan, *Modern Sacred Art* (London, 1938).

O'Connell, J. B., *Directions for the Use of Altar Societies and Architects*, 4 ed. (1933).

—— *The Celebration of Mass*, 3 ed. (Milwaukee, 1940–1941).

Pilkington, Rinaldo, *La Chiesa e il suo arredamento* (Turin, 1937).

Pugin, A. W., *Glossary of Ecclesiastical Ornament and Costume,* 3 ed. (London, 1868).

Rock, Daniel, *The Church of our Fathers,* new ed., ed. by G. W. Hart and W. H. Frere (London, 1903–1904).

Rohault de Fleury, *La Messe,* 7 vols. (Paris, 1883–1889).

Roulin, E., O.S.B., *Vestments and Vesture* (London, 1931).

—— *Nos Eglises* (Paris, 1938).

Schuster, Ildephonus, O.S.B., *The Sacramentary,* 4 vols. (London, 1924–1926).

Truman, Nevil, *The Care of Churches* (London, 1935).

Van der Stappen, J. F., *Sacra Liturgia,* 5 vols. (Mechlin, 1912).

Le Vavasseur-Haegy, *Manuel de Liturgie et Céremonial,* 2 vols., 6 ed. (Paris, 1935).

Viollet-le-Duc, *Dictionnaire raisonné de l'architecture française* (Paris, 1858–1868).

—— *Dictionnaire raisonné du mobilier français* (Paris, 1872–1875).

Walcott, Mackenzie E. C., *Sacred Archeology* (London, 1868).

Wapelhorst, Innocent, O.F.M., *Compendium Sacrae Liturgiae,* 10 ed. (New York, 1925).

Watkin, E. I., *Catholic Art and Culture* (London, 1947).

Wattjes, J. G., *Moderne Kerken in Europa en Amerika* (Amsterdam, 1931).

Webb, Geoffrey, *The Liturgical Altar,* 2 ed. (London, 1939).

Weber, E. J., *Catholic Church Buildings* (London, 1927).

Wigley, G. J., *St. Charles Borromeo's Instructions on Ecclesiastical Building,* translation and annotation (London, 1867).

PERIODICALS

Arte Sacra (Turin).

Art Notes (Oxford).

Bulletin Paroissial Liturgique (Abbaye de Saint-André, Bruges).

Cahiers de l'Art Sacré (1945–1947) (*Editions du Cerf*)

   I) *Reconstruire les églises : L'esprit et les principes*

  IV) *. . . Le plan de l'église et du centre paroissial*

   V) *L'éclairage des églises*

 VII) *Tendances actuelles de l'art chrétien*

  IX) *L'éducation artistique du clergé*

   X) *Reconstruire les églises : Formes de l'architecture religieuse moderne*

Die Christliche Kunst (Munich).

Ephemerides Liturgicae (Rome).

L'Artisan Liturgique (Abbaye de Saint-André, Bruges).

L'Art Sacré (special issues 1945–1947) (*Editions du Cerf*)

   Le Programme de l'église à reconstruire

   Sauvegarde, restauration, digne présentation du Patrimonie sacré

   Le Zèle de la Maison de Dieu

Les Questions Liturgiques et Paroissiales (Abbaye de Mont César, Louvain)

Liturgical Arts (New York).

Orate Fratres (St. John's Abbey, Collegeville, Minn.).

The Church and the People (Prinknash Abbey, Gloucester).

The Clergy Review (London).

CONTENTS

LIST OF ILLUSTRATIONS

CHURCHES
THEIR PLAN *and*
FURNISHING

CHAPTER I

ECCLESIASTICAL BUILDINGS — PLACES OF WORSHIP

DEFINITION OF A CHURCH

According to Canon Law, a church is a "sacred building dedicated to divine worship for the use of all the faithful and the public exercise of religion."[1]

In other words, the principal object of a Catholic church is to provide a suitable building in which the faithful can meet for the offering up of the Sacrifice of the Mass or other liturgical functions and the reception of sacraments and sacramentals.

NECESSITY OF CHURCHES

If we lived on a planet where there is an equable climate, with neither wind, rain, snow, sleet, nor extreme sunshine, there would be no practical reason for building churches. Public worship could be performed in the open air. As this ideal state of things does not exist, some sort of protection from the weather is necessary for decency, reverence, and comfort. Hence the primary object of a church is to cover the worshippers and to protect the objects used in worship. This is the *function* of a church: a building erected for a particular kind of "job" — public worship.

HISTORICAL NOTES

In the first ages of Christianity no special buildings were set apart for public worship. The assemblies of the faithful for the celebration of the Eucharist, prayers, and preaching took place in private houses.[2] By the second century we read of a *Domus Ecclesiae* (house of the church), which seems to have been a building used for all services of the Christian body in a town or city, with an apartment dedicated to worship.

During the third century the *Domus Ecclesiae* had become the *Domus Dei*: a large room or hall, cut off from the rest of the house. During the first three centuries Christian churches, with but few exceptions, appear to have been situated in towns. Country folk had to come in to towns to fulfil their religious duties. Then came mortuary chapels in cemeteries, where funerals and anniversary services were held. Chapels, built over the tombs of martyrs, soon became popular centres where the faithful gathered together, at first on anniversaries, and then other times. So great did the crowds become that larger buildings had to be erected. The Catacombs* at

---

* The ineradicable notion that Christians held their synaxis in catacombs obviously stems from the tales of not very observant pilgrims and pious fiction. One look at the damp, poorly ventilated, narrow, and dark tunnels — to which we should add the fact that the catacombs were being used as burial grounds and

Rome and elsewhere do not appear to have been used for regular services except during times of severe persecution, or for funerals and on festivals of the martyrs. Very little is known about early Christian churches in rural districts. They appear to have been served occasionally by priests from the towns. It was not until the fourth or fifth centuries that resident priests were appointed to country places. Subsequently we find chapels or oratories attached to the villas of the nobility. Finally came the conventual churches of monastic communities.

MODERN CLASSIFICATION

Ecclesiastical buildings are divided into two classes: (1) churches and (2) oratories.

I. CHURCHES

Churches may be: (*a*) Metropolitan, (*b*) Cathedral, (*c*) Collegiate or conventual, (*d*) Parochial, (*e*) Basilica. It should be noted that, strictly speaking, a church is a building set apart *in perpetuity* for the public exercise of worship.

a) Metropolitan

A metropolitan church is presided over by an archbishop. According to whether it is the seat of a patriarch,

primate, or archbishop, it is called patriarchal, primatial, or simple.

b) Cathedral

A cathedral church is presided over by a bishop and contains his throne. Metropolitan and cathedral churches should normally be served by a body of canons or a chapter,* whose primary duty is the public recitation or chanting of the Divine Office in choir. In countries where a lack of clergy makes it impossible to maintain resident canons or chaplains, the Divine Office cannot be celebrated publicly. Originally, the cathedral church was the only parish church for a whole diocese. Country parishes and additional town parishes came later. A survival of this primitive discipline survives in certain Italian cities where only the cathedral church has a baptismal font, in which children of all parishes are baptised. It should be noted that a cathedral is not necessarily the *largest* church in a diocese. It is merely the *bishop's church* over which he presides, in which he teaches and conducts divine worship for the flock under his charge.

c) Collegiate or Conventual

A conventual church is a public place of worship served by a community of regular clergy (canons regular, monks, or friars), who are bound to the recitation of the Divine Office in choir.

---

full of decaying remains on three of four tiers right and left of the passages! — should convince any visitor that no crowds could have attended Mass, especially when we remember that Low Mass and silent, inactive attendance were unknown to the Christians of the martyr Church. The celebrant would have been invisible to anyone but the first two or three faithful standing in "indian file" and spread backwards for unending distances. — *H. A. R.*

---

* American ecclesiastical legislation of the Councils of Baltimore in the nineteenth century, with papal approval, excluded this institution from our soil, with the exception of New Orleans and Eastern Canada and, of course, the formerly Spanish colonies. — *H. A. R.*

d) Parochial

A parish church, strictly speaking, should have a baptismal font, a confessional, and a cemetery, and the normal liturgical equipment for baptisms, marriages, and funerals. In countries where canonical parishes have not been set up, the "mission" or "quasi-parish" churches have practically the same privileges.

e) Basilica

A limited number of churches receive the honorary title of basilica. In pre-Christian times a "basilica" (Greek *basilike–oikias* — a royal house) was a court of justice and a meeting-place for assemblies. Usually it consisted of a long hall with a double row of columns, with an apse at one end. The name was first given to early Christian churches built over the tombs of martyrs. To-day it is merely a title of honour applicable to various kinds of churches.

There are two classes — "major" and "minor." There are four *major basilicas,* all in Rome. They correspond to the four great patriarchates: (1) St. John Lateran is the "Mother and Mistress of All Churches" and the head of the patriarchate of the West. It has the title of archbasilica and is the Cathedral of Rome. (2) St. Peter's represents the patriarchate of Constantinople. (3) St. Paul's Outside the Walls represents the patriarchate of Alexandria. (4) St. Mary Major represents the patriarchate of Antioch. The Basilica of St. Lawrence Outside the Walls formerly held the same privileges.

The title of *minor basilica* is granted

to certain churches by the pope.[3] The serving clergy, secular or regular, take precedence over other priests. In processions they carry certain decorative insignia[4] which indicate their special dependence on the pope. The papal arms are displayed on the exterior.

II. ORATORIES

Oratories are places of worship not intended for the use of all the faithful indiscriminately.[5] Three kinds are recognised in Canon Law: (*a*) public, (*b*) semipublic, and (*c*) private.

a) Public Oratories

A public oratory is primarily used by a religious community as its chapel, but the public have access, at least during times of services, either through the house or through a separate entrance leading directly onto the street or road.[6] A public oratory can be consecrated like a church.[7]

b) Semipublic Oratories

A semipublic oratory is intended for a special community, and is not normally open to the faithful in general.[8] It can be erected only with the permission of the Ordinary.[9]

c) Private Oratories

A private or domestic oratory is generally a room set apart for worship in a private house for the use of the family or an individual.[10] Mass can be offered in private oratories only by papal indult, only one Low Mass may be said daily, even on Sundays, not however on the more solemn feasts. No other ecclesiastical functions are allowed, but the local Ordinary can give permission for Mass on more solemn feasts for special reasons.[11] Private oratories cannot be consecrated — only blessed.

The same rules affecting the building, consecration, blessing, desecration, or reconciliation of a church apply to public oratories, and all ecclesiastical functions can be performed in them, except in certain cases.[12]

Private oratories are not "sacred places" in the strict sense of the word, and they remain the property of the owner of the house or land. They can be used again for secular purposes without technical "desecration." For this reason the furniture in a private oratory should be of a character that can easily be removed; e.g., it would be unsuitable to erect a stone altar, which could not be consecrated.

In the case of semiprivate oratories, the furniture and fittings should be of a more permanent nature, for the building cannot revert to secular use without the authority of the Ordinary.[13]

St. Charles Borromeo has left us some useful ideas regarding the planning of "an oratory wherein the Holy Sacrifice of the Mass is occasionally offered up."[14] He recommends that it should be "of one nave only"; the length of which should not be less than 16 ft. 6 in., its width 13 ft. 9 in., with a height suitably proportioned to the site. The sanctuary should be about 11 ft. wide or more, with length and height which agree with the width. There need be only one step between the nave and the sanctuary, with fixed rails of the form prescribed elsewhere in the *Instructions*. Only two steps are required for the altar, one of them being the predella or footpace. There should be at least 2 ft. 9 in., between the railings and the lower step of the altar. He orders that the windows should be constructed high up "so that a man standing outside cannot look within." He suggests that the door should be opposite the altar, and should be surmounted by a circular window "to be like the eye of the church." The sacristy should be on the south side of the altar, if possible, and proportioned to the size of the building. On the north side of the altar there may be a small turret "not at all resembling a parish steeple; or, at any rate, two piers of stone or brick may be constructed on the top of the wall, so as to support one bell only." If more altars are needed in an oratory where several Masses are celebrated about the same hour, single chapels may be erected on both sides of the nave.*

---

* This indicates, clearly, that there is no justification to multiply chapels or altars without a reason. — *H. A. R.*

NOTES

1. C.J.C. 1161.
2. Acts 2:46; Rom. 16:5; 1 Cor. 16:15; Col. 4:15; Phil. 2.
3. C.J.C. 1180.
4. The golden patriarchal cross on a short shaft, a small bell, and a red and white striped umbrella.
5. C.J.C. 1188, § 1.
6. C.J.C. 1188, § 2.

7. C.J.C. 1181, § 2.
8. C.J.C. 1188, § 2, 2°.
9. C.J.C. 1192, § 1.
10. C.J.C. 1188, 3°.
11. C.J.C. 1195, §§ 1 and 2.
12. C.J.C. 1191, § 2.
13. C.J.C. 1192, §§ 2 and 3.
14. *Instructions*, Chap. XXX.

CHAPTER II

BUILDING AND DEDICATION
OF CHURCHES

A church cannot be built without the express permission of the diocesan Ordinary.[1] This rule dates from the Council of Chalcedon, which forbade religious orders to erect oratories without episcopal consent. It was reinforced in many subsequent councils and synods. The Ordinary may withhold his consent if he is not satisfied that means are available to erect the church, and support the clergy, etc.[2] This again is a very ancient law. Another reason may be that a new church would seriously affect the financial and spiritual status of an existing one. Canon 1162 gives additional reasons. Even religious orders, who have obtained permission to make a foundation in the diocese, must obtain the consent of the bishop before they can erect a church or public oratory in a particular place.[3]

SITE

It is difficult to lay down any rules regarding the site of a new church, because in most instances there is not much choice in the ground available. St. Charles Borromeo states that the site must be chosen by the judgement of the bishop, and from the counsel of the architect whom he will have appointed or approved. The first point is that the site should be a prominent one, if possible slightly elevated, so that there can be three to five steps up to the main entrance. St. Charles attaches much importance to steps, for he goes on to say that the level of the church should be raised if necessary.

As to site, St. Charles advises that a church should not be erected near "stables, vegetable stalls, taverns, smithies, markets, and all places of sale," moreover that it should not be near the quarter of a town where such places abound — rather difficult it would seem! He prefers a definitely isolated site, not connected in any way with secular buildings. He lays down the rule that the "dwellings of the ministers of the church" should be on one side of the building, not adhering to its walls but connected with it by other walls. Very prudently he warns his clergy against erecting churches in damp and marshy places, as well as "near to hills or declivities, whereby either torrent or any other great body of water running down swiftly may occasion any detriment to the edifice." He even goes so far as to give practical advice on building drains so that surface water may be carried off elsewhere. Finally, he tells us that the size of the church should be sufficient to accommodate not only the normal congregation, but also "the quantity of men flocking therein on solemn days."[4]

THE CORNER-STONE

Canons 1156 and 1163 state that the right to bless and lay the corner-stone of a new church belongs to the Ordinary in the case of "secular" churches, and to the major superior in the case of religious.[5]

The corner-stone should be one large block, at least one foot in length, breadth, and depth, with a small cavity in the top, in which are usually inserted souvenirs or "memoranda'" of the event.

The position of the corner-stone is not mentioned in either the *Rituale Romanum* or the *Pontificale*, but it is usual for it to be placed in the foundations near the high altar.[6]

TITLES OF CHURCHES

It is laid down in Canon 1168 that every blessed or consecrated church must have its own title which cannot be changed after dedication. The same canon also states that churches cannot be dedicated to a *beatus* without an indult from the Holy See. The title* may be the name of any person or mystery of the faith that is the object of public

---

* It is to be regretted that so many of us seem to be afraid to maintain one of the finest traditions of our own Catholic Church, namely to use above all the traditional titles and the ones that are more focused on the central truths and mysteries of our faith. Why are Christ's Church, Most Holy Saviour, the Twelve Apostles, the Good Shepherd, the Blessed Trinity, the Holy Spirit, so seldom used? Where are the martyrs now? We have an abundance of secondary titles of our Lady, innumerable churches of one and the same saints in an endless unimaginative and narrow monotony. Only in our million-population cities do we find a rich catalogue of titles. I suspect, however, that there the reason is the great number of churches more than conscious effort to break our monotony. — *H. A. R.*

devotion: e.g., the Holy Trinity or one of the three divine Persons (but not God the Father), Jesus Christ or one of His mysteries, our Lady or any one of her titles, the holy angels, the canonised saints, or any mystery connected with their lives.

DEDICATION OF A CHURCH

Canon 1165 lays down definite rules. No services may be held in a church until it has been solemnly consecrated, or at least blessed.

CONSECRATION

A church cannot be consecrated unless the following conditions are fulfiled:

1. That it is built of stone or brick. Churches of other materials — e.g., iron or wood — can only be blessed.[7] But a reinforced concrete church may be consecrated provided that the places for the twelve crosses on the walls and doorposts are of stone.[8]

2. That the church stands free on all sides. Should there be only minor obstructions at a few places the church may still be consecrated.[9] If the exterior walls cannot be reached, an apostolic indult must be obtained before the consecration.[10]

3. There must be twelve crosses on the inside walls of the church — six on each side. The crosses may be painted directly onto the walls or, if made of stone or metal, attached to it. They may not be made of fragile material. They must be irremovable,[11] as they are the permanent sign of a consecrated church. A bracket to hold a candle is placed above or below each cross.

4. The high altar should be conse-

crated with the church. If it is already consecrated, a side altar must take its place.[12] Should all the altars have been consecrated, an apostolic indult is necessary before the church can be consecrated.[13] One permanent, stone altar is essential.

5. The property must be free of debt.[14]

BLESSING OF A CHURCH

The ceremony of blessing a church is far less elaborate than that of consecration, and consists chiefly in sprinkling the outer and inner walls with holy water. The form is given in the *Rituale Romanum*.[15] All churches and public oratories must at least be blessed, even if they are to be consecrated later on,[16] otherwise they cannot be used for divine worship. The Ordinary may delegate any priest to perform the blessing.

Canon 1165, § 2, lays down that if it can be forseen that a church is likely to be turned to "profane uses" the Ordinary must withhold his consent to its erection and refuse to bless or consecrate it when built. Such an instance might occur in the case of a church or public oratory erected by an individual layman or family on private property, which may be sold or alienated at a future date.[17]

LOSS OF CONSECRATION OR BLESSING OF A CHURCH

Canon 1170 explains that the consecration or blessing of a church is not lost unless the building is totally destroyed, or the greater part of the walls has collapsed, or if the Ordinary has given permission for the building to be handed over for profane uses, which he may do under certain conditions.[18]

DESECRATION OF A CHURCH

Canon 1172 gives the various ways in which a church can be violated or desecrated, i.e., diverted from sacred to profane use. They consist of:

1. The crime of homicide;

2. Injurious and serious shedding of blood;

3. Impious and sordid uses, e.g., heretical worship, secular meetings, use as barracks, etc.;

4. The burial of an infidel or one excommunicated by declaratory or condemnatory sentence.[19]

CONSEQUENCES OF DESECRATION

The result of a violation or desecration of a church is a cessation of all services and the obligation of reconciliation before Mass can be said again or the sacraments administered.[20]

RECONCILIATION

Canons 1174–1177 deal with the matter of reconciliation of which the most important detail is the order that it must take place as soon as possible according to the rites laid down in approved liturgical books. The necessary conditions are much more complicated in the case of a "consecrated" church than of a church which has simply been blessed.

NOTES

1. C.J.C. 1162, § 1.
2. C.J.C. 1162, § 2.
3. C.J.C. 1162, § 4.

4. *Book of Instructions on Church Building,* I, Chap. I.
5. Full details of the nature of a corner-

stone will be found in A. J. Schulte's *Benedicenda* (New York, 1907, p. 1), and in Martinucci-Menghini's *Manuale Sacrarum Caeremoniarum,* L. VII, c. XV, 4 vols. (1911).

6. The two authors mentioned give elaborate instructions concerning the placing of the corner-stone. The rite of blessing and laying will be found in the *Pontificale* (Pars. II) and in the *Rituale* (Tit. VIII, c. 26).

7. C.J.C. 1165, § 4.

8. S.R.C. 4240.

9. S.R.C. 1321.

10. S.R.C. 2687.

11. S.R.C. 1939.

12. C.J.C. 1165, § 5.

13. S.R.C. 3907.

14. Other details concerning the ceremonial requisites needed for consecration will be found in Schulte's *Consecranda. See also* Collins, *The Church Edifice and its Appointments,* pp. 9–15.

15. Tit. VIII, c. 27.

16. S.R.C. 4025.

17. S.R.C. 3546, ad 1.

18. C.J.C. 1187. The definition of "partial destruction" is rather complicated; details may be found in any commentary on Canon Law; e.g., Ayrinhac, *Administrative Legislation in the New Code of Canon Law* (New York, 1930), Fr. Augustine, O.S.B., *Commentary on the New Code of Canon Law* (St. Louis, 1931), Vol. VI, pp. 32, 33.

19. The exact interpretation of these cases may be found in commentaries on Canon Law *ut supra.*

20. C.J.C. 1173, § 1.

CHAPTER III

STYLE AND PLAN

It is outside the scope of this book to deal at length with the controversial subject of "style," which is really so unimportant that it might be better not to refer to it at all. Yet many in authority, when faced with the job of building a new church, make up their minds first of all that they want it to reproduce some favourite features of an ancient building and require the architect to carry out their wishes. More practical details are regarded as comparatively unimportant.

It is not everyone who realises that "architecture is primarily related to the science of construction, and that man, having mastered the fundamental problem of ensuring stability in his buildings, thereafter, and *only* thereafter, proceeded to satisfy his instinctive primal urge to decorate. . . . The reversal of an essentially logical sequence is responsible for the present mass of dishonest architecture, which, unfortunately, appears to meet with general public approbation."[1]

In no sphere of building is there so much "dishonest architecture" as in churches. A large number of churches erected in the past century can only be described as "meretricious shams."

A church, like a house, *should be evolved* in sequence of design *from the inside outwards,* not from the outside inwards. The building itself is funda-

mentally* just a covered-in space to protect the worshippers from the elements. Provided that it fulfils these requirements it does not matter much whether the covered-in space is left plain or decorated. A church will "look like a church" if functional needs of the building are put first and foremost, just as in the case of a garage, factory, aerodrome, or theatre. The primary functions of a Catholic place of worship have not changed much in the course of many centuries, and it does not require any particular shape of arches, windows, or columns to emphasize its function.[2] **

---

* We ought, however, not to forget the intrinsically symbolic character of the church building. If it were only a shelter with a special purpose, we would never reach any more perfection than pure "functionality." From the basilica down to the Baroque abbey churches of Austria and Spain through all the different styles the builders have always seen in their churches a significant form of symbolical content: the royal hall, the house of God mirroring the edifice of the Church, the mystical banquet hall, the "presence" of heaven. These are implicit notions and it is not necessary that they find the obvious and often crude obtrusiveness of the later periods! Man, the imitative creator, has always tried to bring into his churches something of the totality and comprehensiveness of the "kosmos," the adorned universe. — H. A. R.

** The history of ecclesiastical architecture in the United States is not always pleasant to read; e.g., that sad fate of the old cathedral in Boston, built by a great American master like Bulfinch and superseded by a pseudo-Gothic misfit as the present structure. Lately we have been trying hard to do better: our imitations have more "atmosphere," our "taste" has im-

11

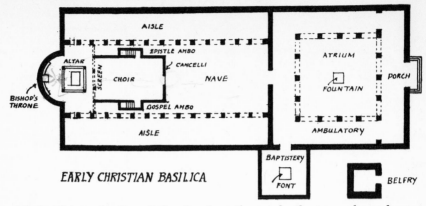

EARLY CHRISTIAN BASILICA

Early Christian basilica: if the altar faces the people, the two ambones have to be exchanged as the Gospel side is always the left-hand side from the celebrant.

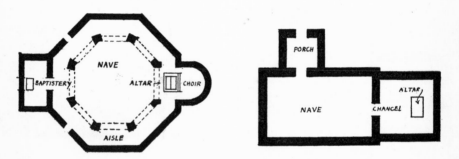

OCTAGONAL PLAN   ANGLO-SAXON PLAN.

Octagonal plan (e.g., San Vitale in Ravenna, Aix-la-Chapelle, i.e., Aachen): here the true emphases are somehow shifted into the wrong place, from the sanctuary to the people's space. The same is true about the Hagia Sophia in Constantinople. — *H. A. R.*

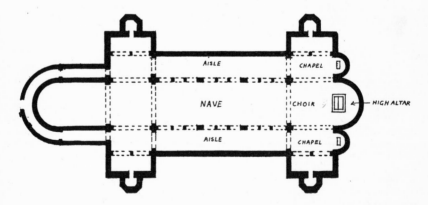

GERMAN ROMANESQUE PLAN   *(Designed on groups of squares)*

German Romanesque shows the first traces of accommodation of the Church to the growing custom of private Masses, here visible in side altars. — *H. A. R.*

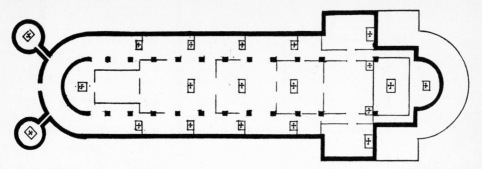

Abbey Church of St. Gall (A.D. 800): note curious arrangement of ~~nineteen~~ twenty altars.

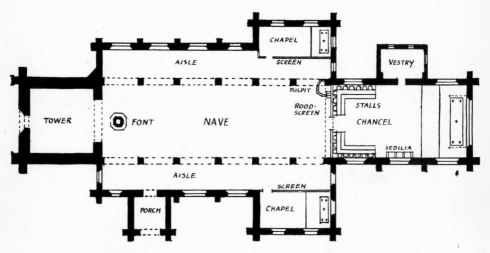

Typical 14th century English parish church; this plan shows usual position of font at lower end of nave, chapels with screens, and chancel largely hidden by rood-screen.

When one reads certain passages in Pugin's works it is difficult to remember that his book, cited below, was pub-

lished in 1841. He tells us that "the two great rules for design are these: (1) that there should be no features

proved, above all, better material is being used and the rubrics are being observed with greater care. A close observer might even say that, as imitations go, our neo-Gothic, neo-Colonial, and neo-Californian is far superior to anything of this kind attempted in Europe. But neither taste, nor imitative and recreative skill, nor the admirable sense of scale and proportion make for creation and originality. Acquired and learned skills observed in the old masters are

not to be contemned, it is true, but more is yet required. Ralph Adams Cram's "lovely," virile and almost atmospheric Gothic is a perfect example of its kind, yet still a profound bow in the direction of the past achievement, despairing of our own future. All the prerequisites for a great flowering of American church architecture are now given. The masters may enter now and take over. — *H. A. R.*

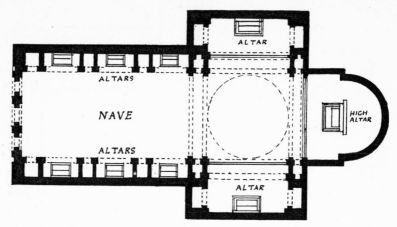

ITALIAN RENAISSANCE PLAN

Italian Renaissance: after the liturgical and architectural confusion of the waning Middle Ages, we find here a clear conception of the first purpose of the church: to house the altar. The accent is still slightly shifted and architectural beauty has it over liturgical appropriateness: the dome is a hollow climax on nothing. This was probably a consequence of the ambition to imitate Bramante's St. Peter, forgetting that in St. Peter's the dome is directly above the *confessio* and the main altar. — *H. A. R.*

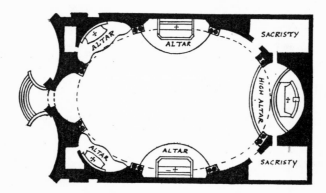

BAROQUE PLAN

Baroque: this plan shows the final stage of Baroque, when all orientation was lost and the charming and almost musical products of this grand style had completely lost their sense of purpose. — *H. A. R.*

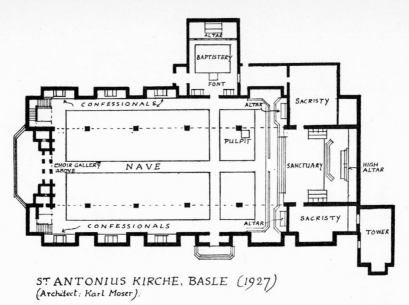

ST ANTONIUS KIRCHE, BASLE (1927)
(Architect: Karl Moser).

St. Antonius: the plan shows nothing startling, but is rather conventional. What shook the architectural world in the twenties when this edifice arose, was the complete honesty in the use of modern technical devices as concrete, glass, and steel. The architect left the imprint of the wooden shell into which the concrete was poured without paint or plaster, thus giving it an interesting texture. — *H. A. R.*

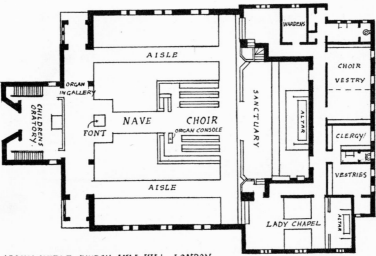

JOHN KEBLE CHURCH, MILL HILL, LONDON.
(Architect: D.F. Martin-Smith). 1936.

Mill Hill Church: the only church known to me in the United States which shows the same arrangement for the choir is St. Aloysius in Chicago. — *H. A. R.*

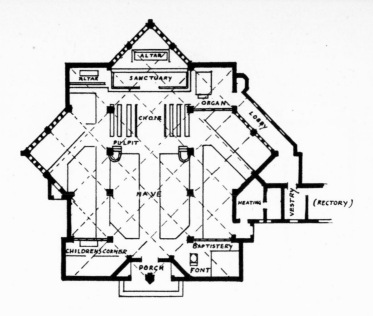

ST MICHAEL & ALL ANGELS, WYTHENSHAWE. 1937.
(Architect. N.F. Cachemaille-Day)

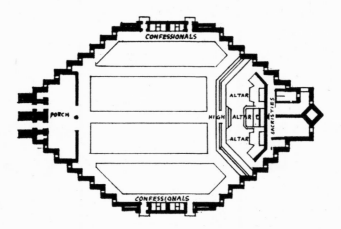

CHURCH OF CHRIST THE KING, CORK. 1956
(Architects. Barry Byrne and Boyd Barrett)

Cork, Ireland: three altars in the sanctuary, otherwise a daring attempt to find a shape commensurate with modern architectural materials and to do away with aisles no longer required, as we can now bridge any space. The architect has a tendency to conceive a shell first and then to cast the church into this newly conceived, however interesting, shape. — H. A. R.

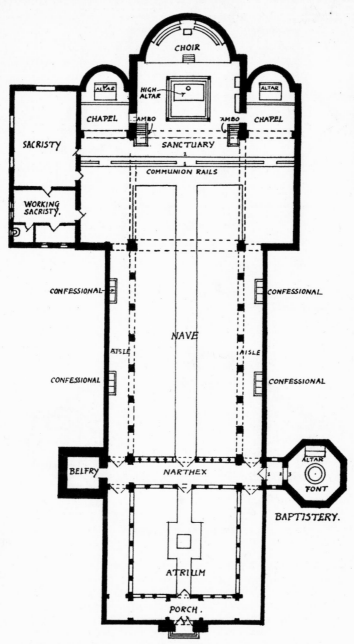

Parish church plan in accordance with St. Charles Borromeo's
Instructions.

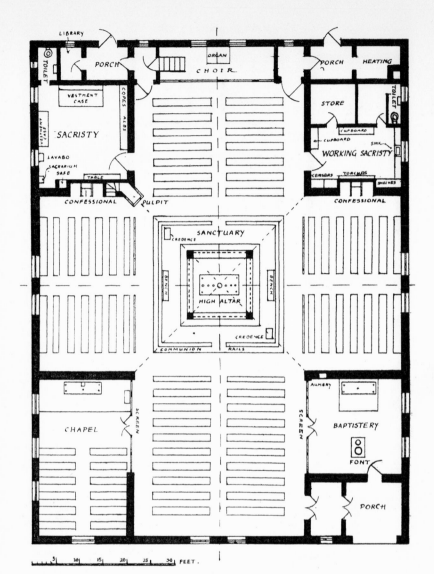

Modern central parish church: In the American editor's opinion a complete misconception of the liturgical purpose of the church. The people in the back of the church see the priest's back; those on the sides, to whom he never turns, his profile; and those behind the altar, his face. To whom will he turn when he sings the *Dominus vobiscum?* What happens to the congregation as an entity? Will there be two Masses on the same altar at the same time? The cruciform shape and the complete novelty of arrangement have it over good practical sense and liturgical correctness. — H. A. R.

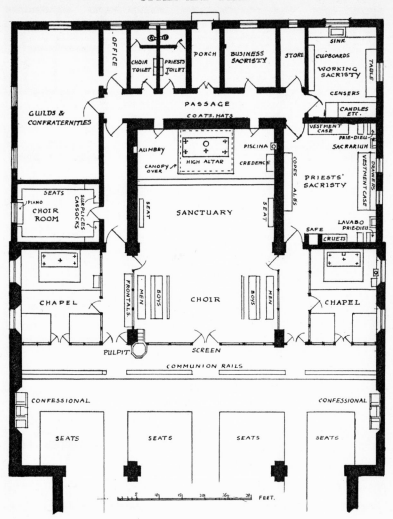

Modern parish church planned on late mediaeval English lines.

about a building which are not necessary for convenience, construction, or propriety; (2) that all ornament should consist of enrichment of the essential construction of the building." He points out that "the neglect of these two rules is the cause of all the bad architecture of the present time. Architectural features are continually tacked on buildings with which they have no connection,

merely for the sake of which is termed effect."[3]

Two years later Pugin issued his *Apology for the Revival of Christian Architecture in England.* Here again he startles us with phrases that are in such complete agreement with the "modernists" of our own times that it is hard to believe that they were written a hundred years ago. He deplores the fact

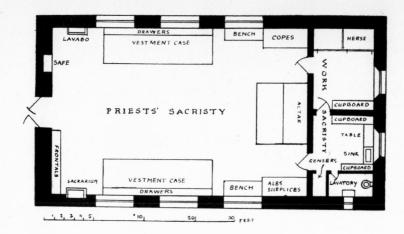

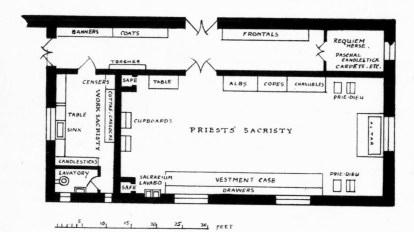

Two plans of large sacristies.

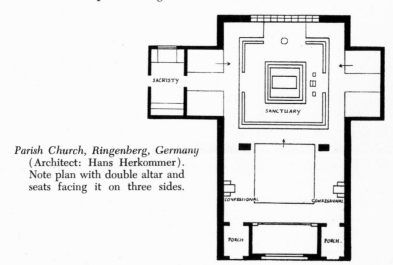

Parish Church, Ringenberg, Germany
(Architect: Hans Herkommer).
Note plan with double altar and
seats facing it on three sides.

that in regard to the public buildings which had been erected during his own lifetime "in no one instance has the purpose or destination of the building formed the ground-work of the composition." He lays down that "architecture and art should be a consistent expression of the period." He voices the feelings of many a later architect when he says that "we do not wish to produce mere servile imitators of former excellence of any kind, but men imbued with the consistent spirit of the ancient architects, who would work on their principles, and

Audaincourt, Doúbs, France.
Typical example of work of Dom Paul Bellot, monk-architect of Solesmes Abbey.

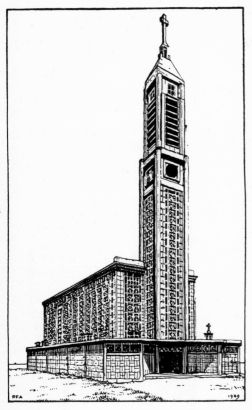

Ste. Thérèse,
Montmagny, Seine-et-Oise, France (1935). Steel and concrete church designed by **A. and C. Perret.**

carry them out as the old men would have done, had they been placed in similar circumstances, and with similar wants to ourselves."[4]

It was not only Pugin who was laying down these fundamental principles a century ago; the Cambridge Camden Society, founded in 1841, was preaching "functionalism" when it laid down in the first number of the *Ecclesiologist* that "the most important requisite in erecting a church is that it be built in such a way that the Rubricks and Canons of the Church of England may be consistently

Benedictine Abbey, Nassau, Bahamas (J. C. Hawes, 1945).

observed, and the Sacraments rubrically and decently administered." It pointed out that "plainness need not be inconsistent with reverence"; "pretence is, and must be"; and that "in God's House everything should be *real*."

P.F. ANSON

1937

St. Philomena's, Middlesbrough, Yorkshire.
German Romanesque in a north of England industrial town.

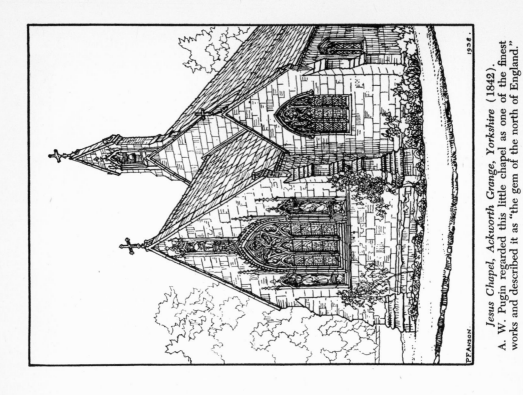

Jesus Chapel, Ackworth Grange, Yorkshire (1842).
A. W. Pugin regarded this little chapel as one of the finest works and described it as "the gem of the north of England."

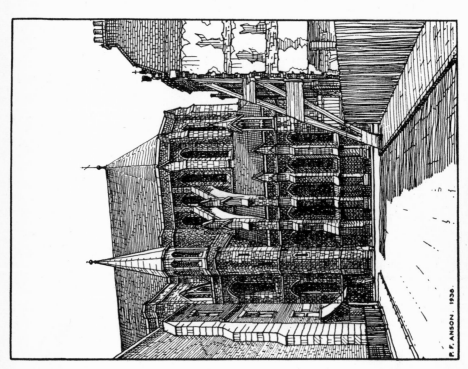

St. James, Spanish Place, London (1890).
This large church, inspired by 13th century French Gothic, was designed by George Goldie.

THE GOTHIC REVIVAL

It was not long before the principles of Pugin and the Camden Society were almost forgotten in a craze for Christian symbolism,* of which John Mason Neale was the chief apologist. Symbolism is always a dangerous hobby and some of the leaders of the ecclesiological movement, both clergy and laity, Catholic and Anglican, were swept off their feet by the fascination of this new field of thought. Their pious dreams were often so far-fetched and fantastically improb-

---

* Since a great deal of this "symbolism" lies in the realm of the far more arbitrary, it may be better to catalogue it under Allegorism. — H. A. R.

Church of Christ the King, Via Massini, Rome. Designed by Piacentini, this new church is a startling contrast to the older churches in Rome.

St. Anthony the Hermit, Rotterdam (1929). A characteristic brick church designed by the famous Dutch architect, Professor Kropholler.

able, that they completely lost sight of the fact that all architecture is based on construction.

So passed the Gothic Revival in England in all its phases. It produced some great architects who have left memorials in the churches which they designed. It also produced some very bad ones. But we need not be ashamed to admire the genius of such great men as Sir Gilbert Scott, George Edmund Street, William Butterfield, James Brooks, J. L. Pearson, G. F. Bodley, George Gilbert Scott, Jr., or J. D. Sedding — to mention but a few of the better-known nineteenth-century church architects. No other country in Europe can show such a number of really out-

New Cathedral, Ballarat, W. Australia (John C. Hawes, 1944).

St. Gerard Majella, Utrecht, Holland. This modern brick church was designed by Jan Van de Leur, a pupil of the late Dom Bellot, the architect-monk of Solesmes.

St. Mary's Filey (1906). This little church, designed by Dom Augustine Roulin, O.S.B., of Ampleforth Abbey, in the style, more or less, of an early Christian basilica, looks somewhat exotic amid the hotels and lodging houses of a popular English seaside resort.

Our Lady, Chapeltown, Glenlivet, Scotland (1908). A satisfactory treatment of a country church on traditional lines in a mountainous part of Scotland.

Our Lady, Star of the Sea, Wells-on-Sea, Norfolk, England. An unusual exterior, inspired by Flemish architecture found in parts of East Anglia.

All Saints, Thropton, Northumberland (1811). A perfect example of an unpretentious, very early "Gothick" Revival building in a remote village in the north of England.

St. Mary, Lea Town, Lancashire (1801). There is much to be said in favor of a simple brick Mass house like this erected with no thought of "architecture" nearly thirty years before Catholics in England gained their emancipation.

St. Mary, Great Eccleston, Lancashire (1835). The stark simplicity of this Catholic chapel in rural Lancashire expresses the solid piety of the people who clung to the "Old Religion" through three centuries of persecution.

Church of the Sacred Heart, Wimbledon, London (1887–1931). Designed by F. A. Walters. A large church decorated in Gothic style, built of flints with stone dressings in traditional English manner.

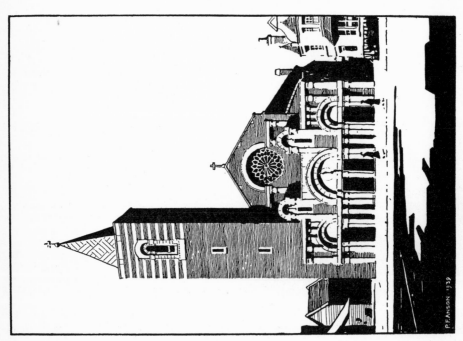

St. Boniface, Tooting, London (1927). Modern brick and stone church in London suburb. Free treatment of Italian Romanesque style.

standing churches erected in the past
century as England, even if to-day some
of us may be inclined to criticise them
unfavourably because their inspiration
is derived more often than not from
mediaeval Gothic, and because they aim
rather at being "period pieces" rather
than what we now term "modern."
Yet, when one considers them seriously,
these nineteenth-century churches are
"modern" in the sense that they re-
flect the spirit of their age in the
same way as do the churches of the
Renaissance period. Nobody could ever

*Freuensfrieden Kirche, Frankfurt,
Germany* (1927). Designed by
Professor Hans Herkommer.

mistake* a nineteenth-century Gothic
Revival church for a genuine mediaeval
example any more than one could suppose that a Renaissance basilica had
been erected during the Roman empire.

---

* True to the author's directions: to object
whenever he disagrees with him, the editor
would like to point out here that he thinks that
the case is very definitely different: the vigor-
ous men of the Renaissance actually created an
entirely new style. Therefore St. Peter's in
Rome and the Pantheon have little in common.
They handled their classical detail with sov-
ereign independence and magnificent creative-
ness. Through their vitruvian façades shone
Gothic dynamism in spite of their serene restraint and their willful this-worldliness. The
neo-Gothics of the nineteenth century, however,
were completely enslaved by their effort to
catch about every smallest detail of their model,
viz., the twelve volumes of Viollet-le-Duc's encyclopedia. The result was that their too correct
imitations can be told at a mile from any
mediocre medieval original by their pale
anemia. — *H. A. R.*

Sainte Jeanne d'Arc, Nice, France
(Jacques Droz). Modern church
made up of intersecting ovoids
completely cast in concrete.

Holy Cross Church, Bornhein, Frankfurt-on-the-Main (1929). Architect: Martin Weber. Characteristic example of post "Global War No. 1" style in Germany.

MODERN METHODS OF CONSTRUCTION

Times have now changed and, whether we like it or not, we cannot ignore the fact that new methods of steel and ferro-concrete construction are superseding "mass wall" building in large covered-in spaces. Again it has to be recognised, no matter how desirable it may be to use local materials for building, that it is often cheaper to employ those which can be obtained from a distance; a serious consideration in the case of a large building such as a parish church in a town. Actually there is no reason why a reinforced concrete church need look any more out of keeping with its surroundings than a brick Byzantine basilica or an imitation mediaeval Gothic church. In towns it seems more logical that a church should not look alien in the midst of domestic and business architecture. The same principle may be applied to villages in the heart of the country. Here, perhaps, a more traditional use of materials may be better. But the builders of red brick "Queen Anne" houses in England never worried about the half-timbered buildings of an earlier period. In fact, as Eric Gill reminds us: "the best works and the best periods (of art) are those in which the nature of the thing to be made is best *known* and most poignantly *expressed*. . . . Bad works are the production of men *who do not know what they are making or who do not care*."[5]

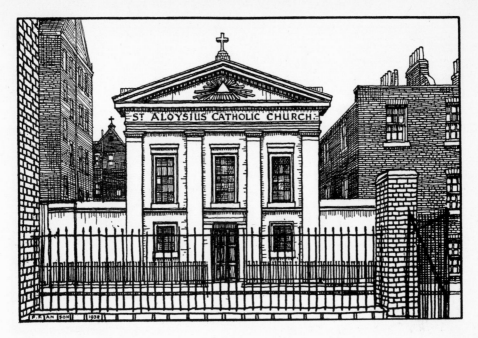

St. Mary's, Somers Town, London (1808). In churches of this type, built by French emigré priests, English Catholics rediscovered their architecture.

PRESENT-DAY NEEDS

The right planning of a church is largely dependent on a knowledge of its functional needs. As these are never quite the same in any two instances, it is difficult to lay down any general principles. Perhaps the most important thing is that there should be a clear view of the high altar from all the fixed seats, whether the building has a nave with or without aisles. Second, the sanctuary should be large enough for the performance of the type of functions that are normally carried out. The larger the church, the more difficult is the planning, especially when the site available is irregular in shape or not level. There is much to be said in favour of the primi-tive Basilican *plan*, with nave, aisles, and apsidal sanctuary. Cardinal Schuster reminds us that "the Roman Liturgy originated and developed in the classical Latin basilica, hence this type of building suits its form and peculiar character better than any other."[6]

Then there is the circular or octagonal style, also adopted by early Christians, with the altar in the centre of the rotunda, in the very midst of the people. Cardinal Schuster thinks that this "offended too intimately that very delicate sense of aesthetic mysticism which everywhere pervaded the Roman basilica,"[7] and the same objection is made to-day although many would like to bring the altar into closer relations

St. Mary's, East Hendred, Berkshire (1865). In some villages of rural England, Catholic churches were erected during the past century that are quite in keeping with their environment. Here is a good example.

with the congregation. "There is nothing whatever in the nature of an altar," writes Eric Gill, "that implies that it should be anywhere else but in the middle. It began as a table around which people sat and partook of the consecrated bread and wine. It remains that thing." The same writer maintains "that the Liturgy must be revived: i.e., made alive again, and to 'revive the liturgy' it is first necessary to disinter it. It is buried beneath a load of mediaeval and post-mediaeval customs. The divorce between clergy and laity, between the people and the altar, has become as wide as the distinction between the artist and the factory hand, the responsible human worker on the one hand and the irresponsible tool on the other. . . . The altar is the centre of the church; it is indeed the church itself. The altar is at hand for those who pray and it assists the hopes of men by granting what they need."[8]

"At the present time it is the custom to place the altar at the end of the church, very often in a specially built apse or chancel, and generally separated from the people by the seats of the ministers, and, in Anglican churches,

St. George's Cathedral, Southwark, London (1848). The tower and spire of A. W. Pugin's cathedral were never completed. Only the walls are left to-day. The building was destroyed by enemy action in 1941 and may never be rebuilt on the original plan.

even by those of the choir. There is thus a monstrous division between the place of the altar and the rest of the church. The sanctuary is ruled off as being not merely a holy place, but a mysterious place — a place in which only professional feet may tread, and a place in which the laity can only enter more or less timidly, when they go up to receive Communion."[9]

It is worth noting that J. N. Comper, an ecclesiastical architect who is violently opposed to what he regards as "modernism" in art, also shares the views of Eric Gill as to the need to bring the altar back into the midst of the people. "The amazing thing," he writes, "is that we go on building on the mediaeval plan, for all the talk about being modern and expressing the age, and for all the architectural poverties which such talk produces." He goes on to say that "the need therefore of our larger parish churches is to bring the altar into direct contact with the people and place the choir somewhere where they will not come between the people and the altar and obstruct the view."[10]

Corpus Christi, Maiden Lane, London (1875). A little, but much frequented church in a back street, jostling with stage doors of theatres, restaurants, and offices. But the bell tower dominates them all!

St. Columba's Cathedral, Oban, Scotland. Sir Giles Gilbert Scott's design for the new cathedral of the diocese of Argyll and the Isles is still incomplete.

The Oratory Church, London (1884). This imposing Baroque church in the Brompton Road was designed by Herbert Gribble on the lines of the Chiesa Nuova, Rome.

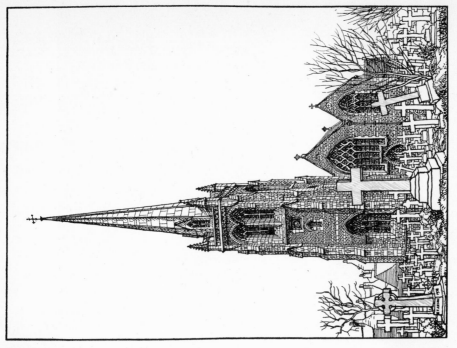

St. Thomas of Canterbury, Fulham, London (1847). So perfect in almost every detail is A. W. Pugin's copy of an English 14th century parish church that it is hard to believe that it is only a hundred years old.

St. Bridget's, Nörrkoping, Sweden (1928). Catholic architecture, as well as the Catholic religion, was dormant in Scandinavian countries for over three centuries. This new church in Sweden shows that a revival has begun already.

from clergy and choir. No matter how beautiful this typical mediaeval English parish church plan may be, it is not suitable for present-day worship. The space is too broken up with columns and piers (erected from purely constructional limitations and not from aesthetic and symbolical reasons).

A long, narrow chancel was a functional necessity in the later Middle Ages when there were choirs of men and boys occupying the stalls; to-day, except in special cases, it is not. Modern materials and constructional methods have made it possible to roof large spaces without

Our Lady Immaculate, Limehouse. A factory-like church in the dock area of London (1934).

St. Patrick's, Soho, London. An 18th century Georgian house, crushed by 19th century Italian Renaissance campanile and a 20th century "Movietone News" office!

The Gothic revivalists of the past century, as indeed many of the clergy and laity to-day, held opposite views. They clung to long chancels, choir-stalls, and an altar raised on steps in the mediaeval tradition. High Church Anglicans remembered the rubric in the Book of Common Prayer: "the chancels shall remain as they have done in times past," and when Pugin and the Cambridge Camden Society started to build new churches about a century since, they planned long chancels, preferably with a rood-screen to divide the congregation columns or piers, so that there is really no need to obstruct the covered-in space, even if the fanciful symbolism of Durandus would have us believe that "the piers of the church are bishops and doctors: who specially sustain the Church of God by their doctrine. . . . The bases of the columns are the apostolic bishops, who support the frame of the whole church. . . . The capitals of the piers are the opinions of the bishops and doctors. . . . The ornaments of the capitals are the words of Sacred Scripture, to the meditation and observance of which we are bound."[11]

Ste. Thérèse de L'Enfant Jésus, Elizabethville-sur-Seine, France (1928). Paul Tournon's famous steel and concrete church. Note the great windows.

The Guardian Angels, London, E. (1901). Modern mediaeval Gothic church in the Mile End Road. It was designed by F. A. Waters, the architect of Buckfast Abbey.

The solution of the problem lies in a happy mean between two views. The altar is, and always has been, the one essential feature of a Christian church — everything else, apart from the font, is secondary. A church should be designed in relation to the altar, not the altar to the church. If the architect bears in mind the definition given in Canon Law: *"a sacred building, dedicated to divine worship, chiefly for the purpose that it may be made use of by all the faithful for public services,"* he cannot go far wrong either in style or planning,

St. Saviour & St. John the Baptist, Lewisham, London. This red brick campanile is an even more prominent landmark today than when it was built in 1909. Nearly every other building around the church has been destroyed by enemy action.

planning it may be worth while to give the rules laid down by St. Charles regarding the form of a church (*Instructions,* c. II). He states that "it can be of great variety," but that "the form of the cross is preferable." He tells us that "the form of construction, which resembles an oblong cross, should be adhered to where it is possible." At the same time he allows any other form suited to the site, granted the permission of the bishop.

St. Charles recommends that an ob-

St. Mary's, Hampstead (1816). Situated in a quiet backwater of 18th century houses in north London, this little church is in perfect harmony with its surroundings.

provided that, at the same time, he observes the laws which are laid down regarding furniture.[12]

He must therefore have a clear understanding what is meant by "divine worship" and the "use" that will be made of the "sacred building" by the faithful for "public services." This knowledge is infinitely more important than a knowledge of the historical "styles" of architecture employed in past ages, and therefore popularly supposed to be "ecclesiastical."[13]

In these days when all sorts of experiments are being made in church long, cross-shaped church should have either one nave only, or three or five naves (i.e., a nave with side aisles). There should be chapels on either side of the sanctuary, with slightly projecting transepts, carried up to the full height of the building. He seems to consider it very important that the church should have an imposing façade, and gives careful directions as to its sculptured decoration. Wherever there is space, and funds permit, an atrium or open court-yard should be built in front of the church, surrounded by cloisters with columns. But if this court-yard is not possible, then there must be a spacious

Eisden-Mines, Limbourg, Belgium. A striking example of modern brick work (A. van den Nieuwenborg).

St. Francis, Glasgow (1881). Gothic details employed in typical example of large 19th century city church (Peter Paul Pugin).

portico, or at least a broad vestibule in small churches.

REMODELLING AND REFURNISHING OF CHURCHES[14]

It is again difficult to lay down general principles. The work must depend largely on the funds available and the character of the building. The essential is to ensure that the altars and other furniture conform to liturgical regulations so far as is possible, and that structural alterations are limited to parts that are awkward or inconvenient. Churches erected in the past century may not appeal to the present generation, but it is probable that our children will regard them differently. Gothic Revival

Effingham, Surrey (1913). A small modern county church with mediaeval details but completely lacking the essential spirit of real Gothic work.

trate on essentials, e.g., lighting and heating, flooring and seating. If elaborate mural decorations are shabby and need renewing, it may be better to do away with them altogether rather than replace them with work done by artists who no longer possess the spirit which evolved the originals. It is a great mistake to suppose that all the furniture of a church must conform to a particular style. Uniformity is often dull and monotonous. So long as any piece of furniture is sincere and honest craftsmanship and not too obtrusive, it will look well in any setting. Common sense should indicate what to avoid. New work should respect its neighbours, but also express the spirit of its own

churches should not be treated disrespectfully because they have gone out of fashion! We deplore the vandalism of eighteenth-century restorers who tried to turn Gothic churches into Classical temples; we are horrified at the recklessness of nineteenth-century architects who destroyed so much good Renaissance church furniture. There is as much danger to-day that we may feel the urge to tamper with perfectly good work erected between 1850 and 1900 just because it has ceased to be fashionable.

If the structure of a church is still good, then leave it. Worn parts can be replaced, cleaned, or repaired. Concen-

S.GIORGIO IN VELABRO.   ROMA.

A typical Italian portico.

St. Anne's Cathedral, Leeds, England (J. H. Eastwood, 1902).
An interesting church designed in "art-nouveau" Gothic.

St. Margaret's Oratory, Comrie, Scotland. An old barn transformed into a public oratory, with Italian Baroque furniture.

time. A house of God feels much more homely and less like a public institution or hotel if the furniture possesses the variety usually found in a house that has been lived in by the same family for several generations. A church should be homely, otherwise those who worship in it will never grow to love it. This quality of homeliness makes churches in Catholic countries so different from so many of our own.

We should therefore concentrate on altering furniture which does not conform to liturgical requirements, provided that the workmanship is of good quality.

Should a church happen to have a good* example of a nineteenth-century high altar, backed by a lofty reredos, bristling with crockets and statues of saints and angels, it would be a pity to remove it. It represents the spirit of the period to which it belongs. All that need be done is to provide frontals, to remodel the tabernacle so that it can be completely covered with a tent-shaped veil, to see that the crucifix does not stand within the permanent throne for exposition, and,

---

* A really good reredos of the nineteenth century would be such a rare thing that for that reason it should be preserved. — *H. A. R.*

St. Mary's, Derby (A. W. Pugin, 1839) described by Cardinal as "without exception the most magnificent thing the Catholics have yet done in modern times in this country, and quite worthy of ancient days. . . . On the whole it would not have done dishonor to Rome."

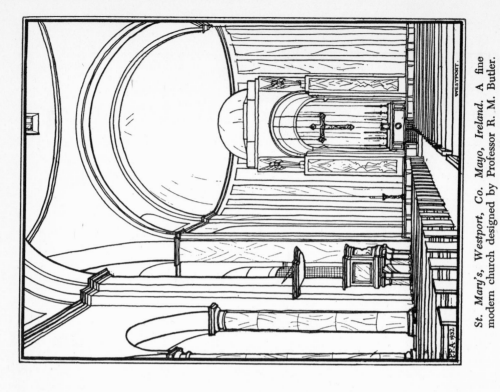

St. Mary's, Westport, Co. Mayo, Ireland. A fine modern church designed by Professor R. M. Butler.

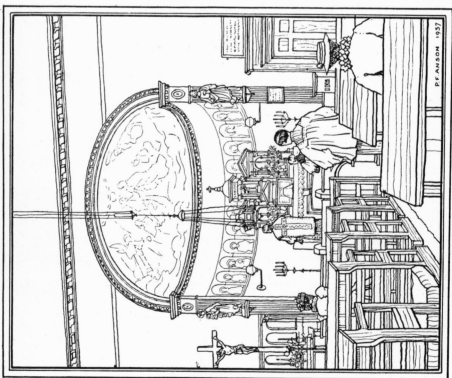

SS. Mary & Joseph, Hedon, Yorks. A characteristic early 19th century Catholic church in England: simple and unsophisticated.

St. Peter's, Gorleston, Suffolk, England
(Eric Gill). The high altar is in the centre
of the building, with seats on all four sides.

always safe to use white or pale cream, rather than a stronger colour. White is the best background for furniture, whether of natural wood or coloured. If the walls of the sanctuary are distempered a vivid blue, red, or green, the result "kills" the colours on and around the altar, which should be the central feature.

Should the windows be filled with tinted glass it is better to remove it and substitute plain white glass. A pale-green or yellow light plays havoc with colours. It is curious that there should

if possible, to erect some kind of canopy over the altar and footpace. A reredos of this type can be greatly improved if well decorated with gold leaf and colour. In most of them the carving is cold and machine-like in quality and will look better when brightened up.

In large town churches it is common to find far too many shrines — some are dedicated to saints whose popularity has waned — and whose statues can be moved or can be removed, especially if they are without merit. In almost every case the statues, if they are plaster, will need to be repainted. The work should be entrusted to capable artists.

If there is doubt as to the colour to use for distempering walls, it is nearly

St. Cuthbert's College, Ushaw, England,
(1884). A remarkable example of an altar being treated as an unimportant base for the exposition throne. Architect: Peter Paul Pugin.

St. Alban's, Warrington, England. This drawing is reproduced, for it is such a perfect example of 19th century good intentions to transform a Classic building into a sort of Romanesque basilica, at the same time breaking almost every rubric concerning altars, etc.!

be such an objection to seeing the sky through church windows!

In almost every case, the lighting and heating and ventilation will need atten-tion, especially in town churches where there are big congregations and many services.

NOTES

1. Leathart, Julian, *Style in Architecture* (1940), pp. 17, 18.

2. So far as Catholic churches in Great Britain are concerned, there was a complete break in ecclesiastical architecture in Britain for about two and a half centuries. It was not until the passing of the Catholic Emancipation Act in 1829 that Catholics were able to resume church building without the fear of having their work destroyed by a mob. Once freedom had been gained there was an epidemic of building, but both clergy and laity had lost touch with native traditions, and mostly sought inspiration from abroad. Augustus Welby Pugin was the first among Catholic architects of the past century to point out that there are funda-mental principles underlying church building. It is not fair to judge this architect by his churches, even the few which have been left unspoilt. Otherwise we may be inclined to look upon him as nothing more than a romantic Mediaevalist. In fact, he was very much the opposite, and, unlike most of his contempora-ries, he fully grasped the fact that the essen-

tials of mediaeval architecture lie in its methods of construction and not in the copying of merely superficial details.

3. *True Principles of Pointed or Christian Architecture*, p. 1.

4. Pugin, *Apology for the Revival of Christian Architecture in England*, pp. 8–22.

5. Gill, Eric, *Beauty Looks After Herself*, p. 245.

6. Schuster, Card., *The Sacramentary*, Vol. I, p. 166.

7. *Op. cit.*, p. 166.

8. Prudentius, *Perstephanon*, c. 2, A.D. 407.

9. Gill, Eric, *Sacred and Secular*, pp. 140–150.

10. Comper, J. N., *Further Thoughts on the English Altar, or Practical Considerations on the Planning of a Modern Church* (1933), pp. 59–75.

11. Neale, J. M., and Web, Benjamin, translation of the *Rationale Divinorum Officiorum* by Durandus (1843), quoted by Basil F. L. Clarke, *Church Builders of the 19th century*, p. 93 (1938).

12. When planning a church for one of the older religious orders, such as the Benedictines, Cistercians, or Dominicans, the architect would be well advised to study their ceremonial customs and traditions, which differ in many ways from those found in churches following the normal Roman rite. For instance, a Dominican church would require a spacious choir, wide aisles for processions, and broad altar steps, for the deacon and subdeacon who must move about and genuflect on them. The Dominican *Caeremoniale* lays the same insistence on the tabernacle being covered with a *conopaeum* as do the decrees of the S.R.C. and a frontal is required on the altar — it must be stretched on a wooden frame and not hang loosely. Riddel posts (*coronides ligneae circa altaris angulos*) are forbidden, although curtains of silk or other rich material are permitted (*Caeremoniale Episcoporum*, L.I, c. XII). Above the altar and footpace there should be a square-shaped tester (*umbraculum*), unless there should be a ciborium of stone or marble. The Cistercians have a definite ceremonial of their own, while the Benedictines and Franciscans conform to the Roman rite in nearly all ceremonial details, though Franciscan tradition logically requires great simplicity in material and design. The general principle is that the older religious orders obey the decrees of the Congregation of Rites in all things which do not affect their peculiar rubrics.

13. The only details given in Canon Law about the plan and construction of a church are: (1) the prohibition of an opening of windows from the church into the house of lay people, (2) that the basement or upper part of the building may not be used for "profane purposes" (Canon 1164, § 2). All other canonical legislation refers to furniture.

14. The American magazine, *Liturgical Arts*, has given much attention to remodelled churches. A study of the numerous illustrated articles, devoted to practical and structural alterations in churches in the United States, will show what can be done with buildings which, at first sight, might appear to be impossible of improvement.

Abbey Church, Nassau, Bahamas (J. C. Hawes).

Our Lady of Good Council, Beverwijk, Holland. Typical modern brick church, designed by Professor Kropholler. Planned to give an unbroken view of high altar from every seat.

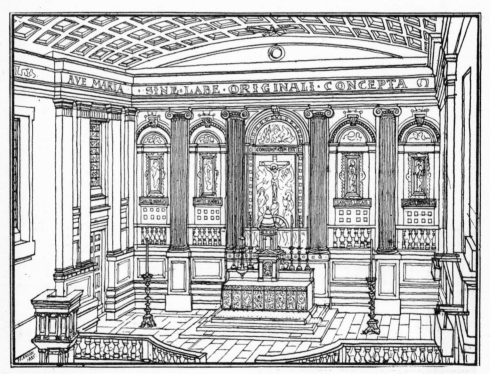

St. Mary's, Wallsall, England. This stately church in the Grecian style shows the type of buildings being erected in England at the date of the "Catholic Emancipation" (1829).

St. Francis, Gorton, Manchester, England. Designed by Edward Pugin, this very lofty church shows the Gothic Revival at its best. It was begun in 1872.

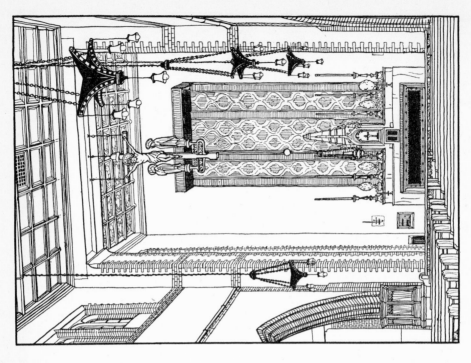

Our Lady of the Assumption, Northfleet, Kent. A typical example of the early work of Sir Giles Gilbert Scott, erected in 1914. Note the unliturgical high altar with the permanent throne, unveiled tabernacle, etc.

St. John's, Holme Hall, Yorkshire. Erected in 1670, this private chapel shows the simple dignity found in many other oratories in the houses of Catholic nobility in England during the Penal times.

The Oratory Church, Birmingham, England (1909–1920). A striking 20th century "period piece" of the Italian Baroque style, designed by Doran Webb.

St. Birinus', Dorchester, Oxfordshire.
A characteristic example of English Gothic Revival (1849).

The High Altar, St. John's, Wigan, Lancashire, England (1819). Striking example of monumental type of Renaissance tabernacle in former Jesuit church.

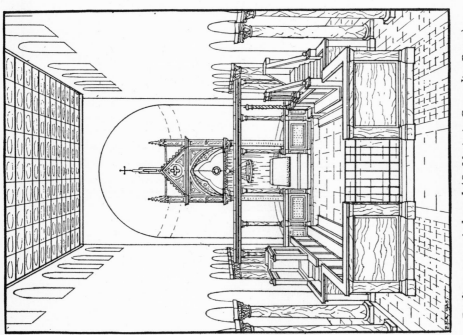

Basilican type of chancel (S. Maria in Cosmedin, Rome). Note Gospel ambo on the right and Epistle ambos on the left, screen, and ciborium.

Church of the Holy Rood, Watford, England (1889–1900). Characteristic example of work of J. F. Bentley, the architect of Westminster Cathedral. Note rood loft without screen beneath it.

The Chapel, Everingham Hall, Yorkshire (1839). The Constable family remained Catholic after the Reformation. To mark the passing of the Emancipation Act in 1829 this magnificent chapel in the Corinthian style was erected adjoining their ancestral home near York.

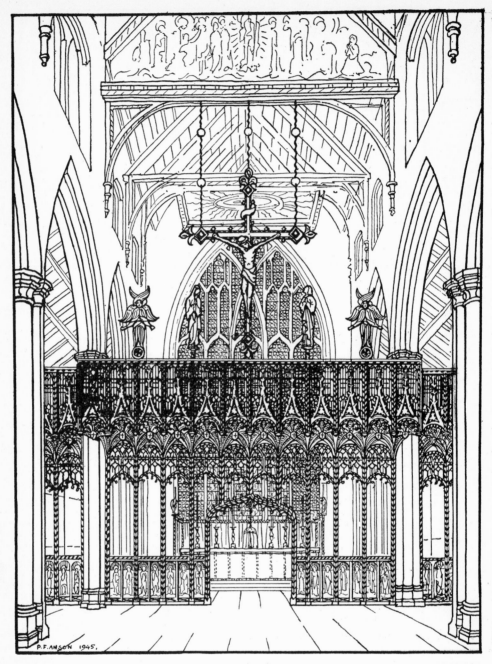

Rood-Screen, St. Cyprian, Dorset Square, London (J. N. Comper, 1903). This Anglican church manages to recapture the atmosphere of a typical late mediaeval building. The screen is gilded and coloured.

Ringenburg, Germany (1935), Hans Herkommer, architect. Mass is said facing the people. There is a smaller altar, not visible in this drawing, with a tabernacle for early Communion Mass, built against the wall that carries the high altar. The large window behind the altar is made of very strongly coloured stained glass, so as to prevent glare.

CHAPTER IV

ALTARS

The Christian altar is a table on which the Eucharistic Sacrifice is offered. Of all the accessories of Christian worship, the altar has always ranked first in dignity and importance. Indeed, strictly speaking, the church is built for the altar, not the altar for the church. The supreme act of Christian worship can be performed in the open air when occasion demands, with no other covering than the sky, although in ordinary circumstances the permission of the Ordinary must be obtained.[1] But the Holy Sacrifice can never be offered up without an altar, no matter how small, simple, and unadorned.* The altar is the *raison d'etre* of the church. It should be made its focal point. In the Latin rite the essential feature is a stone slab, containing relics of a martyr, and consecrated by a bishop, or by an abbot having the requisite faculty. In these days it is common to build a church and leave the altar or altars to be erected later on. It would be more logical and in accordance with the mind of the Church to erect at least the high altar, to have it consecrated, and then proceed with the rest of the building.

HISTORICAL NOTES

During the first centuries of Christianity, the Holy Eucharist was celebrated in private houses on ordinary domestic tables. The word "altar" was carefully avoided by the early Christians because of its pagan associations, and most historians are of the opinion that it does not seem to have been employed before the fifth century. The wooden tables depicted in the frescoes of the catacombs are of various shapes: square, round, and semicircular. Some have three legs, but four legs are more common. Two pieces of one of these primitive wooden tables are preserved in Rome. The Holy Eucharist was also celebrated on or near the tombs of the martyrs in the catacombs from the first quarter of the second century. In this case, the stone slab over the tomb served as the altar, which often occupied a space hewn out of the rock (*arcosolium*), which formed a sort of canopy over it.

---

* The perfect altar consists of the consecrated table without additions of any kind. Such, for example, is the high altar of the chief basilicas of Rome, St. Patrick's in New York, and Westminster Cathedral, London. In parochial and smaller churches, where the Blessed Sacrament is reserved at the high altar, the tabernacle is a necessary addition. . . . [Any addition] may be made only on the condition that they do not interfere with the essential structure of the altar. . . . Very large tabernacles are not desirable since they detract from the importance of the altar itself. . . . Thus Cardinal Vaughan's instructions. Unless they are heeded the present static attitude of adoration, silent and meditative, will be encouraged and our hope for active participation of the faithful in the primary eucharistic worship, the Mass, will be stifled by the secondary one centered in the real presence. Architecture can help one or the other. — *H. A. R.*

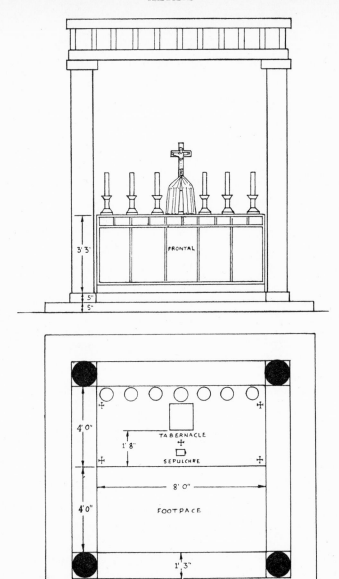

Altar, standing beneath ciborium (civory).
For description, see page 82.

More frequently the altar was detached from the wall and consisted of an oblong or square slab of stone or marble resting on one or more columns.

When Christians gained freedom of worship in the fourth century, permanent altars of wood or stone were erected for the first time in Western Europe. So great was the veneration for the martyrs, especially in Rome, that in

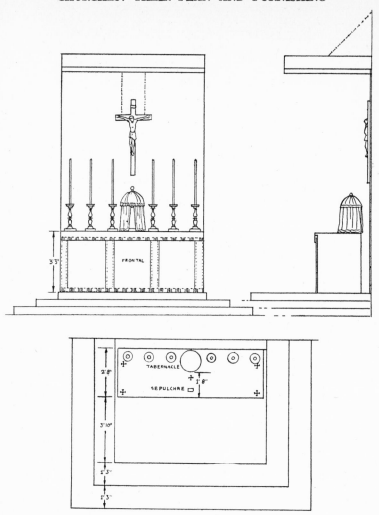

For description, see page 83.

almost every church the altar stood over the tomb of a martyr. It seems that the earliest reference to the obligation of stone altars is in 517 when the Provincial Council of Epaume in Gaul laid down that only stone altars could be consecrated. This rule was enforced by many subsequent councils.

In some of the Eastern Churches a wooden tablet is laid down on the top of the stone altar, thus retaining the idea of the original wooden table. This is the exact reverse of the Western or Latin custom, where, even when the greater part of an altar is made of wood or other material, a "portable altar" of stone must be placed on top.[2]

Nevertheless, wooden holy tables were used in Western Europe alongside with stone altars during the Middle Ages; the altar was often called "God's Board."[3]

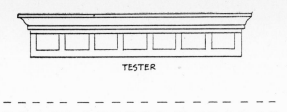

TESTER

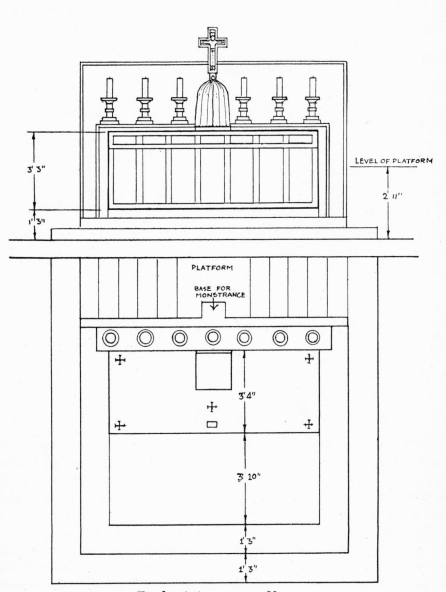

LEVEL OF PLATFORM

3' 3"

1' 3"

2' 11"

PLATFORM

BASE FOR
MONSTRANCE

3' 4"

3 10"

1' 3"

1' 3"

For description, see page 82.

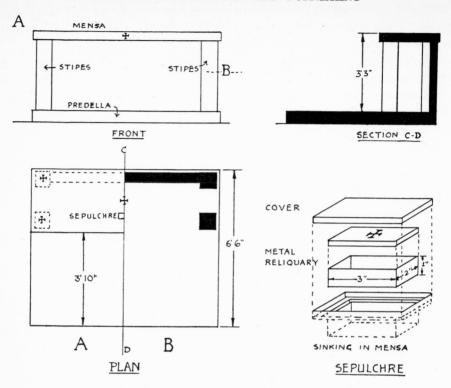

Diagram showing construction of altar.

FORMS OF ALTARS

Various forms have been used in Western Europe during the past fifteen centuries. They include the following types:

1. *Tables,* i.e., a stone slab, supported by one or more columns, either in the centre or at the corners.

2. *Altars over tombs.* Owing to the increasing veneration for the martyrs after the fourth century, wherever possible a church was erected over the grave, with the altar immediately above. The space below and in front of the altar — generally beneath the level of the nave or sanctuary — was known as the *Confessio.* The tomb could be seen through openings, often protected by iron gratings for fear of profanation. Most of the Roman basilicas have high altars of this type.

3. *Tomb-altars.* Later on the body or relics of the saint came to be placed immediately beneath the altar, or were built into the space between the supports. From about the thirteenth century it became common to use the space beneath the *mensa* as a cupboard for valuable objects, e.g., lesser relics, sacred vessels, vestments, etc. This practice was condemned in various decrees from the sixteenth century.

4. *Built-up altars.* From the eleventh

century, and all through the later Middle Ages, the most common form of altar was a solid structure, with the space beneath the *mensa* built up completely between the supports. The chief reason for this form was the great length of mediaeval altars. The early Christian altars were small,[4] often square shaped, table form, as corresponding more closely to the spirit of the Eucharistic liturgy."[6]

Some of the early stone table altars had a low ledge round the four sides, the inside surface being concave. Standing usually on one column they are reminiscent of a modern "bird bath." The

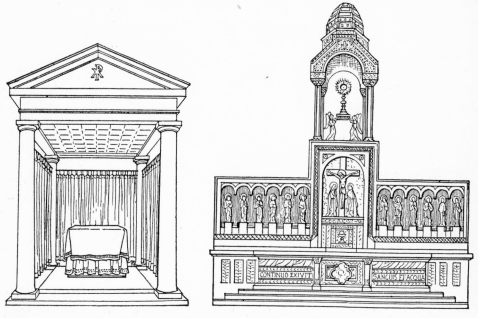

Contrasts. Typical Early Christian altar and 19th century altar (Sacré-Coeur, Montmartre).

but, by the end of the fifteenth century, twelve feet or more was not uncommon for the length of an altar.[5]

Cardinal Schuster thus qualifies the appropriateness of two of the above types: "Each is authorised by liturgical tradition, but since the idea of the *altar tomb* is later in date than that of the simple and primitive *mensa Domini,* and introduces a quite secondary funereal element, so, if one had to select a type of altar suitable for the Blessed Sacrament, one would preferably choose the

"ledge" was to prevent the contents of the chalice from dropping onto the ground if it were spilt, an accident which might easily happen when large chalices were needed to communicate the laity.

About the thirteenth century the custom arose of marking four crosses on the upper surface of the *mensa* where the anointing with the holy oils was made at the consecration. Since the publication of the *Roman Pontifical* of 1597 five incised or painted crosses on the *mensa* are obligatory.

Elne Cathedral, France.

Rome: SS. Vincenzo ed Anastasio, Tre Fontane.

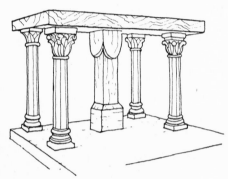

Bologna, S. Giovanni in Monte, 11th cent.

Florence, S. Maria Novella, 15th cent.

Assisi: S. Francesco, 13th cent.

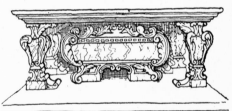

Piacenza, S. Sisto. 17th cent.

Table altars.

NUMBER OF ALTARS

It is doubtful if any church had more than one altar before the fifth century. It is still the custom in most Eastern rites to have but one* altar in a church.

The multiplication of altars was due to the following causes:

altar should be in the sanctuary, but in a chapel sufficiently distinct from the sanctuary so as not to convey the idea that there is more than one altar in the focal center of the church (see Card. Vaughan's Directions, 4 ed., p. 8). — H. A. R.

* Let us remember that even today no side

Tomb Altar, S. Giovanni in Oleo, Rome

Tomb Altar, S. Ambrogio, Genoa

Block Altar, S. Francesco, Assisi

Block Altar, S. Domenico, Arezzo

Block Altar, S. Giovanni degli Incurabili, Rome

SARCOPHAGUS

LOCULUS   LOCULUS

Altar over tomb
S. Ambrogio, Milan.

Altars.

1. The celebration of "private" Masses, which became the rule from about the eighth century. During the ninth century many priests offered Mass several times on the same day. This practice became such an abuse, that by the thirteenth century the multiplication of private Masses was forbidden. At any earlier

period not more than one Mass was allowed to be celebrated the same day on an altar.

2. The provision of a base for reliquaries — a result of the mediaeval cults of saints.

PRESENT-DAY LEGISLATION

According to Canon Law there are two kinds of altars.

Eleventh century canopy over altar.

Sixth century canopy in museum of Perugia.

1. *Fixed* or *immovable* (*immobile seu fixum*).

This consists of (*a*) a *table* (*mensa*); (*b*) a *support* or *base* (*stipes*). The two parts are consecrated together as one whole.[7]

2. *Portable* (*mobile seu portatile*). This consists of a stone, generally of small size, which alone is consecrated, or the same stone with its support which is not consecrated as one whole.[8]

A third kind of altar, referred to by the Sacred Congregation of Rites as *"ad modum fixi,"*[9] is a compromise between a fixed and a portable altar. The altar is a solid or permanent structure of stone or wood or any other suitable material, into the top of which a consecrated stone (a portable altar) is inserted.

It is also stated that the slab or stone table must extend over the whole altar, and be firmly cemented to the support.[12] Five crosses must be incised on the slab; one at each corner directly above the supports, i.e., about 6 in. from both edges, and one in the centre. A sixth cross must be marked on the front of the altar. Where the lower part is open this cross may be incised in the centre of the front edge of the *mensa*.

It is desirable that the front edge of the *mensa* should project at least 2 in. beyond the support to prevent the priest knocking his feet against the lower part. The dimensions of the table are largely regulated by its ordinary functions. An

S. Cecilia, Rome.

FIXED OR IMMOVABLE ALTAR

The *fixed or immovable altar* consists of three parts: (*a*) the table (*mensa*); (*b*) the support (*stipes*); (*c*) the sepulchre (*sepulchrum*).

a) The Table

The flat surface on top must be of a single natural stone in one piece and unbreakable.[10] By "natural stone" is meant marble, granite, sandstone, limestone, slate, etc. All kinds of artificial stones, no matter how durable, are forbidden, also concrete, brick, pumice stone, and gypsum.[11]

S. Marco, Venice.

of one solid block of stone or marble, or of at least four stone columns, which must be directly under the four crosses at the corners of the top slab.[13] The space between the columns may be left open or filled in with stone, brick, or cement. It may not be used as a cupboard, even for sacred vessels, although S.R.C. 3976, ad 1 (1898) allows the custom at Feltre of keeping books in the back of the altar not directly beneath the *mensa*.[14] It is permitted to place the body of a saint beneath the altar.[15] The support must rest on the actual pavement of the church so that it cannot be moved.[16] For the validity of the conse-

Italian Renaissance baldaquin.

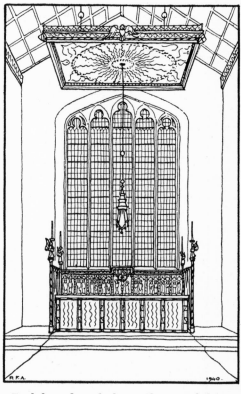

English mediaeval altar with suspended pyx and tester.

altar where Low Mass is the rule need not be so large as an altar where High Mass is frequently celebrated.

b) The Support

This may be of any form provided the following details are observed:

The material must be of natural stone as ordered for the table. It may consist

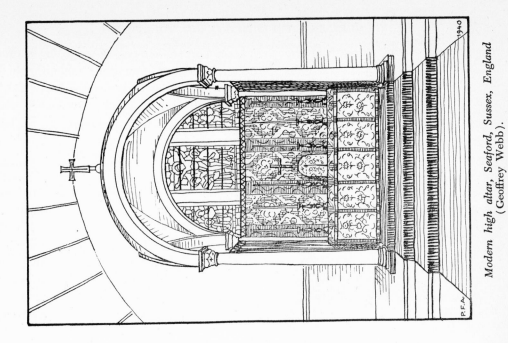

Modern high altar, Seaford, Sussex, England
(Geoffrey Webb).

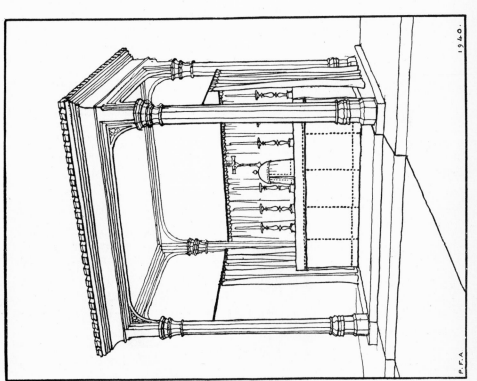

Modern high altar, Braintree, Essex, England (Geoffrey Webb).

St. Thomas', Claughton, Lancashire (about 1800).

cration of an altar consisting of a single solid block of marble or stone, shallow stones at each corner must be provided by way of supports.[17]

c) *The Sepulchre*

The sepulchre is a small square or oblong opening or cavity in which are placed relics of saints.[18] It may be in one of three positions:

1. In the top surface of the *mensa*, in the centre, near the front edge;

2. In the top of the stone base, so that the *mensa* itself forms the cover. This position saves cutting into the solid block of the *mensa;*

3. In the front or back of the base, half-way between the *mensa* and the ground.

The cavity or lid covering the sepulchre must be of one single stone of the same material as the *mensa* if the sepulchre is in the altar slab itself.[19] Otherwise it may be of any stone. It should

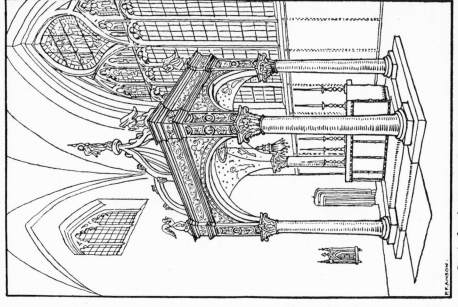

St. Andrew's Episcopalian Cathedral, Aberdeen
(J. N. Comper, 1940).

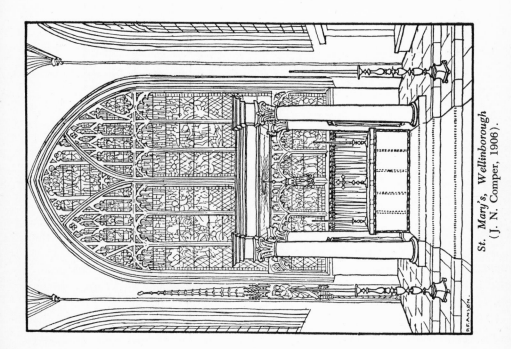

St. Mary's, Wellinborough
(J. N. Comper, 1906).

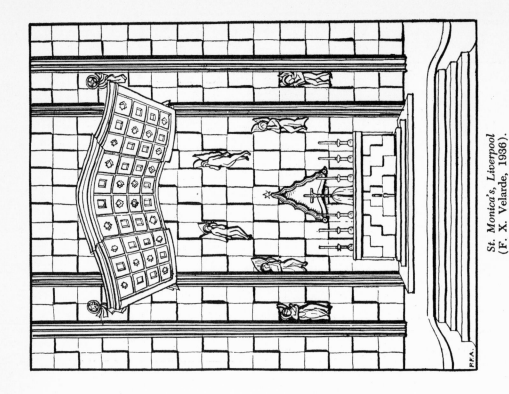

St. Monica's, Liverpool
(F. X. Velarde, 1936).

St. Mary's Catholic Cathedral, Aberdeen (1860).
Typical 19th century Gothic Revival altar.

Church of the First Martyrs, Bradford, Yorkshire, England (1935). Octagonal-shaped building, with altar in centre, and seats all round. The Blessed Sacrament is reserved on a side altar. Archeologically interesting, but rubrically incorrect!

P. F. ANSON. 1937

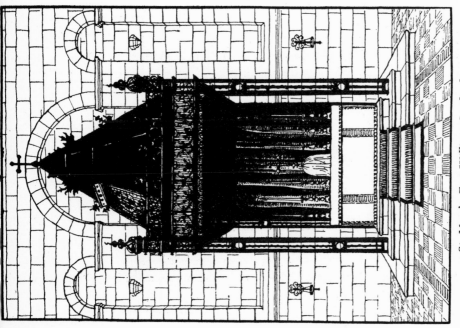

St. Mary's, Fort William, Scotland (R. A. Fairlie, 1934).

Chapel of the Annunciation, Héverlé, Belgium (Fl. Van Reeth).

fit in easily as it has to be cemented in during the consecration rite.

FOUNDATION

It has been stated already that the support of the altar must rest on the actual pavement. Should the floor surface of the sanctuary be of wood, rubber tiling, or any other material not of earth substance, then the altar itself must rest on a foundation of stone, brick, concrete, calytiles, or terra-cotta.

RELICS

For the valid consecration of a fixed altar it is necessary to insert the authenticated relics of two canonised martyrs, even if nameless.[20] The consecration will be valid if one of the two saints is a martyr.[21] For a portable altar the relics of one martyr and another saint are considered sufficient. The relics are placed in a reliquary of lead, silver, or gold. They are usually tied with a ribbon and sealed. Three grains of incense and a parchment with a certificate of the consecration are also inserted.

POSITION

As the bishop, vested in cope and mitre, and carrying a thurible, is ordered to go *round* the altar seven times during the consecration ceremonies, it is important that a fixed altar, or at least the high altar, should stand free of the wall.[22] A space of *at least* 2 ft. 6 in. should be allowed. This is the only rubric that mentions the position of the altar, otherwise an architect can place the altar where he thinks best.[23] Side altars may stand against a wall if there should not be sufficient room to allow them to stand free. This usage, as some authorities point out, is one of those which in certain

*Nordernez, Chapel of Our Lady
Star of the Sea* (D. Böhm).

18 in. on each side. A good average length in a small church is 7 ft. 6 in.

3. *Breadth.* No definite measurement can be given for the breadth of the *mensa,* but a minimum of 20 in. to 24 in. should be allowed from the front edge to the tabernacle — or to the candlesticks where there is no tabernacle. Eighteen inches should be allowed for the tabernacle itself, and at least 9 in. for the crucifix, should it stand immediately behind. Therefore the minimum breadth of a high altar with a tabernacle should be 4 ft.

ALTAR STEPS

In the early ages altars were usually erected on the level of the floor and not raised up on steps. The following steps are now ordered by the rubrics.

places possibly have become customs with the force of law.

MEASUREMENTS

1. *Height.* The height of an altar from the footpace to the top of the *mensa* may vary from 3 ft. 3 in. to 3 ft. 6 in.

2. *Length.* This depends on the size of the sanctuary or side chapel. As stated above, primitive altars were often cube-shaped, from about 3 ft. 6 in. to 4 ft. long. Some mediaeval English high altars were 16 ft. long; those in side chapels less than 5 ft. The shortest altar should be not less than the width of the missal on each side of the corporal, i.e., about

High Altar, Logelbach (Haut-Rhin), 1927.

High altar, Eglise Saint-Léon, Paris (Emile Brunet, 1930).
An outstanding example of disregard of rubrics!

1. The footpace (*predella* or *suppedaneum*) is required for all altars.[24] It is the platform on which the priest stands when he is saying Mass. It should have a depth of at least 3 ft. 9 in. so that the celebrant may genuflect without difficulty. In cathedrals the footpace should be at least 4 ft. deep, for part of the ordination ceremonies take place on it. As a general rule it is more convenient that the footpace does not extend beyond the length of the *mensa* as the deacon is supposed to stand on his step

to turn over the pages at the corner of the altar, and on other occasions. The servers are also supposed to stand on the second step when bringing up cruets.

2. Two more steps should be added for a high altar, not less than 1 ft. 9 in. wide, preferably 2 ft., and not more than 5 in. high. These steps can extend across the whole width of the sanctuary, according to the usual mediaeval practice, which in many ways is more convenient for the sacred ministers and servers, although this means that the servers,

Greyfriars, Walsingham England (1935). Altar with tester and dossal in temporary chapel of Capuchin friary (J. & L. Dagless & P. F. Anson)

etc., stand all the time on the deacon's step. On the other hand, most modern churches have the two lower steps going round the footpace, not only in front, but at the sides. It has been ordered that the footpace should be made of wood, but this rule is not generally observed except in Italy.[25] Nevertheless wooden footpaces might well be adopted everywhere. They are much better than stone.

PORTABLE ALTAR

This must be a single slab of natural stone, entire and not easily broken.[26] It is usually square, and although no definite measurements are prescribed, it should be large enough to hold the chalice, the host, and a small ciborium, if Holy Communion has to be given to a number of people. Although it is customary to have five small crosses incised on the stone, this is not essential for validity.

Portable altars are generally covered with strong linen or calico, waxed on the inside. This custom is supposed to prevent the holy oils from staining the linen cloths, but it is doubtful if the oils remain for more than a week or so! Portable altars are inserted into the

S. Prassede, Rome.
"Confessio" beneath altar.

PFA 12

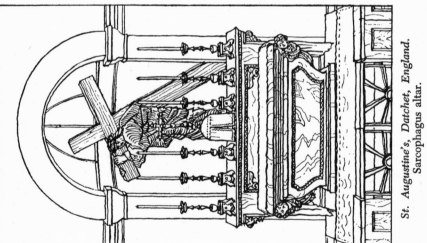

St. Augustine's, Datchet, England.
Sarcophagus altar.

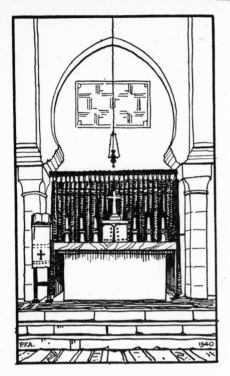

El-Abiod, Morocco. Chapel in monastery of the Brothers of the Sacred Heart founded by Père de Foucauld.

wooden tables of temporary altars so that they are level with the surrounding surface. It is dangerous to have the portable altar resting on a wooden table lest the chalice should upset.

In churches where a fixed altar has been erected, but not consecrated, the best plan is to have a wooden top to fit over the *mensa* into which a portable altar can be inserted. This temporary top should be made as low as possible, otherwise the extra height of the altar itself may be inconvenient to a short priest.

In blessed churches all altars may be portable. In a consecrated church one altar must be fixed and consecrated,

preferably, but not necessarily the high altar.[27]

CONSECRATION AND LOSS OF CONSECRATION

It is outside the scope of this book to describe the elaborate ceremonies connected with the consecration of an altar. It suffices to recall the fact that a fixed altar loses its consecration if the table is separated, even for a moment, from the base to which it has been permanently joined in the act of consecration. The consecration is not, however, lost if the entire altar is moved without the separation of the parts.[28]

If there is a *considerable* break in any part of the altar — fixed or portable —

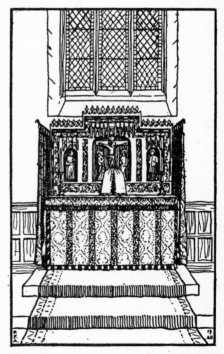

The Slipper Chapel, Walsingham, England. Small modern altar in mediaeval style except for tabernacle (J. E. Dagless).

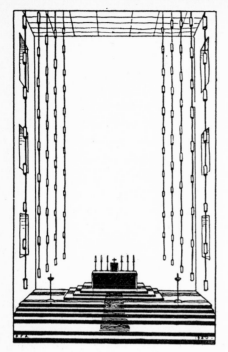

Corpus Christi Church, Aachen, Germany
(Rudolf Schwarz).

would suffice to place the monstrance on the *mensa* in front of the tabernacle. For more solemn exposition the cross would be replaced by a movable stand with its base just above the top of the tabernacle.

On page 63 is shown another type of high altar, with a gradine behind the tabernacle and a low retable above it. It will be noticed that the retable projects slightly behind and above the tabernacle to provide a base for a temporary throne for the monstrance during exposition. To reach this base, steps and a platform are necessary. It is more convenient if there are steps at both sides of the platform. The height from the platform to the base should not exceed 4 ft. 6 in.

Should this type of altar have a civory,

the consecration has to be renewed.[29] This applies, not only to the quantity of the actual material broken, but more particularly to the importance of the part — e.g., one of the corners marked with the four crosses; the removal of the reliquary or its contents in the case of theft; etc.[30]

FURTHER NOTES ON THE CONSTRUCTION AND ARRANGEMENT OF ALTARS AND THEIR FITTINGS

The illustration on page 61 shows the plan and elevation of a high altar in a parish church, standing beneath a civory (*ciborium*). The altar itself is completely isolated, having no reredos. The cross and candlesticks stand in a straight line behind the tabernacle, there being no gradine. For ordinary exposition it

Mediaeval type of altar with suspended pyx.

Baroque (sarcophagus shape).

SUMMARY OF ALTAR DIMENSIONS

High Altar. Minimum length: 7 ft. 6 in.; height from footpace to top of *mensa* (for all altars): 3 ft. 3 in. minimum, to 3 ft. 6 in. maximum; depth from front of *mensa* to front of tabernacle: 1 ft. 8 in. minimum, to 2 ft. 1 in. maximum. Should there be no gradine at least 5 in. should be allowed for the candlesticks and crucifix.[31]

Side Altars. Minimum length: 6 ft.; depth from front of *mensa* to back: 1 ft. 9 in. minimum, to 2 ft. 1 in. maximum.

Footpace. The footpace or platform (*predella*) must have a minimum depth of 3 ft. 9 in., with a maximum depth of 4 ft. 6 in. (useful in cathedral churches).

baldaquin, or tester over it, which is not a matter of choice, but of obligation insisted upon by many decisions of the Congregation of Rites (cf. Rev. J. P. Redmond, *The Clergy Review*, June, 1932, p. 505), there would be no need for a temporary throne. The monstrance could stand on the top of the retable during exposition.

On page 62 is depicted an altar with a dossal tester and hanging crucifix. It stands against the wall.°

° Let us here reprint the directions for altar societies and architects compiled under Cardinal Vaughan, 4 ed., p. 7 f: "In cathedral, collegiate, or conventual churches, where the choir functions are carried out at the high altar, the Blessed Sacrament is to be reserved, as a rule, not at the high altar but in a special chapel. . . . In other churches at least one side altar is necessary, others may be needed if many Masses are celebrated. Side altars should not be multiplied unnecessarily in any church. They are for the celebration of the Mass only. If places be needed for the cult of images or relics, they should take the form of shrines, e.g., a pedestal or a bracket should be used, not of altars." This is clear language based on

clear principles, but how often do we not see churches with a half dozen altars serving as a side board for vigil lights, flower pots, and candlesticks, while Mass is never said on them. With our hourly and half hourly Mass schedules in parish churches, hardly any parish church needs more than two side altars. — *H. A. R.*

Paris Exhibition, 1927.
High Altar in Pontifical Pavilion.
Architect Paul Tournon.

The depth should be measured from a vertical line taken from the extreme projection of the *mensa* to the footpace.

Java, East Indies. Pagan art forms consecrated to Christian usages.

The footpace may be the same length as the *mensa* or about 6 in. to 1 ft. longer. This is recommended by St. Charles Borromeo.

Steps. A high altar should stand on at least three steps, but there may be five or seven. For some curious reason an odd number is ordered. The footpace counts as one. For side altars a footpace suffices. The same may be done with the steps of the high altar, except the footpace. All altar steps should be at least 14 in. wide, with a rise of not more than 5 in. In this case the altar will stand on the back part of the footpace, the depth of both being about the same. St. Charles Borromeo lays down the rule that the bottom steps should be made

Sacré-Coeur, Petit Colombes, Paris. Modern French altar, designed with complete disregard for rubrics.

of stone or bricks, but that the third step ought to be made of wooden boards.[32]

NOTES

1. C.J.C. 822, § 4.

2. It is worth mentioning perhaps that, so far as the Roman rite is concerned, *wooden altars* do not exist and have no official recognition. In Canon Law there is no difference between a rough packing case and an elaborately carved oak table made to *look* like an altar. Both of them are really nothing more than a necessary support for a stone *portable altar*, which is the only essential in either case.

3. The development of the Christian altar may be summed up as follows: first, a small wood or stone table, with the priest standing behind it, facing the people. Then, relics of martyrs placed under the table, so that it becomes a tomb. The cultus of relics grows, and the body of the saint is placed behind the altar. The priest turns round and has his back to the people, facing the shrine. The shrine itself is placed longways — north to south, and the altar is lengthened to be in proportion to it, and is backed by a reredos or low wall. The civory that had hitherto covered the altar is done away with, often giving place to a reredos that extends over the entire east wall. The altar eventually becomes little more than the base of a sideboard arranged for exposition.

4. The early altars were so small that there would have been no room on them for books, candlesticks, or a crucifix.

5. This length was probably due to the introduction of "Low" Mass at which the altar

had to provide an "Epistle" and "Gospel" side in replacement of the ambones.

6. Schuster, Card., *The Sacramentary*, Vol. I, p. 170.

7. C.J.C. 1197, § 1, 1°.

8. *Ibid.*, § 1, 2°.

9. S.R.C. 3162, ad. 1.

10. C.J.C. 1198, § 1.

11. S.R.C. 3675; 4032, ad 2.

12. C.J.C. 1198, § 2.

13. *Ibid.*; S.R.C. 3364, 3698.

14. With reference to the prohibition of cupboards under the altar, Forse informs us in *Ceremonial Curiosities* (p. 9) that in the great cathedral ("La Seo"), at Saragossa, some altars have frontals of painted wood, adorned with arabesques, with a keyhole in the middle, the whole front opening, in hinges, each side, as two doors.

15. S.R.C. 3282, 3126.

16. Van der Stappen, III, Q. 21.

17. Cf. *Directions for Altar Societies*, p. 2.

18. C.J.C. 1198, § 4.

19. S.R.C. 3567, ad 1.

20. S.R.C. 542.

21. S.R.C. 1906, 4180.

22. *Pontificale Romanum, De altaris consecrationis.*

23. It is worth mentioning that altars facing the people are provided for by the rubrics of the Roman Missal. Most authorities maintain that for this reason they are permitted, despite the fact that some bishops, e.g., in Germany, have prohibited them in recent years. A test case would be interesting!

24. S.R.C. 1265, ad 4.

25. S.R.C. 3576, ad 1.

26. C.J.C. 1197, § 1, 2°.

27. *Ibid.*, § 2.

28. C.J.C. 1200, § 1.

29. *Ibid.*, § 2, 1°.

30. *Ibid.*, § 2, 2°.

31. St. Charles' dimensions for a high altar are worth noting. It should be erected at least 2 ft. ¾ in. from the back wall of the church; the breadth 3 ft. 5½ in. or more; the height above the predella from 3 ft. 2½ in. to 3 ft. 3 in.; the length 6 ft. 10½ in. or more. The predella should be at least 2 ft. 9 in. broad, 5½ in. high, and 11 in. longer than the altar itself. All steps should be 5½ in. high, and from 11 in. to 1 ft. 4½ in. wide. He recommends that the altar-table should be not less than 2 ft. ¾ in. broad.

32. *Instructions*, Chap. XI, para. 2.

CHAPTER V

ADJUNCTS OF ALTARS

As we are reminded in the *Directions for Altar Societies and Architects* (4 ed., p. 10): "in parochial and smaller churches where the Blessed Sacrament is reserved at the High Altar the Tabernacle is a necessary addition. Other permissible additions are:

"1) A Reredos, Retable, or Dossal,

"2) Gradines (Altar-ledges),

"3) a Throne for Exposition of the Blessed Sacrament. These additions may be made *only on condition that they do not interfere with the essential structure of the Altar* or of the Tabernacle, as laid down by the rubrics, nor impede the correct position of the permanent furniture of the Altar, i.e., the Cross and Candlesticks."

THE TABERNACLE[1]

Historical Notes

In the early ages of Christianity the Blessed Sacrament was kept by lay people as well as by the clergy in their own houses, especially during times of persecution. Later on the keeping of the Sacred Species was reserved to churches, for the purpose of giving the Viaticum to the sick and dying. There was no uniform method for reserving the Consecrated Species until after the sixteenth century. All that was required was that the Host should be kept in a clean receptacle, of some sort, securely fastened for fear of profanation. The history of development is interestingly given in Dom Gregory Dix's *A Detection of Aumbries* (Dacre Press, Westminster). The chief methods employed before the sixteenth century were:

1. A cupboard or box in the sacristy;

2. A tower, at first in the sacristy, later on at the Gospel side of the sanctuary;

3. A dove-shaped pyx or covered ciborium, with a veil, suspended by a chain and pulley from the tester or "civory" — or from the ceiling;

4. A small casket or coffer placed on the altar;

5. Cupboards (aumbries) in the walls of the sanctuary;

6. More rarely, tabernacles built into reredos and forming part of them.

There is little information about the place or method of reservation before the eleventh century, but most authorities seem to be agreed that the *turris*, or *tower*, was the most primitive. Metal doves (*columbae*) were also used from early times. The use of suspended columbae lingered on in France until the eighteenth century. At Amiens Cathedral the custom has survived all legislation and the eighteenth-century Baroque reredos was designed as a background for the suspended pyx. The first reference to the use of a suspended vessel so far as is known, is in a passage

Suspended Pyxes

Suspended Dove

Dove —
Host inside

'Suspended Dove
with veil

Suspended Pyx, with
Veil and Canopy

Triple Crown
Suspended Pyx

Renaissance Suspended Pyx.

'Sacrament Tower'

Early Box-Tabernacle
(enamelled)

Mediaeval methods of reservation of the Blessed Sacrament.

Italian Renaissance Aumbry Rome

Scottish Aumbry, Kilkeel, Aberdeenshire.

JESVS MARIA

Italian Tabernacle, Modena

Sacrament Tower
Gand, Belgium

Italian Tabernacle, Mantua,

Aumbries, sacrament towers, and tabernacles.

in the life of St. Basil, written by the pseudo-Amphilochius (probably in the ninth century) where it is stated that the saint ordered a golden dove to be fashioned and, having placed in it a portion of the body of Christ, hung it above the altar.[2]

Most liturgical writers are of the opinion that from the twelfth century onwards the usual fashion was suspension in a covered pyx. This was certainly the normal practice in England. The pyx was invariably veiled. There are also occasional references to reservation in the sacristy or in aumbries built into the sanctuary wall, behind or at the side of the altar. This later practice may have arisen during times of strife when a need was felt for greater security.

In Volume V of Rohault de Fleury's *La Messe*, and in Father Braun's *Der Christliche Altar*, there are numerous illustrations of the various forms of vessels used for reservation during the Middle Ages and after — eucharistic doves, towers, aumbries, coffers, and various types of suspended pyxes. The last stage before the introduction of the tabernacle can be seen in the chapel of the Blessed Sacrament at St. Mary Major's, Rome. There is now a wooden tabernacle on the same altar. The original tabernacle is seldom used, if ever. It might be described as a suspended pyx come down to earth.

The modern tabernacle has thus gradually evolved out of the various methods of reservation employed before the Reformation. The name *tabernaculum* — a tent — is simply an interchange of terms, for originally it signified, not the vessel itself, but the tent-like veil or canopy which covered it in almost every instance where the receptacle was suspended. The veiled tabernacle upon the altar is therefore the mediaeval, tent-covered, suspended vessel placed on the altar, for practical reasons — mainly more frequent Communion.[3]

When the laity only received Holy Communion two or three times a year, or even less often, the mediaeval methods presented no practical difficulties. There was no frequent need to raise or lower the pyx, or to unlock tower or aumbry, except to renew the Sacred Species or to take Holy Communion to the sick. Exposition was confined to the Octave of Corpus Christi, and then only during the later Middle Ages. Exposition in a monstrance did not become general until after the Reformation. At the present time, when frequent and daily Communion are normal, it is obvious that mediaeval methods would be awkward in a large parish. It will therefore be understood why it is now ordered that the tabernacle must stand in the centre of the altar.

Yet there are still a few places in Europe where the older methods have survived — e.g., at Amiens, as we have seen, and at the Benedictine Abbey of Solesmes, which retains a suspended pyx; in some Spanish churches aumbries are still used;* and in Germany and

---

* At Zamora Cathedral, Spain, it was the custom as late as 1924, and may still be, to reserve the Blessed Sacrament in an aumbry let into the wall behind the high altar, with a wide passage between the two (Forse, *Ceremonial Curiosities*, p. 76). The same writer mentions "sacrament houses" still being used for reservation at Aussee (Austria); Notre Dame, Malines; St. Pierre and St. Jacques, Louvain; St. John's in Osnabrück, Germany; and elsewhere.

He also tells us that in Santa Maria la Mayor

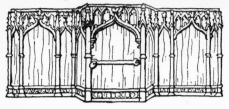

14ᵗʰ century, Germany.   *16ᵗʰ century Italian (Bologna).*

Tabernacles in reredos.

Belgium a few "sacrament houses" — tall towers usually built against the north wall of the sanctuary — survive. In 1863 the prefect of the Sacred Congregation wrote to the Belgian bishops forbidding further use of aumbries or towers for reservation, and ordering tabernacles. This order was not enforced in every diocese where practices which had prevailed for centuries were cherished. From this brief survey it will be realised that although the tabernacle is often regarded as an essential part of an altar, especially of the high altar, this is far from being the case.

RESERVATION OF THE BLESSED SACRAMENT; GENERAL LEGISLATION

According to Canon Law "the Most Holy Eucharist is to be preserved in an immovable Tabernacle placed in the centre of the Altar."[4] The same authority states that the Blessed Sacrament cannot be reserved habitually on more than one altar in the same church, but it may be kept on a second altar for a brief period, e.g., to make it easier to give Holy Communion.[5] The Blessed Sacrament should be kept in a place worthy of it, which is usually on the high altar in parish churches, unless there should be a better altar more conveniently situated and better suited for the veneration and worship of the Holy Sacrament.[6]

In cathedral, collegiate, and conventual churches where the choir functions take place at the high altar, the Blessed Sacrament should never be reserved at the high altar unless absolutely necessary, so that the services are not interfered with.[7] It should be noted that the verb used is *"opportunum est,"* which implies that this is not obligatory.[8] Nevertheless there is at least one instance where the Sacred Congregation of Rites has refused to allow the Blessed Sacrament to be reserved on the high altar of a cathedral, in spite of the reasons put forth.[9] The *Caeremoniale Episcoporum* orders that the Blessed Sacrament is to be removed from the

---

at Ronda, in Spain, the Blessed Sacrament is reserved at an altar at the west end. An arrangement, somewhat similar to that at Zamora, has been adopted at Downside Abbey, where the Blessed .Sacrament is reserved in a tabernacle on a small altar immediately behind the high altar. A curtain is drawn between the altars during conventual Mass and pontifical

functions. A similar arrangement had been made at St. Hedwig's Cathedral in Berlin, now destroyed. The difference was in the fact that the Holy Eucharist was reserved in a mosaic tower of great beauty in a small chapel behind the main altar, visible from the church itself. — H. A. R.

altar at which the bishop is to pontificate.[10] In North America, Great Britain, and other English-speaking countries where "choir functions" seldom take place at the high altars of cathedrals, which are normally used as parish churches, it is regrettable that the almost universal custom is to reserve the Blessed Sacrament on the high altar, instead of in a chapel.

Rectors of churches are ordered to take care that the altar on which the Blessed Sacrament is reserved is more elaborately decorated than the other altars, so that by its very appearance it may inspire the faithful to greater devotion.[11]

Where there is a movable tabernacle and the altar is not guarded by railings, benches should be placed round it.[12]

It is undesirable to have more than one permanent tabernacle in a church or oratory. Should it be necessary to reserve the Blessed Sacrament for a brief period at a side altar, a movable tabernacle can be used. In the case of oratories, a tabernacle should not be fixed on the altar unless permission has been obtained for reservation. Otherwise a tabernacle is superfluous.

The Blessed Sacrament *must* be reserved in the cathedral church, the main church of an abbatial or prelatical territory *nullius,* of a vicariate and prefecture apostolic, in every parish and quasi-parish church, and in the church of a monastery of exempt religious, either male or female.[13]

It *may* be reserved, with the permission of the Ordinary, in collegiate churches, in the principal public or semi-public oratories of charitable or religious houses, also in the chapels of ecclesiastical colleges under the charge of secular clergy or religious orders.[14]

In all other places of worship reservation is allowed only by papal indult. The local Ordinary may grant this permission only for churches and public oratories, and for a just cause, as long as the reason exists (*per modum actus*).[15]

Should the local Ordinary feel there is sufficient reason he may give permission for the Blessed Sacrament to be removed from the church at night, and be kept in a more secure place, but always with due reverence.[16]

POSITION OF THE TABERNACLE

According to Canon Law, the tabernacle must stand on the altar-table in the centre and be firmly fixed to it in such a way that it cannot be unscrewed or removed from the outside.[17] It should not be embedded in a reredos or gradine, since it cannot then be veiled properly (see p. 94). If there is a tall gradine at the back and round the sides, a space of at least 2 in. should be left to allow the veil to hang. The tabernacle should not be nearer than 20 in. to the front edge of the *mensa,* to allow room for the chalice and ciboria. The distance should not exceed 24 in., so that the priest may reach the tabernacle door. About 22 in. is a practical distance.

MATERIAL

Canon Law says nothing about the material of which a tabernacle should be made, but states that it must be skilfully constructed and safely locked.[18] Any durable material, e.g., stone, metal, or wood, therefore, can be used. It must

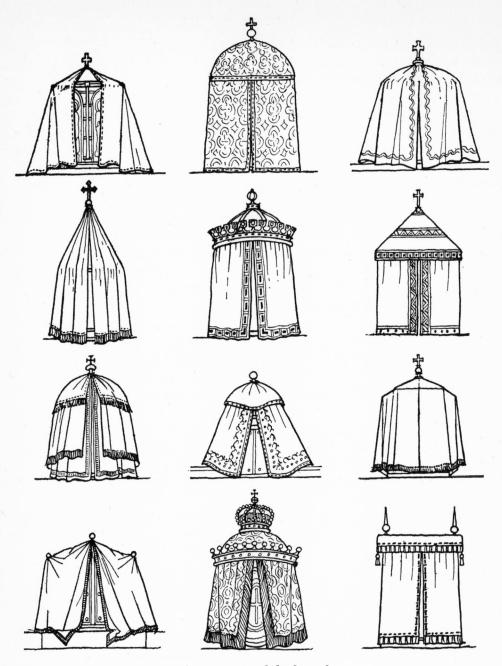

Twelve forms of veiled tabernacles.

however be damp-proof; therefore some kinds of woods are better than others, e.g., maple or linden rather than oak or walnut. It is forbidden to make tabernacles of transparent material such as glass or crystal.[19] If stone or marble is used the interior should be lined with metal or wood. Wooden tabernacles should be gilded on the outside,[20] although perhaps the best type is on the model of a burglar-proof, fire-proof safe.[21] The doors may swing out on hinges or slide back on rollers when the key is turned.

The Friars Minor Capuchin have permission to use wooden tabernacles without exterior decoration.[22]

SHAPE

The tabernacle may be of any shape — round, square, hexagonal, or polygonal.

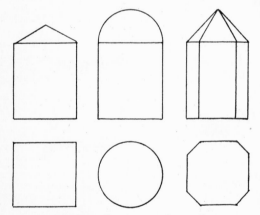

Alternative shapes for tabernacles.

The following points should be noted:

1. As it has to be *completely covered* with a tent-shaped veil,[23] it is desirable that the top should either be domed or pyramidal in shape.

2. A permanent throne for exposition may not be built above it.[24]

Neither relics, pictures, statues, candles, or vases may be placed on the top. In *Directions for Altar Societies*[25] it is stated that, while S.R.C. 4136, ad 2 (1904) seems to allow the placing of the cross on the tabernacle, this is not its correct position, for (*a*) it is contrary to the directions of the ceremonial book of the bishops;[26] (*b*) the tabernacle should be covered even on top with the canopy (*conopaeum*); and (*c*) ought not to be made a stand for anything, not even the cross.[27] If the placing of the cross on the tabernacle is tolerated in some dioceses, it is still strictly forbidden to stand the monstrance on it.[28]

SIZE

This should suit the dimensions of the altar. Very large tabernacles are impractical and obtrusive; they detract from the prime importance of the altar. The tabernacle should be large enough to hold at least two ciboria of a size generally used, also the pyx or lunette for exposition. A good average measurement (inside) is 14½ in. high, 14 in. wide, and 15 in. deep.

EXTERIOR

This, especially the door, may be ornamented in any suitable way. Large tabernacles should have a split or revolving door, so that when opened, the door will not strike the chalice or ciborium. For the same reason the hinges of a single door should be on the right-hand side. Projecting crockets should be avoided, for they prevent the veil hanging properly. The top should be surmounted by a small cross or emblem. If the tabernacle has a flat top this is not practical, although the whole can and should still be covered all over with a veil.

The key, gilt or silver-plated, should be kept in a special small case and carefully guarded.[29] There should always be at least one extra key.

INTERIOR

The interior may be gold or silver-plated or gilded, but if cedar wood or oak is used it must be lined with a white silk cloth.[30] The floor is covered with a corporal, fitted to actual size. It should be changed as soon as it gets the least soiled. Inner curtains are inconvenient and there is no obligation to have them if the door of the tabernacle is lined in gold or silk — these inconvenient inner curtains seem often to replace this lining.[31] It is forbidden to place an electric light inside.[32]

BLESSING

The formula in the *Roman Ritual* must be followed before tabernacles are used.[33] It can be given by priests delegated by the Ordinary.[34]

THE TABERNACLE VEIL

This is *absolutely obligatory* on any tabernacle containing the Blessed Sacrament. The Sacred Congregation of Rites has declared that neither custom, nor the presence of an inner veil, nor the fact that the tabernacle is of precious metal or of rich workmanship, dispenses from the observance of this law.[35]

The Latin word used in the *Roman Ritual* is *conopaeum* — literally, a mosquito net. It indicates what kind of veil is intended, i.e., one which completely

envelopes the tabernacle. Little curtains hung *before* the door of the tabernacle, which have not the least resemblance to a mosquito net, cannot possibly fulfil the law. However, if any existing tabernacle is of such a shape or size that it cannot possibly be covered all over with a veil, e.g., in the major basilicas at Rome, then nothing is gained by spoiling its architectural character with curtains in front or at the sides, although certain liturgical writers maintain that front curtains before the tabernacle are "a gesture in the right direction."[36] Such tabernacles are not "tabernacles" — i.e., tents — in the strict meaning of the word, but are really "sacrament houses" erected on the altar: a survival of an epoch before existing legislation. They are best regarded as "period pieces" and treated with the respect that their age deserves!

MATERIAL OF VEIL

The canopy (*conopaeum*) may be of any material; brocade, damask, or silk poplin are recommended. It may be plain

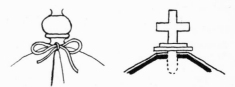

Methods of fixing veil over tabernacle.

or edged with braid. The shape will depend on the form of the tabernacle. The veil may fit tightly, but it is better to allow it to drape loosely. In the former case the veil can be lined with other material, but nothing should prevent the material from falling gracefully. The most simple form consists of a single piece of material with a hem on top,

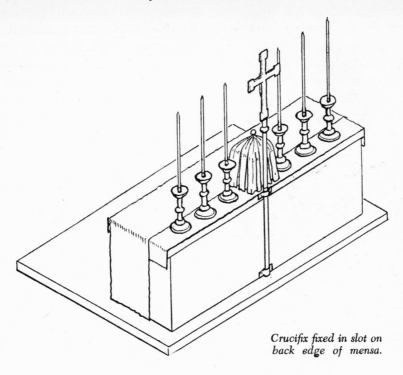

*Crucifix fixed in slot on
back edge of mensa.*

through which a ribbon or tape is passed. This is tied up, allowing enough room to slip the veil over the small cross or emblem on the top. If the small cross or emblem is removable, the *conopaeum* may be neatly fitted and kept in position.

Normally the veil is open all the way in front, unless it is thought better to sew the top part. But if not sewn it is easier to turn back the veil and open the tabernacle door.

COLOUR OF VEIL

The veil may be white, or it may conform to the liturgical colours.[37] Black never may be used, so violet is substituted at requiem Masses.[38] Should a church possess frontals of liturgical colours it is more fitting that the *conopaeum* should match them.

GRADINES

These are steps or shelves erected on the back part of the altar, now generally used for candlesticks and flower vases.

It is probable that gradines were evolved from low, wooden shelves for the display of relics and sacred church plate. They seem to have first been used in France, Germany, and the Low Countries during the latter part of the Middle Ages. There are references to shelves on or above altars in several pre-Reformation inventories of English parish churches, and a few examples of permanent stone shelves above late mediaeval altars have survived in England. Most historians are agreed that gradines did not become general until the sixteenth century, and even then were not regarded as essential.

*Bronze tabernacle in St. Mary Major's,
Rome* (16th century).

Little can be said in favour of gradines, except perhaps in churches where there is perpetual exposition of the Blessed Sacrament, for it is more convenient to place the extra candles on gradines than on the *mensa*. An altar is first and foremost a *table*, and should not look like a dining-room sideboard, or a flower show! The Roman custom consists of a single low shelf behind *side* altars, for there is never a gradine on the high altar in the greater basilicas. The candlesticks and crucifix stand on the *mensa* and not on gradines. Some liturgical purists would wish to abolish gradines, but as they are not forbidden and custom tolerates their use, there is no positive reason against having them, but the obvious objection is that they detract from the dignity and function of the altar.

Gradines must be kept quite clear of the tabernacle, as we said above. They may be used for extra candlesticks at exposition, and for vases, or reliquaries.

BACKGROUND

"The ideal Altar — standing well away from the surrounding walls — needs no background other than the wall of the apse in which it stands."[39] In other words, an altar is a *table*, not a sideboard, and, as we have already seen, a table for a Sacrificial Meal — the Holy Eucharist.

If the holy table is placed close to or against the wall, it may need a special background. This may consist of:

a) Altar-Piece

An altar-piece may be a painting or sculpture framed or suspended from the

Tabernacle on high altar, Siena Cathedral
(15th century).

wall, or a group of sculpture above the altar. When the painting is divided into two or three partitions it is called a *diptych* or a *triptych*.

b) Dossal

A hanging of rich material, tapestry, or brocade, extending the length of the altar or beyond, is known as a *dossal* or *dorsal*. It may be plain or embroidered with sacred images or emblems. It can form the background for a large suspended crucifix. An altar crucifix is not required if there is a suspended crucifix or if the crucifix is the chief feature of the reredos or altar-piece.[40]

c) Reredos and Retable

A *reredos* is a larger form of *retable*, which may or may not be of the same material as the altar. Sometimes it is built against the altar or, which is better, entirely separate. It must not interfere with the essential structure of the altar as laid down by the rubrics, i.e.:

1. It must not prevent the use of a ciborium or baldaquin above the altar, especially where the Blessed Sacrament is reserved.

2. It must not prevent the cross and candlesticks from standing in the same straight line and on the same place.

3. It must allow the tabernacle to stand free on all sides.

4. There must be space between the tabernacle and the reredos for the crucifix, and for the seventh candlestick should the Ordinary sing High Mass. When there are seven candles, they should stand in a row with the crucifix in front of the centre candlestick.

THE EXPOSITION THRONE

The throne of exposition is a small platform with a canopy (unless the altar has one), erected above the altar upon which the monstrance is placed.

HISTORICAL NOTES

Exposition and Benediction of the Blessed Sacrament were comparatively

Silver tabernacle, N. D. du Léman, Vonge, Haute-Savoie, France.

infrequent until the sixteenth century, except during the Octave of Corpus Christi and other special occasions. After the Reformation such devotions, as the Forty Hours' Prayer, Mass before the Blessed Sacrament exposed, and Perpetual Exposition, became popular, probably because of the instinct of protest against unbelief and sacrileges committed by heretics — although the origin of these devotions seems to be found in the need for special prayers against the Turks and to expiate sins committed during the carnival season before Lent. The result was that altars were backed with permanent thrones — tower-like structures rising above the tabernacle, and provided with a ledge, either a niche or more often a stone or wooden canopy in which the crucifix was placed when not occupied by the monstrance. This arrangement was a further adaptation of the "sacrament house" (see page 89). As time went on the throne of exposition became the chief feature of many altars, so that in some churches it is difficult to discern the altar which is dwarfed by a huge reredos, a big tabernacle, and an imposing throne.

NECESSITY AND FORM

A throne is not needed for exposition. The monstrance may stand on the *mensa*, which is the place prescribed in the rubrics dealing with the procession on the Feast of Corpus Christi.[41]

There is no liturgical authority for the use of a small portable throne (*thabor*) placed on the *mensa* in front of the tabernacle. It may increase the visibility of the monstrance in a large church. Should there be any civory or canopy above the altar there is no need for a second canopy above the throne, either permanent or temporary.

A *throne* is required for solemn exposition. It may be placed on or over the tabernacle.[42] It should have a base on which the monstrance will stand, and a back surmounted by a canopy on two or four posts, unless there is a permanent canopy above the altar. In this case only the base is required.

A temporary throne is best made of wood or metal. It should be as light as possible, so long as it stands firmly. The size will depend on the dimensions of the tabernacle and altar and monstrance.

When the temporary throne is placed behind the tabernacle, the crucifix will be removed.[43]

PLACE FOR PERMANENT THRONE

The best place for a *permanent throne*, which is only necessary in churches having a perpetual exposition, is a niche built into or projecting from the reredos. It must not be placed directly above the tabernacle.[44] At the same time it must not be too far from the altar, with which it ought to form a unit.[45] This may involve steps and platform behind the altar. Four or five steps, not less than 2 ft. wide, will usually be sufficient from the same level as the footpace. The steps may be on the "Epistle" side of the altar so that the priest or deacon can place the monstrance on the throne with the right hand and, if necessary, hold on to a rail with the left hand. It is better if the hand-rail continues right round the platform. If the steps are on both sides of the altar, it is unnecessary to turn round on the platform after the monstrance has been enthroned.

The base of the throne should be about 7 ft. above the footpace, and its depth, breadth, and height should fit the monstrance in use. If there is a canopy over the altar, all that is needed is a shelf projecting from the reredos. In churches where it is impossible to have steps behind the altar, the only expedient is to use movable steps on the footpace, which are most inconvenient, ugly, and dangerous.[46]

On the side of the throne candlesticks may be placed, but not behind it.[47] No electric light or mirrors may be fitted inside.[48] A corporal must be spread on the base to receive the monstrance. Should the tabernacle have a flat top on which, despite the rubrics, the crucifix stands, it is still forbidden to place the monstrance there.[49]

NOTES

1. Cf. St. Charles Borromeo, *Instructions,* Chap. XIII.

2. *ASS,* June, Vol. II; cf. de Fleury, *La Messe,* Vol. V, p. 78.

3. When St. Charles Borromeo issued his *Instructions on Ecclesiastical Building* in 1599, he prescribed fixed tabernacles on altars which, except for a few minor details, conform to those ordered to-day by Canon Law and the decrees of the Sacred Congregation of Rites, but he does not mention veils.

4. C.J.C. 1269, § 1.

5. C.J.C. 1268, § 1.

6. *Ibid.,* § 2.

7. *Ibid.,* § 3.

8. In doubtful matters of ceremonial it is always wiser to follow the *Caeremoniale Episcoporum* than the *Codex Juris Canonici,* if explicit directions are given.

9. S.R.C. 3335.

10. *Caer. Ep.,* Tit. I, c. 12, n. 8.

11. C.J.C. 1268, § 4.

12. S.R.C. 3525 ad 4.

13. C.J.C 1265, § 1, 1°.

14. *Ibid.,* § 1, 2°.

15. *Ibid.,* § 2.

16. C.J.C. 1269, § 3.

17. *Ibid.,* § 1.

18. *Ibid.,* § 2.

19. S.R.C. 2564, ad 2.

20. S.R.C. 3697, ad 13.

21. S. Cong. Sac. 1938.

22. S.R.C. 3697.

23. *Rit.,* Tom. IV, c. I, n. 6; S.R.C. 2067, ad 10; 2740, ad 1 and 5; 2906; 3966.

24. S.R.C. 4268, ad 4.

25. Fourth ed., p. 24, n. 5.

26. *Caer. Ep.,* L. I c. XII, n. 11.

27. Cf. S.R.C., Vol. IV, p. 203.

28. S.R.C. 3576, and 4268, ad 4.

29. C.J.C. 1269, § 4.

30. S.R.C. 4035; S.R.C. (1941), p. 358, and (1938), July–Dec., p. 170.

31. S.R.C. 3150.

32. S.R.C. 4275.

33. S.R.C. 4034, ad 4.

34. C.J.C. 1305.

35. S.R.C. 3520; 3150; 4137.

36. Cf. Collins, *The Church Edifice,* p. 83.

37. S.R.C. 3035, ad 10.

38. S.R.C. 3562.

39. *Handbook for Altar Societies,* 4 ed., p. 14.

40. S.R.C. 1270, ad 2. The *Caeremoniale Episcoporum* recommends a dossal for altars standing close to or up against the wall (L. I, c. XII, n. 13).

41. *Rit. Rom.,* IX, c. 5, n. 5; *Caer. Ep.,* L. II, c. XXXIII, nn. 24–27.

42. S.R.C. 4268, ad 4.

43. An exposition veil is essential in all churches where sermons are given at the time of exposition of the Blessed Sacrament. It consists of white material, about 3 ft. square, and is best hung like a banner from a wooden or metal stand. It should be high enough to hide the monstrance when standing on the throne or on the *mensa* of the altar.

44. S.R.C. 4268, ad 4.

45. *Ibid.,* ad 5.

46. *Portable steps* are an unfortunate necessity in those churches where the throne for Exposition is built high up above the altar. They can be made so that the upper portion of the steps folds over the altar. It is important that the steps should be covered with carpet fastened on the upper surface. Needless to say that such steps are not to be regarded as permanent furniture of the sanctuary. They should be kept out of sight when not in use.

47. S.R.C. 3780, ad 4.

48. S.R.C. 2613, ad 5.

49. S.R.C. 3576, ad 3.

CHAPTER VI

THE ALTAR CANOPY

HISTORICAL NOTES

For more than a thousand years the Christian altar retained its primitive simplicity. Little or no attempt was made to change its original form or to decorate it, but, to emphasize its importance as the chief accessory of worship, it was invariably surmounted by a civory of stone, marble, or wood, resting on four columns.

The earliest forms of civories were based on those which sheltered statues of the Roman deities (*aedicula*) – semicircular in shape – or from the complete civory on four columns which stood over pagan altars or tombs (*peristerium* and *tegurium*). In pagan basilicas a civory over the chief magistrate's seat was a symbol of his authority derived from the emperor. The word ciborium (*kiborion* – the seed-vessel of the lotus, with a secondary meaning, a cup) hardly seems to suggest either of these meanings when applied to a civory over an altar, and does not seem to have been employed until the sixth century.[1] It is not easy to discover how the civory became known as a ciborium, for none of the early examples are cup-shaped – unless the domed ones can be said to resemble inverted cups.

Altar civories are to be found almost everywhere in southern Europe in churches dating from the ninth century. There are references to their use from the fourth century, when the Emperor Constantine had one erected over the high altar of the Lateran Basilica in Rome. The oldest surviving example is probably at S. Apollinare in Classe, Ravenna (806–816).

During the second half of the Middle Ages the use of altar civories spread all over Europe. As Gothic architecture supplanted early Christian and Romanesque, the style of the ciborium changed, while the structural features remained unaltered. The disappearance of the four-columned civory was due: (1) to the increasing length of altars in proportion to *depth* in the later Middle Ages; (2) to the placing of altars against a shrine of a wall, which resulted in the erection of reredoses or retables to build up the shrine or fill up empty wall space.

In some countries the ciborium – civory is mediaeval English – survived as a flat or curved canopy, known as a *tester* (old French *teste*, i.e., *tête* – a head). The variously shaped canopy was suspended from the ceiling or vaulting. The four columns that once supported it survived as posts at the corners of the altar.[2] Upon the posts, candles were often placed and between them on the sides and at the back, curtains were hung (*riddels* in mediaeval English). It is generally supposed that riddel curtains are an adaptation of the curtains that once hung round the ciborium.

100

During recent years there has been a wide-spread revival of this mediaeval type of altar with riddels and posts, especially in the Church of England. Numberless Anglican cathedrals and parish churches have what are called "English altars" — a misnomer, as neither riddels nor posts were a necessary adjunct of the pre-Reformation altar in England.[3] Some of these modern examples are dignified and practical, others are as shut in as a box bed. Should such an altar have curtains at the side, they should be made to draw back, and be placed at least 1 ft. from the sides of the *mensa*. Mediaeval pictures show the riddels and posts at a distance leaving plenty of room to get at the altar ends. In some cases too, the curtains are shown drawn back or looped up.

Even after the sixteenth century and the remodelling of the Renaissance, the ciborium, later termed *baldaquin*,[4] retained its importance in Italy and elsewhere in southern Europe. In Spain it gave place to an immense reredos, or *retablo*, often reaching from the floor to the roof and covering the east wall of the sanctuary. North of the Alps we find Renaissance and Baroque altar canopies in France, Belgium, and Germany. In recent times they have been frequently revived, though many have a strong prejudice against them. It is often objected that — like the rood-screens — a civory over the altar prevents it being well seen by the congregation.

NECESSITY

The Sacred Congregation of Rites laid down in 1697 that *every* altar should be covered with a civory or canopy.[5] More recently (in 1846), that at least the altar of the Blessed Sacrament should be so respected.[6] However, the editors of the General Index of the Decrees of the S.R.C. and certain modern liturgical writers maintain that, owing to the wide-spread neglect of this discipline, even in Rome itself, these decrees no longer bind. On the other hand, many authorities insist that the decrees are still in force for the high and Blessed Sacrament altars.

It is still the mind of the Church that a civory is the best way to emphasize the dignity and majesty of the altar as representing Christ Himself. Geoffrey Webb reminds us that a canopy "is the most effective way of expressing honour due to royalty; and there is nothing which can replace it as the most expressive manifestation of the Altar's true dignity and majesty."[7] Van der Stappen explains this principle: "The mind of the Church is that over all altars should be constructed a civory on columns, or shrine of wood or stone or marble or, in the absence of a canopy (i.e., civory) on columns, should be hung a canopy which they call a baldaquin, square in shape, covering the altar and its footpace. If a (civory) on columns, or a baldaquin of this kind is fitting over any altar, it is certainly most of all fitting over the altar in which the Most Holy Sacrament is reserved; and not only is it fitting, but the S.R.C. has established that a baldaquin should definitely be placed."[8]

FORMS OF ALTAR CANOPIES

1. The *ciborium* (*civory*) consists of a solid structure of metal, stone, marble,

or wood, erected over the altar and foot-pace, and supported on four or more columns. It will vary in size, style, and ornament according to the church. The roof may be domed, spherical, or flat.

2. The *baldaquin*[9] is a smaller and lighter structure in metal or wood, or merely a light frame covered with silk, brocade, or some other rich material. It consists of a canopy projecting over the footpace as well as the altar, with a dossal at the back. Any colour may be used. Its canopy is hung over the altar by chains, attached to the wall by a bracket, or supported on two posts like the canopy over a king's throne.[10]

3. The *tester*, in mediaeval England, was usually of wood, either with moulded panels or a flat surface of boards within a carved cornice. A tester is suspended from the ceiling, and may be rectangular, oblong, round, or conical. The essential point is that it should cover the footpace as well as the altar. Like the baldaquin it can be made of rich fabric, stretched over a metal or wood frame, with a deep valance on the lower edges.

In view of the wide-spread neglect of the rules laid down about canopies over altars, it cannot be insisted too strongly that even the most simple church, where the Blessed Sacrament is reserved, should not be without some form of canopy over the altar. Cardinal Schuster writes: "In the minds of the early Christians the Altar could never be without the halo of its sacred nature — that is, the Ciborium or Baldaquin in marble or in silver. The Altar in its entirety constituted the true Tabernacle of the Most High, who assuredly could not dwell *sub divo* without a special roof of His own under the lofty vaulting of the *naos*."[11], *

---

* To sum up: the general term ought to be canopy (from the Latin *conopaeum*) for anything that roofs the altar. If the canopy rests on four columns (or more) it is a *civory*. If it is fastened to the wall or reredos or dossal behind the altar, it should be called a *baldaquin*. If the canopy is suspended from the vault or ceiling above the altar it should be called a *tester*. — H. A. R.

NOTES

1. Braun, *Der Christliche Altar*, II, p. 190.

2. It is possible to find a link between the original ciborium and the mediaeval posts which became separated from the canopy in some of the Spanish churches, e.g., at Palma, Majorca, and at Gerona. In the latter church the curved canopy is supported by four slender posts of metal, with the aid of tie-rods. Much the same arrangement is to be seen at Palma, where there are also four posts holding up a tester. (Cf. Comper, *op. cit.*, p. 39.)

3. As Comper reminds us (*Further Thoughts on the English Altar*, p. 37): "One of the most notable inferences of this Collection (*English Altars from Illuminated Manuscripts*, by Sir William St. John Hope, Alcuin Club Collections), therefore, is that it was unable to produce any definitely English examples of posts round the altar. It also shows more altars without side curtains than altars with them. . . . I do not for a moment suggest that there were no examples in England of the four altar posts; for they were as certainly continental as they were almost certainly English, too. But, most definitely, neither riddels, nor posts are a necessary adjunct of the English altar, and it is a misnomer to call them 'English' in that sense."

The same authority points out (p. 38) that "what matters is not whether the altar should have posts or not, or whether the posts should be confined to the high altar, but that the altar should so fit its surroundings as to look, but for the newness of its materials, as if it had always been there and could not be removed without the surrounding architecture looking the poorer for its absence."

4. From *Baldacca*, cloth of Babylon or Bagdad.

5. S.R.C. 1966.

6. S.R.C. 2912.

7. Webb, Geoffrey, *The Liturgical Altar*, 2 ed., p. 78.

8. *Sacra Liturgia*, 2 ed., Vol. IV, q. 155, 4. The same writer says too (with reference to the *Nota* in the Index of the S.R.C. decrees that the canopies above altars are no longer obligatory): "according to some this *Nota* is to be understood as referring to a baldaquin to be erected over Altars (in general) but it cannot be understood to refer to a baldaquin to be erected over the High Altar, and over an Altar of the Most Holy Sacrament, where the two are not identical. And so a baldaquin, or canopy, ought to be hung over the High Altar of a church, and over the Altar in which the Most Holy Sacrament is reserved, unless a canopy on columns has already been set up above the Altars" (*ibid.*, 2 ed., Vol. III, q. 69). See also, "*Regulae speciales pro Visitationis Apostolicae Urbis*," etc., 1905, ref. "Baldachino"; in *Acta Sanctae Sedis*, XXXVIII, 1905, p. 183.

9. The original Italian spelling is "baldacchino" (with two c's). Since our spelling is neither Italian nor English (baldachino), why not use the accepted spelling of *baldaquin*?

10. The *Caeremoniale Episcoporum*, L. I, c. XII, n. 13, directs that if the baldaquin is against a wall, it should be square, and should follow the colour of the vestments, also that it should be "similar to and more splendid" than the canopy over the bishop's throne.

11. Card. Schuster, *The Sacramentary*, Vol. I, c. 12. Another great liturgical writer, Edmund Bishop, says: "The canopy served for honour: the existence of a covering over, and marking the seat of the ruler, magistrate, pontiff, existed in the general instinct of the peoples; it was surely fitting to render the same honour to the seat of Majesty of the King of kings." Lastly, as Bishop reminds us: it also served for "strict use and requirement: the Altar must be veiled: here was a convenient means for hanging up veils or curtains" ("On the History of the Christian Altar" in *Liturgia Historica*).

CHAPTER VII

THE ALTAR CRUCIFIX, CANDLESTICKS, AND SANCTUARY LAMPS

THE ALTAR CRUCIFIX

Historical Notes

Although it is usually stated in liturgical books that the crucifix is the principal ornament of the altar, it is not always realized that a cross is probably the least ancient of altar ornaments. There would seem to have been no universal obligation to set a cross on the altar before the Reformation period, although it had become common before the sixteenth century in most parts of Europe where the Roman rite was in use.

In the first centuries of Christian worship nothing was allowed on the holy table other than the necessary objects used in the divine mysteries — one or more cloths, bread and wine, chalice, and paten. In the ninth century Pope Leo IV gave permission for relics of saints to be placed on the altar. The frontal was a common ornament three hundred years before that. In the tenth century candles stood round, if not on the altar. The cross was suspended above the altar in some places. In others the processional cross (not a crucifix), when not in use, was rested against the holy table or near it. Most pictures of pre-Reformation altars show nothing on them except one or perhaps two lighted candles. In mediaeval England, parish churches were supposed to have a processional cross, but few old inventories refer to any special altar cross. It was not until after the sixteenth century that a crucifix on or above the altar became obligatory in the Roman rite, and "altar" crucifixes became an outstanding feature in the Lutheran churches of Germany and Scandinavia.

NECESSITY, POSITION, AND SIZE

According to the rubrics of the Roman Missal a crucifix should be placed in the midst of the altar on which the most Holy Sacrifice of the Mass is to be celebrated.[1] This rule is confirmed in the rubrics of the *Caeremoniale Episcoporum*,[2] and in another part of the Roman Missal.[3]

There are two exceptions to this rule: (1) the crucifix may be dispensed with provided that the principal feature of the altar-piece, painting, or sculpture, is the Crucifixion;[4] (2) when the Blessed Sacrament is solemnly exposed the crucifix should be removed, although if this is not the local custom, it may remain.[5]

The crucifix should normally stand on the *mensa,* if possible, in a line with the candlesticks, or on the gradine if there is one.

It may *not* stand: (1) on the perma-

Processional Cross. 7ᵗʰ century   13ᵗʰ Century   14ᵗʰ century. 14ᵗʰ century

16ᵗʰ century, German Renaissance.   20ᵗʰ cent.(H.Rivir. 'L'Arche)

18ᵗʰ century. Baroque.

Modern French   H.Charlier   Audaincourt, France
(Dom Bellot)

Crucifixes.

nent throne of exposition;[6] (2) in front of the tabernacle door.[7]

It *may* stand on top of the tabernacle should the latter be built in such a way as to make this possible, i.e., with a flat top or with a ledge over it.[8] However this is merely the toleration of an abuse, and is contrary to the normal rulings of the Sacred Congregation of Rites.[9]

The crucifix may be suspended over the altar between the candlesticks,[10] a convenient arrangement when there is a canopy.

Should the *mensa* be too narrow to allow the crucifix to stand behind the tabernacle on an altar where the Blessed Sacrament is reserved, the most satisfactory solution of the problem is to use a cross like a processional one, the shaft of which rests in a slot, or attachment on the back edge of the *mensa* or gradine.[11]

The altar crucifix should be large enough to be seen easily by the congregation as well as by the celebrant.[12] A small crucifix above a tabernacle is not sufficient.[13] The *Caeremoniale Episcoporum* lays down that the base of the crucifix should be of the same design and height as that of the largest candlestick, and that the figure of the Crucified must exceed the height of the candlesticks,[14] a detail not always observed in practice.

There is no definite rule as to the material of the crucifix, but according to the *Caeremoniale Episcoporum* it should be made ordinarily of the same material as the candlesticks (gold, silver, brass, etc., for feast days, less precious metal or wood for penitential seasons and Requiems).[15] It would seem that there is no prohibition of a wooden crucifix or candlesticks even on feast days.

The altar crucifix must be covered with a purple veil from the first vespers of Passion Sunday until the unveiling of the cross on Good Friday. During the Mass on Maundy Thursday it is veiled in white. It may be covered in purple or black on Good Friday, according to local custom.[16] But black is really the correct colour. Purple only came in because it was considered superfluous to provide a special veil for one day in the year! The veil must cover the whole crucifix, not merely the figure.

An altar crucifix may be blessed, but this is not essential, and the blessing can be given privately (not solemnly) by any priest without special permission.[17]

ALTAR CANDLESTICKS

Historical Notes

There would seem to be no documentary evidence that lighted candles were placed *on* the altar before the tenth century or even later. In the early centuries of Christianity, lights were certainly placed round and near the holy table, but they were suspended from the ceiling or from the ciborium over the altar, or on brackets round the walls. Sometimes the lights were arranged in the form of a corona or cross, even of a tree or animals. The first altar lights were the processional candlesticks carried by the acolytes, which were placed on the steps of the altar when not in use. This is still the normal position for altar lights in some Eastern churches. During the Middle Ages, as can be seen from pictures and

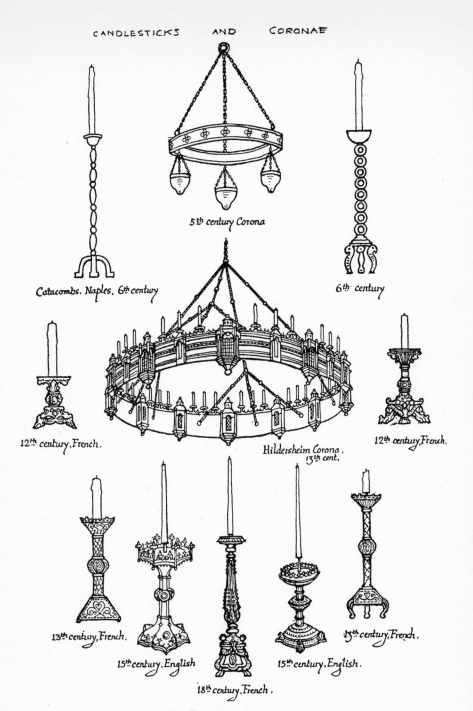

5th century Corona

Catacombs. Naples. 6th century

6th century

12th century, French.

Hildersheim Corona,
13th cent.

12th century, French.

13th century, French.

15th century, English

18th century, French.

15th century, English.

15th century, French.

Candlesticks and coronae.

illuminated manuscripts, two candlesticks were generally placed on the altar during Mass. Even one candle was considered sufficient, and it was sometimes held by the server. On greater festivals the number was increased, and there appears to have been a wide diversity in local customs; odd numbers, such as five, seven, and nine, being quite common. But these lights were not always placed *on* the altar, more often than not they stood round it.

How the present six candlesticks came into vogue is uncertain, but it is more than probable that when a large standing crucifix became the rule, the *seventh* candlestick (still ordered at a pontifical High Mass of a bishop in his own diocese) was removed for reasons of convenience and effect. There is evidence that when the popes were at Avignon during the fourteenth century, as the chapel of the papal palace was so small, the candles borne by the seven acolytes before the pope were put *on the altar* during Mass, instead of on the pavement. This seems to be the origin of the seven or six candles on the altar — at least for Rome.[18]

NUMBER OF CANDLESTICKS

The following rules are laid down:[19]

1. On *every altar*, at least during Low Mass, there must be *two* candlesticks, one on each side of the crucifix.

2. On the *high altar*, or any other altar where High Mass or solemn functions occur, there must be *six* candlesticks, three on each side of the crucifix.[20] Two or four smaller candlesticks may be placed there and used at Low Mass, instead of the larger ones, but they

should not be left there, as they do not form part of the regular furniture.[21]

3. The general rubrics of the Roman Missal (Tit. XC), order that a third candlestick should be placed on the Epistle side of the altar during Low Mass, and lighted from the Consecration until after the priest's Communion. It should not stand on the altar itself, but on a bracket on the wall, on the credence table, or on the floor. This third candle is no longer obligatory,[22] and has been given up* in most places. But it is still used in Dominican churches, and in those belonging to certain other religious orders.

4. The seventh candlestick, used at a bishop's pontifical Mass in his own diocese, though not at a pontifical Requiem, also at a Low Mass of ordination (as a substitute for a pontifical Mass) should be placed behind the crucifix on the altar or gradine, in line with the other six candlesticks.

5. On *side altars* there should be two or four candlesticks.

6. Extra candlesticks, on branches or single, are only needed for exposition and Benediction. Twelve is the minimum number required.[23] The *Instructio Clementina* orders that at least twenty candles should be lit for exposition. When "simple" exposition with the pyx or ciborium is given, at least six candles should be lighted, so there is no need to provide extra ones.

---

* There is no reason why in this eucharistic age this Sanctus candle should not be reintroduced, where it has been neglected. Its reintroduction has everywhere been accompanied by a great reverence and closer participation in the sacred mysteries by the faithful. — H. A. R.

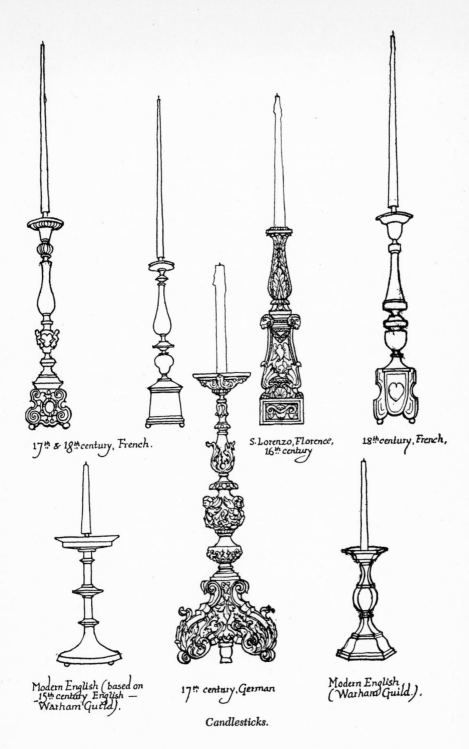

17ᵗʰ & 18ᵗʰ century, French.

S. Lorenzo, Florence,
16ᵗʰ century

18ᵗʰ century, French,

Modern English (based on
15ᵗʰ century English —
Warham Guild).

17ᵗʰ century, German

Modern English
(Warham Guild).

Candlesticks.

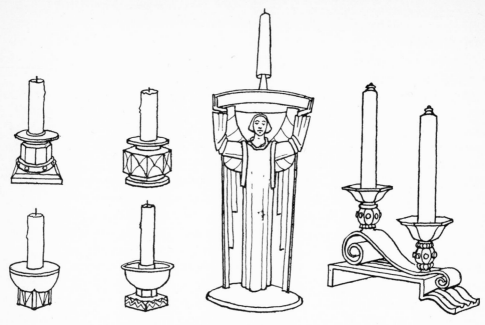

Modern candlesticks.

SIZE, SHAPE, AND MATERIAL

Candlesticks must be single, each having its own base and not part of a branch.[24]

An altar candlestick consists of five parts: the foot, the stem, the knob, the bowl (this should be large enough to prevent grease from spilling on the altar-cloths), and the pricket or socket into which the candle is fixed or inserted. The size, shape, and material will depend on the church and the altar.[25] According to the *Caeremoniale Episcoporum* the candlesticks should not exceed the base of the crucifix in height.[26] The same authority states that the six candlesticks on the high altar should be of various heights, the highest nearest the crucifix.[27] The Sacred Congregation of Rites has declared that this rule need not be observed,[28] and it is now usual to have candlesticks of a uniform height. None of the Roman basilicas observes this obsolete rule.

Altar candlesticks may be of any metal or of wood, and of the same material as the crucifix, if possible. The advantage of wooden candlesticks is that they are easier to keep clean than metal, especially brass, which tarnishes. Where economy has to be considered, painted or gilt wooden candlesticks are strongly recommended.

The *Caeremoniale Episcoporum* mentions silver for great feasts when possible, but forbids the use of silver candlesticks on Good Friday.[29] On this day, and at solemn Requiems, when unbleached candles are used, the candlesticks should be wood, painted black or dull red; wrought iron is effective.

CANDLES

Historical Notes

Candles were often used in pagan worship, and were adopted by the Church at a very early date, almost from the apostolic times. Writers, such as Eusebius and Prudentius, mention the "pillars of wax" that turned night into day in the Christian basilicas. St. Jerome tells us that candles were lit, even during daytime, when the Gospel was read, as a sign of joy. Lighted candles were associated with baptismal ceremonies on Easter Eve in Italy, Gaul, Spain, and elsewhere, certainly from the fifth century, probably much earlier. They were also used at funerals as far back as the third century, as well as during ordination functions. The acolytes carried candles which were placed on the altar steps from the seventh century. The practice of burning candles before shrines can be traced back to the early Middle Ages. To sum up, it may be said that the Christian use of candles in worship is an adaptation of the carrying of tapers before the highest dignitaries of the Roman empire. It is certain that from an early period candles were used whenever the pope or a bishop went in procession to the altar, or when the deacon carried the gospel book to the *ambo* or pulpit. The obligation of using bees-wax goes back to remote times.

SIZE, SHAPE, AND MATERIAL

There is great diversity of opinion as to the shape, size, material, and aesthetic value of tall or short candles. The rubrics have nothing to say on the matter, the only requirement is that the candles used at Mass must contain a definite percentage of bees-wax, the amount being left to the discretion of the bishops. According to one authority, the decree of the Sacred Congregation of Rites,[30] concerning the quantity of bees-wax required for altar candles, may be interpreted as follows: the candles for Mass and the Paschal Candle should be of bees-wax to the extent of 67 to 75 per cent; other candles used on the altar should contain 51 per cent.[31, *]

It is better to use real candles and not "dummies" (i.e., painted wooden or tin stocks with small candles on a spring inside) although the latter are tolerated by the Sacred Congregation of Rites.[32] Dummies can be made covered with wax. The use of imitation candles, fitted with a brass socket hidden behind a shield, is no better, perhaps worse, for the shields break up the line of the candles. But the whole question is difficult, because candles *will* burn at different levels and make a mess, while dummies or shields avoid this!

The height of candlesticks and candles should really be decided by the architect. The cost of large candles, even if they are not burnt down to about two or three inches from the socket or pricket, can be minimized by returning the ends to the makers who will pay for them.[33] On tall candlesticks, tapering

---

* The candles used in the United States permit an admixture of other matter than bees-wax. However those used at liturgical functions and for the exposition of the Holy Eucharist must contain more than 50 per cent beeswax. All other candles used on the altar must have a considerable amount of true wax of bees. (Normally all dealers are anxious to fulfill these regulations and advertise the fact that they conform to these rules.) — *H. A. R.*

candles look better than those of uniform diameter, although they are more costly.[34]

ELECTRIC LIGHT ON OR ROUND THE ALTAR

It is strictly forbidden to use electric light anywhere on or near the altar in place of or in addition to the prescribed candles either at Mass, Benediction, or exposition.[35]

In 1932 the Cardinal Vicar of Rome ordered that electric chandeliers, brackets, or standards must not be placed near or above the altar, so as to form part of its decoration or to complete its design. Both these rulings include the use of candles fitted with electric bulbs. At the same time it should be mentioned that most liturgical authorities permit portable electric lamps on the altar if required to read the missal.[36]

SANCTUARY LAMPS

Historical Notes

There is little or no evidence that lamps were lit in honour of the Blessed Sacrament before the twelfth century, and it was not until the sixteenth century that a perpetual light before the reserved Sacrament was recognised as a strict obligation. Lamps were hung round the ciborium or from great chandeliers, or burned before relics during the early Middle Ages. The first "apostle of the Sanctuary Lamp" — as he might be called — was a certain Eustace, Abbot of Fleay, who went about preaching in England and France during the first years of the thirteenth century, that there should be in every church, where

possible, a burning lamp or some other perpetual light before the Lord's Body.[37]

NUMBER, MATERIAL, AND FORM OF LAMPS

The *Caeremoniale Episcoporum* states that there should be at least one lamp burning before the Blessed Sacrament, but if there are more the number should be uneven.[38] Canon Law lays down that "at least one lamp must burn night and day before the Tabernacle in which the Blessed Sacrament is kept." For this lamp olive oil or bees-wax should be used; if no olive oil is available, other oils may be used, according to the prudent judgement of the Ordinary, but they should, if possible, be vegetable oils.[39]

Nothing is said about size or shape. They can be made of any suitable metal. They may be suspended on chains or pulleys, for convenience in lighting and cleaning, or placed in brackets on the side walls of the sanctuary, so long as they are in front of the altar and within the sanctuary itself.[40] Lamps may not be placed on the *mensa,* or even directly above the altar.[41] For obvious reasons lamps should not hang over the footpace or altar steps, and, wherever they hang, should be at least 7 ft. above the floor.

Most liturgical authorities recommend that the glass vessel in which the oil is contained should be white; this being the colour associated with the Blessed Sacrament, according to Roman usage. The Sacred Congregation of Rites has tolerated lamps of coloured glass — e.g., red, blue, green.[42] In any case, other lamps in a church are better if provided with glass of a different colour from that used before the Blessed Sacrament.

The usual Roman form has a glass vessel to contain the oil that is lowered into the container so that only the lighted wick is visible. In the French model the whole of the glass container is visible — the cuplike base often being used to

hold the burnt-out wicks or matches!

The *Caeremoniale Episcoporum* recommends that lamps should be lit round other altars in a church on the greater feasts, and that they should burn all day, or at least during the times of services.[43]

NOTES

1. *Rub. Gen. Miss.,* XX.
2. L. I, c. XII, n. 11.
3. *Rit. Celeb. Miss.,* IV, n. 2.
Even to-day the altar crucifix is sometimes removed on certain feasts although contrary to the rubrics. For instance, in Italy and Sicily one sometimes finds a figure of the Risen Christ at Easter placed on the altar, or a "Bambino" in a crib at Christmas — both interesting survivals of a not too ancient tradition, though quite un-rubrical! On the other hand it is quite legitimate and legislated for to place a "Bambino" in front of the crucifix.
4. S.R.C. 1270, ad 2.
5. S.R.C. 2365, ad 1.
6. S.R.C. 3575, ad 3; 4136, ad 2.
7. S.R.C. 4136, ad 2.
8. *Ibid.*
9. St. Charles Borromeo's *Instructions* allow the crucifix to be "permanently fixed on the top of the tabernacle" when there is no other place for it (Chap. XIII).
10. S.R.C. 4136, ad 2.
11. See Geoffrey Webb, *The Liturgical Altar,* 2 ed., p. 52. St. Charles prescribes that the high-altar cross should be the processional cross of the church, at least in places where there is no room for a special cross on account of the space taken by the tabernacle (*op. cit.,* Chap. XIII).
12. S.R.C. 2621, ad 7.
13. S.R.C. 1270, ad 1.
14. *Caer. Ep.,* L. I, c. XII, n. 11.
15. *Ibid.*
16. *Mem. Rit.,* Tit. V, c. 1.
17. *Ibid.,* Tit. VIII, c. 25.
18. Bishop, Edmund, "Of six candles on the Altar: an enquiry" in *The Downside Review,* Vol. VI (XXV), July, 1906, p. 189 seq.
19. *Rub. Gen. Miss.,* Tit. XX.
20. *Caer. Ep.,* L. I, c. XII, n. 11.
21. Despite the rulings of the Sacred Congregation of Rites and the rubrics of the Missal and *Caeremoniale* there still exists a considerable diversity in the number of candles on the high altars, and the number lit for High Mass. In Spanish cathedrals little attention is paid to

these rubrics. At Seville the number varies from four to six. In both cathedrals at Saragossa it is usual to find no more than two small candlesticks set on the extreme front edge of the *mensa,* where they are chained to the altar, with a Lavabo towel tied onto the candle at the Epistle side! (Cf. Forse, *Ceremonial Curiosities,* p. 3.) On the high altar at Milan Cathedral (Ambrosian rite) there are only two large candlesticks; in San Petronio, Bologna — with a very long high altar — four candlesticks. What is even more interesting is that Chartres Cathedral still retains the six candlesticks standing on the steps of the high altar, not upon it. This, alas, so that the meretricious reredos may not be obscured!
22. S.R.C. 4029, ad 2.
23. S.R.C. 3480.
24. S.R.C. 3137, ad 1 and 4.
25. As a general principle it may be laid down that large candlesticks and tall candles look best when there is no reredos, and when the altar stands beneath a ciborium or baldaquin — the background being then open. It is unreasonable to hide a fine reredos or altarpiece with six tall candlesticks. The tops of the candles should therefore be below it. On the other hand, a very long altar with a low dossal or retable often gains by having large candlesticks and tall tapering candles. See Comper, *Further Thoughts on the English Altar,* pp. 57–58.
26. *Caer. Ep.,* L. I, c. XII, n. 11.
27. *Ibid.*
28. S.R.C. 3035, ad 7.
29. *Caer. Ep.,* c. XXV, n. 2.
30. S.R.C. 4147.
31. Ryan, Edward, Rev., *Candles in the Roman Rite.*
32. S.R.C. 2448, ad 13.
33. It is not very difficult to join on a small piece of wax candle to the large one if it is thought better always to have tall tapering candles on a high altar.
34. Many awkward problems would be solved if chandlers and candlemakers would treat prickets as normal. The insistence on

sockets in English-speaking countries may be a
survival of the penal days when domestic
candlesticks were used on improvised altars.
Prickets take candles of any thickness without
paring or packing, and save infinite trouble in
cleaning out candle-ends from sockets.

35. S.R.C. 3859, 4097, 4275.

36. Cf. O'Connell, *The Celebration of Mass*,
Bk. 1, p. 249.

37. See article "Lamp" by Fr. Herbert Thur-
ston, S.J., in *Catholic Encyclopedia*, Vol. VIII,
p. 769.

38. *Caer. Ep.*, L. I, c. XII, n. 17.

39. C.J.C. 1271.

40. S.R.C. 3576, ad 4.

41. S.R.C. 4035, ad 6.

42. S.R.C. 3576, ad 5.

43. *Caer. Ep.*, L. I, c. XII, n. 17. On great
feasts large standard candlesticks can be placed
in the sanctuary, fitted with one candle or with
branches. In Carthusian churches four large
candlesticks are always placed on the sanctuary
steps on more solemn feasts. Should there be
a screen or screens, lights can be hung from
them.

CHAPTER VIII

ALTAR-CLOTHS AND FRONTALS

HISTORICAL NOTES

It seems as though it has always been the custom for the Christian altar to be clothed or vested during the celebration of the divine mysteries, at least from a very early date. We find references to altar-cloths from the third century onwards. For instance, St. Optatus of Mileve wrote (about 375) that every Christian knew that during the celebration of the mysteries the altar is covered with a cloth. In the *Liber Pontificalis* attributed to St. Silvester, it is stated that the sacrifice of the altar ought not to be celebrated on a silk veil or a coloured fabric, but only on a cloth made of linen.

From early in the fifth century there are references to "palliums," i.e., "vestments" for the altar made of silk or other rich material. From the written details and from the representations of altars in mosaics at Ravenna and in some of the Roman basilicas, it seems that the pallium either covered the whole of the altar or was hung round the four sides from hooks.

The original altar vestment, like the pallium, enveloped the whole of the table, reaching to the ground on all four sides. But as this arrangement involved awkward folds at the corners, sooner or later the large cloth was cut into two

pieces, or else into one long piece of linen that merely covered the *mensa* and hung down at the sides, leaving the front and back showing the pallium underneath. This is the origin of the frontal or *antependium*. Most of the Eastern Churches have retained the close-fitting vesture of the altar; the typical altar covering (endyton) being made of brocade or embroidered silk.

The doctrinal purpose of clothing the altar is officially recognized in the office of ordination of subdeacons. Here the bishop reminds the candidates that "the cloths and corporals of the altar are the members of Christ, God's faithful people, with whom the Lord is girded as with precious robes." Later on the bishop states that "St. John in the Apocalypse saw the son of Man girded with a *golden* cincture, that is the multitude of saints." This obviously refers to the coloured clothing of the altar.

As early as the seventh century English altars were fully draped. In the life of St. Wilfrid (634–709) we read that: "the Altar also with its vases they dedicated to the Lord and vested it in purple woven with gold." Another interesting reference to the doctrinal significance of clothing the altar is given by Amalarius (d. 859). "The Altar signifies Christ, as Bede narrates. The robes (*vestimenta*) of the Altar are the Saints of Christ."

At a later date the pallium was reduced to a single piece of rich fabric which hung in front of the altar only. There is at least one reference to vesture of this type as early as 800, when Pope Leo III (795–816) gave a red veil to hang before the altar, and which had a cross in the middle.

In the first instance the linen cloth was used to cover the offerings of bread and wine that were placed on the altar at the offertory at Mass. It was found more convenient as time went on to have more than one cloth, and from the ninth century the use of three altar-cloths became almost universal in Western Europe, although it was not obligatory.

We find that frontals were not always made of silk or brocade during the Middle Ages; metal or painted wood hangings being quite common, not only on the front, but also on the sides and back of the altar.[1] These metal frontals were real *antependia*, for they could be removed in penitential seasons.[2] From the Renaissance period the use of frontals disappeared in most places, although they were still retained in the Roman basilicas and elsewhere in Italy. Elsewhere the base of the altar was generally decorated with sculpture or elaborately carved. But frontals were retained in the Church of England after the Reformation, and a "carpet of silk or other decent stuff" is mentioned in the Anglican canons of 1603 as one of the obligatory ornaments of the holy table during the administration of the Lord's Supper. The Lutheran churches of Scandinavia have also preserved the mediaeval frontal almost everywhere. They have likewise retained the primitive custom of re-

moving the linen cloths from the altar after Mass, leaving only the frontal, which generally covers the top of the altar as well as the front and sides.

Although it would appear that the original purpose of the pallium or frontal

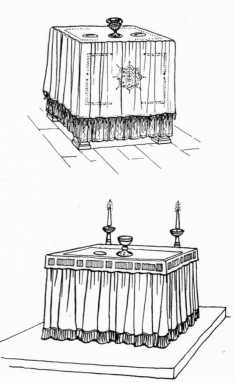

The original altar vestment enveloped the whole of the table, reaching the ground on all four sides.

was purely practical — i.e., a sort of ornamental dust sheet — it must be admitted that a naked altar tends to do away with all the teaching power of the liturgical seasons, and the note of colour provided by a frontal helps to make the altar stand out from its surroundings. It has always been the mind of the Church that, in a mystical sense, the altar *is* Christ, and that, like the priest who celebrates Mass, it should be clothed in precious vest-ments on account of its dignity. What is even more significant is that the frontal is one of the most ancient of all the furniture of the altar. Indeed, it may be said that of all the ornaments now per-taining to the altar, only the *vertical draperies* are original — all the rest, e.g., cross, candlesticks, tabernacle, flower vases, etc., are later innovations.[3]

When one studies the evidences of the almost universal use of frontals in the first sixteen centuries of Christian wor-ship it is difficult to understand why they should have been partially given up after the Renaissance period, espe-cially when the rubrics had prescribed them with such decisive finality at a time when this tendency was just beginning. Various reasons can be found for the temporary neglect of frontals, the chief of which was the desire to display the skill of Renaissance sculptors. "The mag-nificent marble coating already favoured by Italy in the seventeenth century for embellishing altar supports, the effective reliefs decorating the front elevation, the brilliant effect of the marble veneer imposed upon it, made a frontal seem, not only superfluous, but even inappro-priate."[4] But the disuse of frontals may have been due not only to the skill of carvers, but to the eclipse of frontal designers, even more probably to the evolution of a new type of worship that was not based on the liturgy and which concentrated more on private devotions: a withdrawal of emphasis from the doc-trine of the Mystical Body to other doc-trines more characteristic of the Renais-sance. A shifting of doctrine led to a change of symbolism.

ALTAR-CLOTHS

Number, Size, and Material

The altar must be covered with three cloths, which may be made of either linen or hemp.[5] No other material may be used.

The top cloth must cover not only the entire surface of the *mensa,* but the two ends must hang down to the ground, but not on it.[6] The two undercloths, or one large cloth, folded in two, should only cover the actual surface of the *mensa.*[7]

An extra cloth should be laid on the altar if candles stand on it during Bene-diction or exposition of the Blessed Sacrament.[8]

Ornamentation

It is preferable that altar-cloths should be quite plain, without any ornamentation, other than a linen-thread fringe at the bottom edges of the upper cloth where they hang on the ground.[9] There is no actual prohibition against lace[10] being tacked onto the front edges of the top cloth and hanging down several inches.[11] but there is always the risk of its getting torn or frayed, for which reason this is about the most un-suitable place to use such a delicate material, especially if it is old and of valuable quality. A rather better form of ornamentation is coloured embroi-dery, provided the patterns are not too obtrusive.

Position

It is recommended that the top altar-cloth should not hang down over the edge of the *mensa,* but lie along the edge. If it hangs over, it gets rubbed, dirty, and crumpled.

In the case of an altar where the tabernacle stands directly on the *mensa,* without gradines, a certain difficulty may arise in spreading the cloths. Geoffrey Webb explains how this can be overcome: "To one of the cloths is attached the frontlet (see page 120), which hangs over the front edge of the *mensa* as an orphrey covering the frontal rod. It is usually found convenient to stitch it to the lowest cloth, which should be either of coarser linen or of ordinary linen somewhat starched, to prevent the frontlet from sagging or the cloth from slipping. A U-shaped space may be cut out of its back centre to fit on either side of the tabernacle: the whole back edge of the cloth may hang some few inches over the back of the *mensa,* and may be provided with an ample slot. When the cloth is in position, a metal rod may be passed through this slot and across the central gap. The weight of the rod hanging over the back keeps in position both the cloth itself, where it divides round the tabernacle, and also the frontlet attached to its front edge. When there is a Reredos, clips may be attached to it to keep this rod in position. The two other cloths may be similarly cut."[12]

It must be admitted that this method is rather awkward. In Rome a frontal is always formed of one piece of silk or other material stretched on a wooden frame. If necessary the frame can be fastened to the sides of the altar by cords or wires, which are hidden by the cloths. It is also the custom in Rome to have a long piece of wood or metal running the whole length of the back of the altar. This keeps the cloths in position. The rod can be divided if necessary should there be a tabernacle on the altar.

It should also be mentioned that the Roman Pontifical, Pars II, orders that a waxed linen cloth (*chrismale*) should be spread beneath the altar-cloths, so long as any traces of the holy oils remain on the surface of the *mensa.* In Rome the *chrismale* is always kept on the altar.

FRONTALS

It has already been explained that the frontal (*pallium* or *antependium*) cannot be dissociated from the altar-cloth, since it is really nothing more than a fourth cloth which, in earlier ages, completely enveloped the four sides of the holy table.

Obligation

The Church's legislation for the use of the frontal is quite clear and definite. The rubrics of the Roman Missal, drawn up in 1502, direct that (in addition to the three cloths) the altar "is to be adorned with a frontal of the colour appertaining, so far as is possible, to the feast or office of the day."[13] It is also stated that "the clothing of the altar, of the celebrant, and of the ministers must be of the colour conforming to the Office and Mass of the day, according to the use of the Roman Church, which has the custom of using five colours. . . ."[14]

Gold may be used as a substitute for white, red, or green, although it is not a liturgical colour. These remain five in number only.

The *Caeremoniale Episcoporum,* drawn up ninety years after the Missal, add two more details — the number of colours is increased to six by the addition of gold; and the back of the altar, if free of any wall as the ceremony of its consecration requires, is to have its own frontal: "the frontals strengthened with cut and squared lathes called battens (*telaria*) so that they do not appear rucked or puckered, but stretched tight in a more fitting way."[15]

Most liturgists agree with Van der Stappen that "a frontal should be placed on every altar, unless the acutal structure of the altar, either in stone or wood, is ornamented with metal decoration, or precious stone, either with figures, or formed in the style of a sepulchre. Nevertheless, on more solemn feasts the decoration of a more precious frontal is required, or is at least expedient, even for this kind of altar."[16]

But there are other writers, e.g., Wapelhorst,[17] who maintain that the obligation ceases if the altar is constructed like a tomb, or if the front is ornamented with metal, precious stones, or figures. The objection to a "precious altar," as mentioned by this writer, is that on Good Friday the altar should be stripped of all its covering and ornaments, and such an altar cannot be stripped of its *ornament,* at least.

It is difficult to understand why so many priests who are most punctilious about veiling tabernacles, or at least providing them with front curtains (for which there is no obligation!), ignore the rubrics concerning the proper clothing of the altar.

Material and Colours

The rubrics do not require any particular material for frontals, so any suitable fabric can be used. Figured silks or mixtures of silk and wool, provided that they are in bold designs, look effective. Linen can also be used. It is safer to avoid embroidery unless the very best work can be obtained. Even then strong, bold designs are more satisfactory. The colour of the frontal should be the same as that used for the vestments of the feast "so far as possible."[18] This does not mean that one colour may be used instead of another, but that more precious frontals of gold, silver, or brocade, can be put up on greater feasts, even if they do not correspond with the colour of the feast.[19] Or again, a poor church may not be able to afford a complete set of frontals.

Precious frontals of silver or silver-gilt, or of wood, carved, gilded, or coloured, may also be used on great feasts.

There are several exceptions to the rule that the frontal must correspond with the colour proper to the feast or office of the day:

1. It must be white when the Blessed Sacrament is exposed, even though the Mass celebrated requires vestments of another colour.[20] If, however, exposition takes place immediately after Mass or vespers, the frontal need not be changed if the celebrant does not leave the sanctuary before exposing the Blessed Sacrament.[21]

2. The frontal must be the same colour as the vestments at a solemn votive Mass.

3. Should the Blessed Sacrament be

reserved on the altar where a funeral or solemn requiem Mass is celebrated, the frontal must be purple, otherwise it may be black.[22]

In St. Peter's, Rome, a black frontal is often seen on the altar of the Blessed Sacrament when certain annual Requiems have to be celebrated there.

Position and Shape

The frontal should cover the front of the altar, and if the back is also visible, e.g., in churches where the celebrant faces the people, it must also be covered. The frontal ought to hang well beneath the *mensa*, otherwise the priest will touch the lower edge with his feet and rub the upper part with his vestments.

As has been mentioned already, the Roman form of frontal consists of a light wooden frame, on which is fastened down the actual material. The upper part (*aurifrigium*) — about 8 to 10 in. deep — generally has twice as many divisions as the lower, made up of bands of braid, with a broad band of braid between the upper and lower divisions. A band of gilt braid surrounds the entire frame, running along the bottom, being wider than the rest. The number of divisions varies according to the size of the altar, but it looks better if they are uneven, otherwise there is a line down the middle of the altar. A frontal of this type can be slipped into grooves made under the *mensa*, and near the foot of the altar, or it can be hooked onto the corners of the altar. The edges of the wooden frame should be rounded off lest the frontal material gets torn.

A loose frontal should be made with a backing of coarse linen or sailcloth and interlined. This ensures a flat surface. The *Caeremoniale Episcoporum* requires that there should be no ruck or folds.[23] It can hang by small rings about 2 in. apart from hooks screwed under the altar slab. It does not need a rod or wooden lath, a frontal looks better with a 2-in. fringe along the bottom and at the sides — about 1 to 1½ in. deep. The fringes should be of strongly contrasted colours, which looks far better than plain gold — the effect of which is lost when seen from a distance.

The *frontlet* — sometimes called a superfrontal — is a strip of material, with fringe or without, about 6 to 7½ in. deep, extending along the top of the altar. It is a practical necessity when the frontal itself is hung on rings beneath the altar slab, in order to hide the hooks or rod, should these be used. It may be tacked onto one of the under altar-cloths. It should be strongly mounted on coarse linen, and will thus prevent the cloths from slipping. It has been explained already (page 118) how the undercloth to which the frontlet is attached can be kept in position by means of a rod at the back of the altar. Should the altar stand close up to the wall or reredos it is difficult to say which is the best way to keep the cloths in position, but should it be a portable altar, made of wood, thumbtacks can be stuck into it. On the other hand, should there be no gradines, the weight of the candlesticks and cross will help to keep the cloths straight. It is forbidden to *fix* wooden frames on the altar to keep the cloths in position.[24]

Another method is to hang frontals

back to back on rods, giving two to each rod. They hang on iron pieces, fixed to the masonry. Superfrontals can also be fixed by large dress studs to a cloth under the altar-cloths. This makes them very easy to change.

It is doubtful if the frontlet need conform to the colour of the frontals, and for the sake of convenience and economy a plain red frontlet will suffice for ordinary occasions — red being the colour that will go best with white, green, and purple. Roman frontals do not need a frontlet, for they preserve a relic of it in the strip of gold lace with a fringe below it which traverses the width of the frontal. For this reason they are much more practical and convenient. Moreover, Roman frontals usually come up to the level of the top of the *mensa*.

THE ALTAR-COVER

A dust cover of coloured linen or other richer material is needed for every altar. It should tone with the hangings or decorations round the altar. The altar-cover is not a liturgical ornament and should be as inconspicuous as possible. It should be made a little longer than the *mensa* and should hang down a few inches at the sides, also in front if the altar-cloth hangs over the edge. In this case it is permissible, but not generally recommended, that the edges are scalloped, embroidered, or ornamented with fringes. A violet cloth is appropriate for penitential seasons.[25] Some liturgical writers maintain that green is the "correct" colour for ordinary occasions.

Small Linen Cloths

Besides the three large linen cloths covering the *mensa* there are certain small linen cloths which are used in connection with the altar at Mass.

1. *The Corporal.* The corporal (from *corpus, corporalis* — the body, concerning the body) is the cloth on which the Sacramental Species lies during the Mass. It is a linen cloth, about 18 or 20 in. square, upon which are placed the chalice and the Sacred Host. In the early ages of Christianity, when altars were much smaller than they are now, the corporal covered the entire altar slab, and was really the only altar-cloth. The back part was drawn up over the chalice when it had to be veiled. About the eleventh or twelfth century, when very large corporals were still in use, it became the custom to cut them up into two pieces of linen, so that there were actually two corporals. The second corporal served to cover the Host and chalice. By degrees this corporal was reduced to its present size, and eventually became nothing more than a small piece of starched linen which could be laid on the top of the chalice. It is interesting to note that the Carthusians have always retained a single large corporal which is drawn up at the back over the chalice, as in early days, and this is also the custom in the ancient rite of Lyons, in France. It was only after the corporal had been reduced in size that the three altar-cloths, now prescribed, came into use.

The corporal must be made of pure linen. It is better that it should be left quite plain, except for a small, centred cross embroidered in front, although even this is not necessary. Decoration on a corporal makes it difficult to purify if a Host has been standing on that part. After it has been washed, a corporal is folded into three equal parts always inwards, so that any fragment of the Host may be enclosed within it.

2. *The Pall.* The pall (from *palla,* a mantle — originally a veil or piece of stuff) is really a simplified and conventionalized form of the second corporal, which, during the Middle Ages, was placed on the top of the chalice instead of using part of the large corporal of earlier times.

The pall must be about 5 or 6 in. square, and is best made of a piece of linen folded twice or three times and well starched, so that it can support the chalice veil without being bent. The custom of putting a piece of cardboard or celluloid inside a pall to make it stiff is not recommended. The undersurface must be left quite plain, but it is permissible to put embroidery on the upper side. It is, however, better to leave both sides plain. Lace, sewn round the edges of both corporal and pall, is not actually prohibited, but is a doubtful addition. The same applies to cord sewn round the edges of the pall, which is, however, better than lace.

In Rome the pall is merely a square of single linen, highly starched, and surrounded by a narrow band of lace, also starched.

3. *The Purificator.* The purificator is a small linen cloth used for cleansing the chalice. It superseded the maniple which was originally used for this purpose (see page 187). The rubrics do not lay down any definite size, but a purificator is usually from 12 to 18 in. long and from 9 to 10 in. wide. It is folded in three lengths when not in use. In churches where the finger towels are about the same size as the purificators, it is a good thing to have a small cross sewn on the latter so that the two can be easily distinguished.

4. *The Finger Towel.* The finger towel, or Lavabo cloth (*manutergium*), may be of any size, but it is better to have it rather large than too small. A small cloth remains wet if in frequent use, and a real towel — about 20 in. by 16 in. — is much more convenient. But there is no reason why it should not be even larger. Finger towels are sometimes folded in three, like purificators. Neither is blessed before use.

5. *The Communion Cloth.* Since the obligation of having a metal communion plate came into force in 1929, it has been supposed by many persons that there is no longer any need to retain the linen cloth which is prescribed in the rubrics of the Missal, X, n. 6, and the *Caeremoniale Episcoporum,* L. II, c. XXIX, n. 3, to hang over the communion rails, or to be held beneath the chin of those who kneel to receive Holy Communion. No definite instructions having been issued to the contrary, it seems reasonable to continue to use the communion cloth as formerly, at least to cover the rails.

NOTES

1. The papal altar at St. Peter's still has two frontals, one on each side.

2. Metal or carved wooden frontals are still fairly common in Italy, e.g., St. Mark's, Venice.

3. For the history of altar-cloths and frontals, see Joseph Braun, S.J., *Der Christliche Altar*, Vol. II, pp. 9–125.

4. Braun, *op. cit.*, Vol. II, p. 31.

5. S.R.C. 2600, 3868.

6. *Rub. Gen. Miss.*, V, XX; S.R.C. 4029, ad 5 (1899).

7. *Rub. Gen. Miss.*, XX.

8. De Herdt, I, n. 179.

9. Roman tradition does not favour a linen-thread fringe at bottom edges of upper cloth, although the papal altar at St. Peter's has this in gold thread.

10. S.R.C. 3191.

11. In the Roman basilicas the altar-cloths do not hang over the front, but are level with the top of the *mensa*.

12. Webb, Geoffrey, *The Liturgical Altar*, p. 72.

13. *Rub. Gen. Miss.*, Tit. XX.

14. *Ibid.*, Tit. XVIII, 1.

15. *Caer. Ep.*, L. I, c. XII, n. 11.

16. *Sacra Liturgia*, 2 ed., Vol. III, Q. 44.

17. *Compendium Sacrae Liturgiae* (1931), p. 29.

18. *Rub. Gen. Miss.*, Tit. XX.

19. Van der Stappen, III, Q. 43.

20. S.R.C. 1615, ad 7.

21. S.R.C. 2673.

22. S.R.C. 3201, ad 10; 3562.

23. *Caer. Ep.*, L. I, c. XII, n. II.

24. *Ibid.*, L. I, c. XIII, n. 11; S.R.C. 4213, ad 1; 4253, ad 1, 2.

25. *Caer. Ep.*, L. I, c. XII, nn. 8, 16.

CHAPTER IX

ALTAR FURNITURE

I. RELIQUARIES

Historical Notes

During the Middle Ages the veneration of relics of the saints developed to such an extent that again and again the Church had to step in to prevent superstitious abuses which had risen. The cult led to the making of magnificent vessels for holding relics. Sometimes they were in the shape of a coffer, in other instances, one finds triptychs, lanterns, small castles, or cylinders of crystal. In the case of a whole body of a saint, it lay in a great tomb-like structure, very often placed behind the high altar of a cathedral or large church, e.g., the still existent shrine of St. Edward the Confessor in Westminster Abbey. On great festivals all the relics possessed by a church would be brought out and displayed either on or above the altars.

Authentification and Approbation of Relics

According to Canon Law[1] documents of authenticity and approbation must be obtained before a relic can be venerated. The former can be issued by cardinals and local Ordinaries, and a bishop can delegate this power to the vicar-general by a special and express mandate. The latter has to be obtained from the local Ordinary, and a bishop may reject relics if he doubts their genuineness.[2]

Use of Relics

The presence of relics on altars is recognised in the rubrics of the Roman Missal where they deal with the incensation of the altar at Mass.[3] Together with flowers, relics form the "occasional decoration of an altar."[4] The *Caeremoniale Episcoporum*[5] says that reliquaries "may be placed between the candlesticks so long as the length of the altar allows it." From this wording it would appear that there should not be normally more than four reliquaries on the high altar, and they should only be used as ornaments on feast days.

Relics of the cross and passion must be kept separate from other relics, and given a special place of honour.[6] When relics are exposed, at least two lights must be burning.[7] Reliquaries should therefore be covered with small cloths when standing on the altar and the ordinary candles are not lit. No relics may be placed on top of the tabernacle or in front of it.[8] They may not be exposed on the same altar where the Blessed Sacrament is exposed, nor venerated during exposition.[9]

Reliquaries: Form and Material

Reliquaries may be of any suitable material — metal or wood. The only prescription regarding their form is that they should not resemble too closely the

124

monstrance in which the Blessed Sacrament is exposed.[10] They can also be made in the shape of small busts or statues. Their size should conform with that of the candlesticks on the altar.

II. FLOWERS

Historical Notes

Floral decorations seem to have been used in Christian churches from an early period, but they were confined to garlands hung from the walls and columns, or strewn upon the floor. During the Middle Ages it was a common custom to strew sweet-smelling herbs, such as rosemary or bay leaves, on the pavement. So far as it is known, the first reference to flower vases as part of the furniture of the altar appears in the *Caeremoniale Episcoporum* (cap. XII), first issued by Clement VIII in 1600. But all it says is that "on very great feasts, garlands of flowers may be used to decorate the ciborium of the Altar and the doors of the Church," and that "vases may be used on the altar, too, carefully decorated with blossoms, and leaves of sweet fragrance or artificially made of silk."[11] There is another reference to floral decorations in the *Memoriale Rituum,* drawn up by Benedict XIII in 1725. Here we are informed that "if customary, flowers may be used on the altar for the Mass on the Feast of the Purification, on Maundy Thursday[12] and on Holy Saturday,[13] and for the decoration of the 'altar of repose' on Maundy Thursday." The general rubrics of the Missal say that "nothing whatsoever is to be put on the altar which does not pertain to the sacrifice of the Mass, or to the ornamentation of the altar

itself." Flowers cannot be included in this category.[14] Apart from the authorities given above there is no mention of flowers on the altar in any liturgical books.

Use

"Flowers should be used in church and especially on the altar (particularly the high altar) with the *greatest restraint.* They are an ornament — and, though they may be and are very beautiful, they are entirely subsidiary — and their use is intended to mark a special degree of festivity. It is very unbecoming to make the altar — which, as the hallowed stone of sacrifice and the dwelling place of God under the Sacramental Species, should be a place of awe and dignity — a mere stand for flowers."[15]

The proper place for vases of flowers on the altar is between the candlesticks.[16] Should there be a gradine it is preferable to stand the vases on it rather than on the *mensa.*[17] Vases must not be placed on the top of the tabernacle or in front of the door.[18]

But it should be remembered that flowers are offerings, not mere decorations. Their position should indicate this. They should stand before or round the altar — not on it.

In Roman basilicas there are no flowers on the altars, but masses of them adorn the *confessio* on feast days of the martyrs buried below the high altar.

Vases: Shape and Material

It cannot be insisted on too strongly that there is no special reason to use *brass* vases on altars. Plain glass or earthenware vases are much less obtrusive. A flower vase is not a "sacred vessel" even when it is used on the altar, otherwise it would have to be blessed!

Although they are going out of fashion, tin holders for flowers are still used in some churches. They should be avoided.*

Arrangement of Flowers. Flowers should be arranged in bold masses, and with a conservative amount of green. They look best when they are arranged naturally and gracefully, not packed tightly together. Some species of flowers are quite unsuited for altar decoration because they are too small or fade quickly. Their life can be prolonged by (*a*) adding a pinch of salt to the water, (*b*)clipping the end of the stems each day, (*c*) crushing the stems with a mallet (in the case of flowers or foliage that need to absorb much water).[19] There is no reason why the flowers should conform to the liturgical colours of the feast. As a matter of fact, it looks

—————

* Many liturgical authors, e.g., Van der Stappen, III, 62, III, maintain that no potted flowers ought to be used on the altar. (They all seem to agree that they are permissible on the floor of the sanctuary near the altar.) There seem to be valid reasons for this objection, one practical and one symbolical. A flower pot may contain more than the plant — namely worms and insects and remnants of fertilizer, thus for practical reasons a flower pot seems to be out of place. As to the symbolical value, may we point to the beautiful symbolism of the burning candle that consumes itself while it sheds its warm light, an idea no electric bulb can render plausible. The cut flower, too, has more of the self-sacrificing idea than a growing potted flower. The finality of the gift of flowers, too, is better expressed in cut flowers than in the pot which can be taken to the greenhouse for more production. — *H. A. R.*

much better if red, yellow, or blue flowers are used when there are white vestments, tabernacle veil, and frontal.

Other Places for Flowers

The high altar will really look more dignified if flowers are not placed on the *mensa* or gradine, but on either side of it. A few large earthenware vases, or jars, standing on the pavement or on low stools are an effective decoration on great festivals. Vases may also stand on the window sills and ledges. They may be used to decorate round the font or be placed at the ends of the communion rails.

Artificial Flowers

The *Caeremoniale Episcoporum* sanctions the use of artificial flowers on the altar,[20] but an Instruction of the cardinal vicar for the churches in Rome dated June, 1932, definitely forbids the use of artificial flowers of whatever material, bronze, cloth, brass, earthenware, and orders their removal from churches and oratories. This order applies only to Rome, so there is no positive reason against artificial flowers if it is desired to use them. But they should be well made — the *Caeremoniale Episcoporum* implies that the material should be silk,[21] and cheap paper or calico flowers should be avoided. The best artificial flowers are of metal or gilded wood. They look very effective, and last longer than those made of silk.

Prohibition of Flowers on Altars

Flowers are not allowed on altars during: 1. solemn requiem Masses and funeral ceremonies;[22] 2. Advent and Lent,[23] except on:

a) The third Sunday of Advent (Gaudete Sunday);[24]

b) The fourth Sunday of Lent (Laetare Sunday);[25]

c) The Mass on Holy Thursday and at the altar of repose;[26]

d) The Mass on Holy Saturday;[27]

e) The First Communion of children;[28]

f) During the Forty Hours' Prayer.

III. STATUES

Statues or images of the saints are recommended in the *Caeremoniale Episcoporum* as suitable ornaments to be placed on or above the altar on greater feasts. But it is stated that they should be of silver or some other precious metal, and of suitable size.[29] This would seem to exclude large plaster figures from being displayed on or above the altar. Statues — like reliquaries — should normally stand between the six candlesticks on the high altar. Statues may not be placed on top of the tabernacle.[30]

With regard to statues and images in other parts of the church as well as those which may be placed on or above the altar, it is worth quoting Canon Law: "It is never lawful to exhibit in church, even those of exempt religious, an unusual (*insolitam*) image, unless the approval of the Ordinary has first been obtained.[31]

"The Ordinary shall never allow any sacred images to be publicly displayed for the veneration of the faithful, unless these images are in keeping with the approved practice of the Church." By the word "unusual" is meant an image that represents persons or events in a manner which has no justification either in Holy Scripture or Tradition. It refers more to the details of the composition rather than to the style of painting or carving or the medium used by the craftsman. For instance, it is not allowed to display publicly pictures of the Sacred Heart of Jesus alone without the rest of the body, although such pictures are tolerated for private devotion.[32] Statues of our Lady, dressed in priestly vestments, also come under the ban of "unusual images"; so, too, the Blessed Trinity depicted as a man with three hands, or by a man with two heads and a dove between them; or the Holy Ghost in human form.[33] On the other hand statues of our Lady are often vested in copes, which although not a "priestly vestment," might appear so to the uninitiated!

Lastly, the Ordinary must never allow images to be displayed in church which may encourage false doctrine or which offend against decency, or which are capable of leading the ignorant into dangerous errors — e.g., encouraging the veneration of someone who has not yet been declared or acknowledged a saint.[34]

Canon 1281 lays down that "images of great value, either because of their age, or by reason of their artistic merits, or by the veneration given to them, and which have been exposed in churches and public oratories for the veneration of the faithful, if in need of repairs, must not be restored without the written consent of the Ordinary, who before he gives his approval, should seek advice from prudent and competent authorities."

Canon 1281 states that "important images and relics or those of great value, as well as any other relics or images in a church which are honoured by the people with special veneration, must not be alienated or transferred from one church to another without permission of the Holy See."

Veiling of Statues and Pictures

According to the rubrics of the Roman Missal, Breviary, and *Caeremoniale Episcoporum,* all crosses, statues, and pictures of our Lord and of the saints on the altars and elsewhere in a church to which cultus is given with the sole exception of the crosses and images of the Stations of the Cross, must be covered with purple veils, not transparent or ornamented in any way, from before the first vespers of Passion Sunday until after the Gloria in the Mass on Holy Saturday, no matter what feast may occur.[35]

Statues on or above the altar where the Forty Hours' Prayer takes place, should be veiled. No special colour for the veils is prescribed, but it seems more appropriate that it should be white.[36]

Historical Notes

The origin of the custom of veiling statues and pictures during Passiontide can be found in the once almost universal practice of veiling, not only images, but also the altar during the whole of Lent as a sign of mourning and penitence. The colour for Lenten veils was usually white — not purple, and in some parts of Spain, in southern Italy and the Cathedral of Freiburg (Baden, Germany), it is still the custom to hang an enormous veil in front of the sanctuary, which is a relic of the primitive practice of concealing the altar with curtains during the more solemn parts of the

Mass. Mediaeval church inventories make frequent references to white linen veils for Lent, although blue was sometimes used.

IV. OTHER ALTAR FURNITURE

a) Altar Cards

It would seem that the human memory must have become less reliable during the past three hundred years, for until the sixteenth century printed cards, containing certain prayers and blessings which the priest is supposed to know by heart, had not become the almost essential accessory of worship that they are to-day. When the Roman Missal was revised by Pius V in 1570, only one card, the *tabella secretarum,* was ordered by the rubrics.[37]

During the seventeenth century another card with the Gospel of St. John which is recited at the end of Mass, unless another Last Gospel is ordered by the rubrics, was introduced, and then, probably for the sake of symmetry, a third card, containing the prayers said by the celebrant when blessing the water at the Offertory and when washing his hands. This was placed on the Epistle side of the altar.

During the seventeenth and eighteenth centuries it became the fashion to insert altar cards in very ornate frames — some of which in the Baroque style are magnificent pieces of craftsmanship.

There is still no obligation to have more than the one card mentioned in the rubrics of the Missal. This card should be placed against the crucifix or tabernacle during Mass only. The two other cards can be supported against the candlesticks, or against the edge of a shelf or reredos, should there be one. The most important thing about altar cards is not the frame, but legibility. The type used should be bold and clear. Illuminated cards, written in a mediaeval script, are often quite useless to the priest. Except in rare cases illuminated altar cards with elaborate borders, whether hand-painted or printed, are a doubtful addition to the dignity of the altar. As no altar cards were used during the Middle Ages there can be no logical reason for making an imitation mediaeval-looking article. The cards, whether framed or unframed, should be removed from the altar after Mass.

Altar cards are not used at a bishop's Mass, or that of any lesser prelate who has the right of *Pontificalia*. The prayers usually printed on the cards are contained in a separate book, known as the *Canon Episcopalis*.

b) Missal Stand

The general rubrics of the Roman Missal,[38] as well as those of the *Caeremoniale Episcoporum*, state that a cushion is to be used to support the Missal.[39] But a wooden book-rest is now more common, which is also mentioned as an alternative in the *Caeremoniale*. Metal reading desks can be used, if preferred, but if they are adorned with projecting spikes, they are both dangerous and inconvenient. If a cushion is used, it should be about 18 in. square, and stuffed with wool or down, not too lightly, and made up with cord. Tassels at the corners add to the dignity. Altar cushions are still found in Spain and Austria, as well as in other parts of Europe where old traditions have survived. They are also used in Carthusian churches. During the later Middle Ages it was very common to have two cushions on the altar, and it would seem that there is no rubric that forbids this practice. The advantage of two cushions is that it lessens the weight to be carried by the server — a serious matter to a small boy whose arms may not be too strong. According to the *Caeremoniale*, both the cushion and the Missal should be covered in silk of the colour of the feast.[40] Cushions are still used for High Mass at the Lateran and St. Peter's, Rome. In some places it is the custom to cover the missal stand with a piece of silk the same colour as the vestments. Some priests prefer a missal stand resting on a pillar, fixed into a fairly broad, round base, but this is unknown in Rome. Missal stands should not be too low, otherwise the marker ribbons get in the way. In most Roman basilicas the Missal, Epistle and Gospel books, are covered in silk, to match the colour of the vestments worn at High Mass.*

c) Cruets

In primitive times the two cruets or vessels for holding the wine and water used at the Holy Eucharist were generally made of metal, very rarely of glass or crystal. Some of them were much larger than those used to-day, and of the most elaborate workmanship. To distinguish the contents, the two cruets

---

* At Amay-sur-Meuse (Belgium) the venerable old custom of keeping the Missal (or rather the Gospel book) lying on the *mensa* of the altar, day and night, has been revived, symbolizing the presence of the Son of God, *sub aliena Specie:* in the sacrament and in His word. — *H. A. R.*

were often marked with the letters *V* and *A* — *vinum* and *aqua*. It was not until the period of the Renaissance that glass cruets became common. Many of them were mounted in gold or silver.

The rubrics of the Roman Missal order that the cruets should be made of crystal or glass, but metal ones are still tolerated (Tit. XX). Loosely fitting stoppers are important to exclude dust or insects. A glass saucer should be provided for the cruets to stand in, as well as a separate bowl into which the priest can wash his hands. The rubrics of the Missal also mention a small wicker basket (*fenestrella*), in which the bell, cruets, basin, and towel are placed; the basket itself (in accordance with the practice which still prevails in Rome) being carried to the altar by the server when he accompanies the priest from the sacristy.

d) Bell

The practice of ringing a bell at the more solemn parts of the Mass seems to have originated with the introduction of the mediaeval ceremony of the elevation of the Host during the twelfth century — a northern custom which did not spread to Rome until two hundred years later, at least not officially. Ivo of Chartres (d. 1115) mentions the ringing of one of the church bells at the Elevation. Later on it became almost universal in Northern Europe for the server to ring a small hand bell at the Elevation, and in the later Middle Ages "Sanctus bells" were often hung up above the roof of the chancel, so that people outside might know when the Elevation took place.

All that is stated in the Roman Missal is that "the server rings the little bell with his right hand at each elevation, or continuously until the priest lays the Host on the corporal, and at the same way again at the elevation of the chalice."[41]

The *Ritus Servandus* orders that the little bell is to be rung at the Sanctus as well, but these two ringings are the only ones prescribed by the rubrics. All other ringings are merely local customs which have grown up during the centuries. The only two extra ringings which are tolerated by the Sacred Congregation of Rites are as a warning just before the Consecration,[42] and at the *"Domine non sum dignus"* — where it is the custom.[43]

The rubrics of the Missal (XX), the *Ritus Servandus* (VII, 8), and the *Memoriale Rituum* (IV, i, and VI, i) all speak of a small bell — *parva campanula* — also the *Rituale Romanum* (IV, 4–13). The Sacred Congregation of Rites mentions a *tintinnabulum*, which is merely another kind of small bell, "such as is hung round an animal's neck."[44]

The only kind of altar bell which is recognised by the rubrics is a small hand bell with one tongue, made of silver, bronze, or other metal, although chiming bells do not appear to be forbidden. Indian gongs, or the more common upturned, basin-shaped brass instrument, fixed to a shaft and base, are definitely prohibited.[45] There is no reason to leave the bell on the altar steps. When not actually in use it is better to keep it on the credence table.

NOTE. In St. Charles' *Instructions* (Chap. XV, para. 4) it is laid down that a small bell should be attached next every altar to the side wall on the Gospel side, and that there should be suspended from the bell a string sufficiently long to enable the server to use it to ring therewith "a certain number of strokes during the elevation of the Body of Our Lord."

On the other hand, since it is presumed that the high altar will be covered by a canopy and stand some distance from any wall, it is explained that a portable bell brought from the sacristy will be more convenient.

NOTES

1. C.J.C. 1283, § 1.
2. Cf. Dooley, *Church Law on Sacred Relics* (1931), pp. 75, 78.
3. *Rit. Celeb. Miss.*, Tit. IV, n. 5.
4. Cf. O'Connell, *The Celebration of the Mass*, Bk. I, p. 246.
5. *Caer. Ep.*, L. I, c. XII, n. 12.
6. S.R.C. 2647; 2854; 4186.
7. S.R.C. 2967, ad 9; 3029; 3204.
8. S.R.C. 2740, ad 1; 2613, ad 6.
9. S.R.C. 4059, ad 2.
10. Van der Stappen, *Sacra Liturgia*, IV, Q. 365.
11. *Caer. Ep.*, L. I, c. XII, n. 12.
12. *Memoriale Rituum*, Tit. IV, c. I, para. 4, n. 1.
13. *Ibid.*, Tit. VI, c. I, n. 10.
14. Cf. O'Connell, *op. cit.*, Bk. I, p. 246, note.
15. *Directions for Altar Societies and Architects*, p. 22.
16. *Caer. Ep.*, L. I, c. XII, n. 12.
17. S.R.C. 2613, ad 6.
18. S.R.C. 4000, ad 1; 4136, ad 2.
19. Cf. *Directions for Altar Societies*, p. 22.
20. *Caer. Ep.*, L. I, c. XII, n. 12.
21. *Ibid.*, L. I, c. XII, n. 12.
22. *Miss. Rom.*
23. *Caer. Ep.*, L. I, c. XII, n. 12.
24. *Caer. Ep.*, L. II, c. XIII, n. 2.
25. Mem. Rit., IV, c. 1, 4, n. 1.
26. *Ibid.*, IV, c. 10.
27. *Caer. Ep.*, L. II, c. XX, n. 1.
28. S.R.C. 3448, ad 11.
29. *Caer. Ep.*, L. I, c. XII, n. 12.
30. S.R.C. 2613, ad 6; 2740, ad 1.
31. Canon 1279, §§ 2, 3.
32. S.O., 26 Aug., 1891; Coll. P. F., n. 1767.
33. Holy Office, March 16, 1928.
34. C.J.C. 1279, § 3.
35. S.R.C. 3638, ad 11.
36. Inst. Clementina.
37. *Rub. Gen. Miss.*, Tit. XX.
38. *Rom. Miss.*, I, Tit. XX.
39. *Caer. Ep.*, L. I, c. XII, n. 15.
40. *Ibid.*
41. *Rit. Celeb. Miss.*, VIII, 6.
42. S.R.C. 4377.
43. S.R.C. 5224, ad 9.
44. *Directions for Altar Societies*, ed. 1912, p. 25.
45. S.R.C. 4000, ad 3 (1898).

CHAPTER X

THE SANCTUARY

The *sanctuary* is that part of a church which encloses the high altar and extends to the communion rails. The portion of the sanctuary reserved for the clergy, who are assisting at Mass or taking part in the recitation or chanting of the Divine Office, or for a choir of men and boys, is called the *choir,* or quire. It may be situated either before or behind the high altar, or in special cases, in a transept looking onto the sanctuary. The word *chancel* signifies the space between the high altar and the nave, and separated from the latter by a screen (L. *cancelli* – a screen).

HISTORICAL NOTES

The sanctuary, in early Christian times, was confined to the apse or semicircular east end of the church where the clergy had their seats, and in front of which the altar stood beneath a ciborium on four columns. It became too small to hold the increasing number of higher and lower clergy, so part of the nave in front of the altar was enclosed by screens and became part of the sanctuary. This arrangement can still be seen in S. Clemente and other Roman basilican churches. During the early Middle Ages, some large churches had two sanctuaries: one at the east and the other at the west end or in the middle of the building. The sanctuary underwent many modifications during the later Middle Ages. In some places it was pushed outwards into transepts; in others further down the nave to accommodate the choir.

In most parish churches in England before the Reformation the invariable arrangement was to have the choir, with returned stalls for the senior clergy facing the altar (with their backs to the people), enclosed by screens. The chancel, as it was called, consisted of that portion of a church either beyond the transepts or sometimes occupying the eastern bays of the nave where there were no transepts.

The Renaissance architects abandoned screens and favoured wide short sanctuaries with low communion rails, giving an unbroken view of the high altar.

More often than not, chancels were raised above the nave, though there are exceptions to this rule as will be explained later. Sometimes chancels had aisles on either side, sometimes not. In the East one does not find raised chancels. There is usually one step before the iconostasis, but none to the holy table itself. In the continental countries of Northern Europe raised chancels are very common, sometimes having crypts beneath them, especially in cathedrals and large churches.[1]

SIZE

In a large number of modern Catholic

churches the sanctuary is far too small to permit liturgical functions being carried out with ease and dignity. It may be said with truth that a sanctuary can never be too large to satisfy a master of ceremonies! Between the lowest step of the high altar to the communion rails there should be a clear *unbroken* space of at *least* 11 ft. in an average-sized church. Even in a small chapel with only one altar it is better to allow a depth of at least 6 ft. between the altar steps and the communion rails. For a large church 20 ft. or more should be the minimum, when there are no choir stalls in the sanctuary. Should there be a ritual choir in front of the high altar much more space will be needed.

Compare any typical late mediaeval parish church in Europe with the average modern Catholic church, and it will be realized how much is lost by providing too small a sanctuary.

STEPS

Both mediaeval and Renaissance builders understood that it is by no means *essential* that a sanctuary should be raised above the nave. In many pre-Reformation churches in England the nave and chancel are on the same level, and in some cases there is a descent of one or more steps into the chancel. This arrangement has the advantage of bringing the eye level of those seated in the nave to the top of the high altar, should there be the usual three or five steps leading up to it as are recommended by the rubrics.[2]

In many modern churches the congregation have to strain their necks to see the high altar properly owing to it being perched up on an over-lofty sanctuary floor. Indeed there is something to be said in favour of the floor of the nave gradually rising up from the communion rails, so that the view of the worshippers at the back is not obstructed by the heads of those in front of them; in other words, that the levels of the floor of a church should be arranged like those in a theatre or cinema.*

There should be an unbroken space between the communion rails and the bottom step of the altar. It is impossible to carry out any liturgical function properly if the clergy and acolytes have to be going up and down steps all the time. If one breaks up even a large sanctuary with two or three different levels, there will be not enough space left for ceremonies.

If it is desired to raise the sanctuary above the level of the nave, it will be sufficient to have two steps: one in front of the communion rails, the other just inside them, with sufficient space for the priest to move up and down when giving Communion to the people.

---

* We are so proud of our discoveries in modern architecture, but imagine the surprise of Dom Adalbert Schippers, O.S.B., when after laborious excavations and restorations he discovered that the famous abbey minster of Maria Laach (Rhineland) had a floor sloping so gradually down to the steps of the high choir and sanctuary that one entering the doors of the church was exactly on the same level as the sanctuary floor, in spite of its seven or eight steps up from the floor in the front part of the minster. The slope was so gradual that it was unnoticeable when walking toward the altar. The result was that everybody in that long Romanesque edifice of the thirteenth century came away with the feeling of having miraculously been saved from craning his or her neck and yet of having been able to see every detail of the liturgy, even in the rear of the church! — *H. A. R.*

FLOOR SURFACE

In no instance should the floor of the sanctuary be of any highly polished material. There is always the danger that a priest may slip when making his way to give Holy Communion, and a a similar accident may easily happen to the deacon or subdeacon at High Mass. Unlike the acolytes, who in some places are put into slippers when serving Mass so that their boots may not scratch the floor, the clergy are not in the habit of taking off their outdoor foot-wear before taking part in a liturgical function.[3] It is recommended that the centre of the sanctuary should be entirely covered with a carpet, matting, or other kind of floor-cloth. Rubber is a useful material for this purpose and many attractive kinds can now be obtained. At the same time there is always the danger of grease marks from the acolytes' candles, or hot charcoal being dropped by the thurifer — boys will be boys! So it is better to put down some kind of floor covering that can easily be cleaned.

CHOIR-STALLS[4]

Not many modern Catholic churches are provided with choir-stalls in the sanctuary, and unless a mediaeval type of chancel is built, they crowd up space which ought to be left empty. Nothing looks so bad as to see what might otherwise be a decent-sized sanctuary filled with stalls, no matter how good the actual design may be. Sometimes these stalls are not used by "singing men and boys" at all, but are filled with superfluous acolytes at High Mass and Benediction, whose only function is to walk

in and out at the beginning and end of the service. Where a church has a surpliced choir of men and boys, then by all means let them sit in stalls on either side of the sanctuary, otherwise it is advisable to insert no other furniture than is absolutely necessary.

Perhaps an even better place for the body of singers is behind the high altar, but not many modern churches make provision for this arrangement.

FURNITURE OF THE SANCTUARY

A sanctuary should not be crowded up with statues, flower pots, cushions, prie-dieus, gongs, books, and chairs. The following are the essential articles of furniture.

1. *Bench*° *for the sacred ministers.* There should be a long bench for the celebrant, deacon, and subdeacon at High Mass, placed at the Epistle side of the sanctuary. It should be long enough to seat three persons, and, if there is a back, it should be low enough to allow the vestments to hang over it, i.e., not more than 18 in. in height. On Sundays and feast days it may be covered with a cloth of the appropriate liturgical colour.[5] On Good Friday and at Requiems it should be left bare. In Rome

---

° One of the greatest surprises any visitor of this country experiences in church is to see ordinary straight chairs as seats in practically all sanctuaries. Most of our priests and our faithful have by this time accepted these makeshift things as the rule. Not only are they preposterously out of place, ugly, and undignified, but — since it is hard to argue this point — they have been repeatedly and sternly forbidden by the Sacred Congregation of Rites, i.e., A.D. 1614, 1704, 1822, 1861, and finally in 1893. Since forty years' untrammeled use may establish a "custom," it may already be too late for protest. — *H. A. R.*

the bench has no back as a rule. At Mass it is often covered with green baize, or when violet vestments are worn, with a cover of the same colour. The addition of a canopy or the use of separate chairs for the sacred ministers has been forbidden by the Sacred Congregation of Rites. The picturesque mediaeval *sedilia*, with its three canopied seats built into the south wall of the sanctuary, is hardly practical, even if it were allowed, for it provides no means of preventing the back of the vestments from getting crushed when the clergy are sitting down. Cushions are not permitted unless the celebrant has the right to use "*pontificalia*."[6]

2. *Stools or benches* for the acolytes — not more than are required for the actual number who assist at High Mass — are necessary furniture, so that the men or boys can sit down during the sermon. However, it is hard to see why we cannot accept the good old Roman custom of sitting on the steps of the altar, the throne, or the sanctuary. In the Sistine Chapel of the Vatican as well as St. Peter's not only the altar boys and lower ministers sit on the steps, but also the deacons, subdeacons, and assistants of both the pope and the celebrant.

3. *Credence table.* A table, large enough to hold everything needed for certain liturgical functions, also the chalice covered with the humeral veil at High Mass, should be placed against the south wall of the sanctuary. It should be covered with a white linen cloth, reaching to the ground, both in front and at the sides.[7]

4. *Piscina.* It is recommended that there should be a piscina or *sacrarium*, built into the wall on the Epistle side of the high altar. It consists of a basin with a pipe running into the ground, and is intended for the disposal of water that has been used for any sacred purpose. It can be combined with a shelf above the basin upon which the cruets can be placed, and is generally used as a credence table at Low Masses. The diameter of the basin should be about 9 in., and 4 in. in depth. The shelf above should be about 1 ft. in length and about 6 to 9 in. deep.

AUMBRY

On the Gospel or Epistle side of the sanctuary[8] there should be a small cupboard (aumbry) to contain the holy oils, which must not be kept in the presbytery, except for some special reason. It may be built into the wall or hang against it. On the door, which must be kept locked, the words *Olea Sacra* should be inscribed. A veil may be hung before the cupboard door; white or violet if all three oils are kept there; violet if only the Oil of the Sick is within. Should the sacristy be definitely part of the church, the holy oils may be kept there in a similar aumbry.[9]

CARPETS

A carpet down the middle of the sanctuary has been mentioned already. There is no special reason why any particular colour should be used, although the *Caeremoniale Episcoporum* recommends that the carpet on the predella or footpace of the altar should be green.[10] There is very little to be said in favour of carpets supposed to be of "ecclesiastical design," i.e., covered with sacred emblems. Carpets are removed from churches after the stripping of the altars on Maundy Thursday and put back again on Holy Saturday.[11]

COMMUNION RAILS

Communion rails, such as are now almost universal in churches where the Roman rite is followed, are a comparatively modern innovation. They are a sort of compromise between the mediaeval chancel screen and the low wall which enclosed the chancel in the Roman basilicas. There is no evidence that fixed communion rails were found in pre-Reformation churches. No matter what material is used for their construction — stone, marble, wood, wrought iron, stainless steel, or chromium plate — they should not exceed 2 ft. 6 in. in height, otherwise it is difficult for a priest to give Holy Communion to small children. The breadth at the top should be from 9 to 12 in. A wooden kneeling bench is more convenient than fixed rails, for it enables the communicants to kneel on a slightly higher level than that on which the priest stands. Should there be fixed rails, the kneeling step should be provided with long cushions on either side of the entrance to the sanctuary. Even if there should be a structural rail or low wall between the nave and the sanctuary, there is much to be said in favour of separate kneeling benches for communicants in a large church. They can be placed outside the sanctuary. No more than one step should ever be placed at the communion rail, for more than this number may lead to accidents, and extra steps are very awkward for old people and children.

The entrance to the sanctuary should always be provided with a gate of some kind that can be kept locked. A cord is not sufficient protection.

The *episcopal throne,* usually on the Gospel side of the sanctuary, is a permanent piece of furniture in a cathedral church. It should be erected on three steps, and surmounted by a canopy, so constructed that it can be covered with hangings of the liturgical colour of the Sunday or feast day. (Cf. *Caer. Ep.*) The chair may also be covered with hangings of the colour of the day. Space on either side should be given for stools for the deacon and subdeacon, with room for another stool for the assistant priest, just below the right side of the deacon, i.e., farthest from the bishop. A temporary throne of the same type must be put up in a parish church on the occasion of the visitation of the Ordinary, or of a cardinal or other higher ecclesiastic who pontificates at the throne with the permission of the Ordinary. The return of the throne to the apse, behind the altar, is something to hope for.

CHANCEL SCREENS

Practical Necessity

If one considers the matter from a purely utilitarian point of view, a barrier or screen between the congregation and the sacred ministers at the altar is an obvious necessity. The priest does not want to be distracted by crowds pressing round him. In spite of all the mystical and symbolic meanings attached to roodscreens by certain devout authors of the past century, the much more probable explanation of their origin is to be found in an attempt to secure privacy for those who were engaged in the choir office or in the celebration of the Liturgy.

Historical Notes

In the basilican churches of Southern Europe and Northern Africa, which were erected in the first centuries of Christianity, the clergy sat in the apse behind the altar. The celebrant faced the people. The altar was usually shrouded by curtains which were closed during the more solemn parts of the Mass. Very often there was an open screen round the sanctuary or sometimes a low wall surmounted by a cross-beam. In the churches of the Eastern rites these screens came to be filled in, and so developed into the *iconastasis* of mediaeval and modern times. In those Mediterranean countries where the Roman rite is found, the basilican arrangement of the chancel has survived to a greater or lesser degree. In cathedrals and monastic churches the clergy or monks still occupy stalls behind the high altar, but in most parish churches the high altar is usually placed near the east wall. Only a low balustrade separates the laity from what is going on in the sanctuary. Publicity rather than privacy is the result.

Christian churches were usually developed on quite different lines in Great Britain and certain other Northern European countries. Most of them owed little or nothing to the Mediterranean basilica, except those which were erected by missionaries from Rome, e.g., at Canterbury. Our earliest places of worship were small chapels, some of which still survive — e.g., the Saxon church at Bradford-on-Avon, Somerset,

the village church on Caldey Island, and the famous "seven churches" at Glendalough, in Ireland. The invariable feature in all of them is a narrow chancel arch, merely a doorway in a solid stone wall between the nave and the sanctuary. So narrow are those openings that it would be impossible for more than a few worshippers to see anything of what was going on at the altar. Certain archaeologists are of the opinion that in the first instance there was no "nave" to these little chapels, which merely consisted of what is now the sanctuary, and that the chancel arch was the west door on the outside of the building. As time went on and larger churches were needed, a nave was added, with the result that the original door became a chancel arch.

In later ages the separation of the laity from the sanctuary was still retained by more-or-less open screens, constructed of wood or stone. In the case of cathedrals and monastic churches there were usually two solid screens — the "choir-screen," separating the choir from the transepts, and a "rood-screen," separating the latter from the nave. The name "rood-screen" is due to the great crucifix (called "rood" in old English) which stood on or above this screen.

The monks or canons carried on their own worship in private, while a "people's altar" was set up in front of the rood-screen, sometimes with a light wooden screen in front of it. So, in cathedrals and monastic churches there might be two or more almost distinct places of worship under the same roof.

No country in Europe can show such a wealth of mediaeval screens as England. In spite of the havoc wrought by the sixteenth-century Protestants, hundreds of them have been preserved, although in most cases the rood-lofts which once surmounted them have been destroyed. The "rood-loft" was a gallery which stood above the screen and which, in parish churches, often served as a musician's gallery. Sometimes a small altar was placed in the rood-loft. In cathedrals and monastic churches there was a similar gallery over the choir-screen. Screens have never regained their popularity among Catholics in Britain, despite the efforts of Augustus Welby Pugin and other architects of the Gothic Revival of the past century. National traditions of worship had been forgotten as the result of nearly three hundred years of persecution. When it was possible to start building churches again most of the ecclesiastical authorities preferred to look to France and Italy for inspiration, suspecting everything English as being "Protestant." In fact, some of the best rood-screens erected in Catholic churches during the nineteenth century were taken down afterwards, with the result of completely spoiling the interior of the buildings. In other places a compromise was arrived at by retaining the rood-beam and dispensing with a screen.*

---

* It is a controversial question, whether or not rood-screens and iconostaseis were a healthy or unhealthy development. Certainly the fact that the Eastern Church developed a screen does not prove that it should have developed it, as little as the fact that England and the Saxon parts of Germany had rood-screens proves that they were doing the right thing. This development came in the waning Middle Ages, a time which was not outstanding for its liturgical spirit — though very notorious for its individualistic trend in mysticism and its fear

Present-day Problems and Requirements

As the conditions of present-day Catholic worship differ so greatly from those which existed in Europe before the Reformation it is doubtful if it is desirable to have a rood-screen between the congregation and the sanctuary, although this is a venerable tradition which one may regret to abandon. There is much to be said in favour of a certain mystery in worship, for it encourages reverence and devotion. On the other hand, there are persons who maintain that what is far more needed to-day is to emphasize the *corporate* aspects of public worship, and that the best way to achieve this end is to bring the high altar down into the midst of the people, so that they can follow every movement of the Mass without any obstacle being put in their way.[12]

Maybe the solution of this difficult problem lies in a happy mean, and what we should aim at is a revival of the primitive basilican type of sanctuary with the clergy behind the altar, which should stand beneath a ciborium

---

of externals. The Roman basilicas which have preserved their high *cancelli*, like San Clemente, Santa Sabina, Maria in Cosmedin, and many more, indeed hide the chanters, the schola, and the lower clergy from the eye of the laity, but by no means the celebrant and his assistants. The celebrant in all these churches not only faces the people, but is high up on the predella and made more conspicuous by the fact that only he and the deacon are plainly visible during the sacred action. As the people bowed deeply during the *canon actionis* and raised their head only for the (old) elevation during the great doxology before the *Pater Noster* there was no danger of distraction at this time. Besides, the priest is not supposed to gaze into the congregation, even when he turns to them (*dismissis oculis!*). — H. A. R.

or baldaquin in accordance with the rubrics, and a fairly open screen in front of it. When in doubt, no safer rule can be found than to follow the example of Rome itself, and this was the original Roman practice.

SIDE CHAPELS AND ALTARS

Strictly speaking there is no need to have more than one altar in a church unless it is served by several priests who may be obliged to say Mass at the same time, e.g., in the case of a religious community or large town parish. Altars are not intended for arousing devotion but for the purely functional purpose of celebrating the Holy Eucharist. A shrine is quite a different thing and it is not essential that the statue or picture which is the central feature should have a small altar set up in front of it.

On the other hand, it is useful in large churches to have at least one side chapel or side altar. For Mass can be said here on occasions when only a few worshippers are likely to be present and when it is not necessary to give Communion from the tabernacle, which according to present-day custom, is usually on the high altar. It is better that a comparatively small congregation should not be scattered about over a large church. To gather them together in a side chapel enables them to take a more active part in the liturgy, especially if a dialogue Mass is celebrated.

No matter where the side chapels or altars are located the architect should give them a secondary character lest they compete with the sanctuary and high altar. Details of side altars are given in another chapter (p. 83).

SHRINES

It is difficult to lay down any general principles regarding the provision of shrines in churches, except that they should not obtrude themselves too aggressively so as to detract attention from the high altar. The purpose of a shrine is to encourage private devotion towards a particular saint or Christian mystery, not to decorate the church with a work of art. They offer a legitimate opportunity for the laity to express their devotion in whatever way that appeals to them, and as there is practically no legislation affecting shrines, at least in their design, it is wiser to allow full liberty where it is permitted by Canon Law and the Sacred Congregation of Rites. The statues or pictures that form the central feature of a shrine must be "devotional," i.e., capable of inspiring devotion in the average worshipper, yet this does not mean that it is necessary to purchase the most vulgar type of machine-made article sold by church furnishers. Nevertheless it is doubtful[*]

---

[*] The fact that all the older shrines of our Lady are of the icon type and as austere as a Rouault (Monserrato in Cataluna, Czestochowa in Poland, the famous shrine in Sant' Alfonso in Rome, hundreds of others in Italy, Greece, Russia, Austria, and France) seems to me to contradict this doubt. Bernadette Soubirous did not like the statue in Lourdes, as it lacked that majesty which she had seen, and our plaster Lourdes Madonnas are infinitely worse than the original. The market is filled with statues of the whole heavenly court, from angels in long nightshirts to Saviours looking like well-groomed preachers, all sweetness and commonness. A good dose of austerity can only help to bring us back the reverential attitude required by the mystery that the liturgy calls "tremendum." At least that is the flavor of all our liturgical language. Should not pictorial and sculptural art agree? — H. A. R.

if the ordinary Catholic is roused to feelings of piety when confronted by what may be a liturgically correct *ikon* or an austerely "modern" sculpture. There are no regulations about flowers or lights before shrines — they can be as plentiful as possible. The recent legislation regarding votive lights before shrines enforced by the cardinal vicar in Rome has not been made obligatory elsewhere.

Shrines should not be placed in the sanctuary or anywhere else in the church where they conflict with the view of the high altar. The best place for them is in the aisles or transepts. There is no definite reason why shrines need be permanent. Many churches are so overcrowded with them that they are often ignored. If they are not used for the purpose for which they were erected they might as well be removed. They merely collect dust. The picture or statue of a particular saint can be set up on the feast day or in connection with a novena as is usual in Catholic countries.

NOTES

1. The typical sanctuary that one finds in most modern Catholic churches in English-speaking countries is based on the Renaissance type — broad and shallow — even if the style of architecture of the church is an almost literal copy of mediaeval work. If one may be allowed to express a personal opinion, it would have been better if certain architects had studied the planning of mediaeval churches more carefully rather than the details of the architecture. It would be a great gain so far as sanctuaries are concerned.

2. "Care should be taken to keep the levels as low as the vicissitudes of the site will allow. True to the custom of the earliest Christian churches, the first ascent is frequently eastwards of the choir, and not at the entrance to the chancel. By this means the steps are concentrated upon the altar itself without the sacrifice of their real dignity, which is spaciousness and not height, and the table does not lose the prominence due to that most important part of the altar by being raised above the level of the eye" (J. N. Comper. *Further Thoughts on the English Altar*, etc., 1932, p. 31).

3. There are some sacristans, especially nuns, who seem to think that the surface of a sanctuary floor should resemble that of a ballroom or skating rink.

4. See Chap. XX, "The Organ and Choir."

5. *Caer. Ep.*, L. I, c. XII, n. 22.
6. S.R.C. 2621, ad 6.
7. *Caer. Ep.*, L. I, c. XII, n. 19.
8. S.R.C. 1260 (1663).
9. *Rit. Rom.*, II, i, 53; cf. C.J.C. 735.
10. *Caer. Ep.*, L. I, c. XII, n. 16.
11. Cf. Fortescue, *Ceremonies of the Roman Rite* (7 ed.), pp. 313, 318, 337.
12. Eric Gill has expressed these views in an essay entitled "Mass for the Million" reprinted in his *Sacred and Secular* (J. M. Dent, 1940). He reminds us that "Pope Pius XI said that the greatest scandal of our time is that the church has lost the masses, and it is obviously true that the masses of the population in the industrialised countries of Europe and America are not practising Christians." He argues that "there is nothing whatever in the nature of an Altar that implies that it should be anywhere but in the middle. It began as a table around which people sat and partook of the consecrated bread and wine. It remains that thing." Gill believes that "the monstrous division between the place of the Altar and the rest of the church" must be abolished; the altar placed in the midst of the people and surrounded by them. Only in this way can the liturgy be made alive again, for it "is buried beneath a load of mediaeval and post-mediaeval customs."

CHAPTER XI

THE FONT AND BAPTISTERY

HISTORICAL NOTES

The baptistery or font should be placed near the main entrance of a church. During the first centuries of Christianity the sacrament of Baptism was often administered in rivers, pools, or on the sea shore or at other times in the bath-chambers of private houses or in the catacombs* when there was fear of persecution. The practice of open-air Baptism continued until long after Christians had obtained freedom of worship. We are told that, even in the sixth and seventh centuries, St. Augustine of Canterbury and St. Paulinus of York baptised large numbers of converts in rivers.

The original form of baptistery was based on the typical Roman bath-chamber, with a tank in the middle, to which a flight of steps led down from the floor level. The water entered through pipes. On the edge of the tank was a platform on which the priest stood when baptising the catechumens, i.e., converts under instruction before Baptism. One of the earliest permanent baptisteries which exists is adjoining St. John Lateran in Rome. It was erected during the reign of the Emperor Constantine.

This type of baptistery, built out from a church or entirely separate from it, survived until late in the Middle Ages

* See note on pp. 3–4.

in Italy and Southern European countries as well as in the Eastern Church. They are generally round or octagonal in shape. Fine examples are those at Pisa, Florence, Parma, and Cremona. The font was usually surrounded by a railing for the sake of privacy. Sometimes there was a baldaquin over it.

About the eighth century infant Baptism had become the normal custom. The font was moved into the church itself, or else placed in the narthex, or inner porch. In many of the earlier baptisteries the font is large enough to hold several adults, who stood or knelt in the water during the actual ceremony of Baptism.

It would appear that separate baptisteries were very rare in Northern Europe during the Middle Ages. There are only few in existence. The font was invariably placed at the bottom of the church, either at the west end of the nave or in a side aisle. So, just as the high altar dominated the east end of a church, the font became the most prominent feature at the west end. Unlike the primitive Christian baptismal tank, the mediaeval font was usually raised on one or more steps instead of being below the floor level. To protect the baptismal water from dust and dirt the basin of the font was generally surmounted by an elaborately carved wooden cover. The earliest type of font covers were merely flat lids.

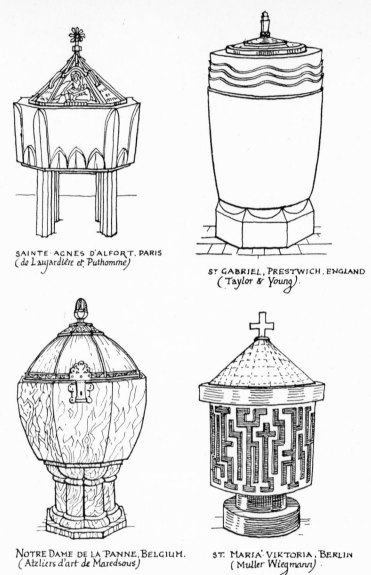

SAINTE·AGNES D'ALFORT, PARIS
(de Laujardière et Puthomme)

ST GABRIEL, PRESTWICH, ENGLAND
(Taylor & Young).

NOTRE DAME DE LA PANNE, BELGIUM.
(Ateliers d'art de Maredsous)

ST. MARIA·VIKTORIA, BERLIN
(Muller Wiegmann).

Modern fonts.

In England a dwarf spire became the most popular type, usually octagonal in plan, and in the form of a pyramid with moulded ribs at the angles, and finished off with crockets. Sometimes they were light enough to be lifted off by hand, more generally it was necessary to suspend them from the roof by a chain and pulley. The spire-crowned font covers in East Anglia are perhaps the finest of all pre-Reformation ones in England.

Youlgreave, Derby

Dolton, Devon

St. Michael, Southampton

Howden, Yorkshire.

Bodmin, Cornwall.

St Stephen Walbrook, London

Calella, Spain,

Peterborough Cathedral.

France (17th century)

Fonts.

NECESSITY

According to Canon Law there should be a baptismal font in every *parish* church, unless for some particular reason.[1]

"Public oratories are governed by the same law as churches . . . *all* sacred functions can be held there which are not forbidden by the rubrics."[2] The Ordi-nary of the place may give permission or order in certain cases that a font be erected in non-parochial churches or public oratories within the boundaries of a parish.

POSITION

No definite position is assigned for the font in the legislation of the church. It can stand either in a baptistery quite

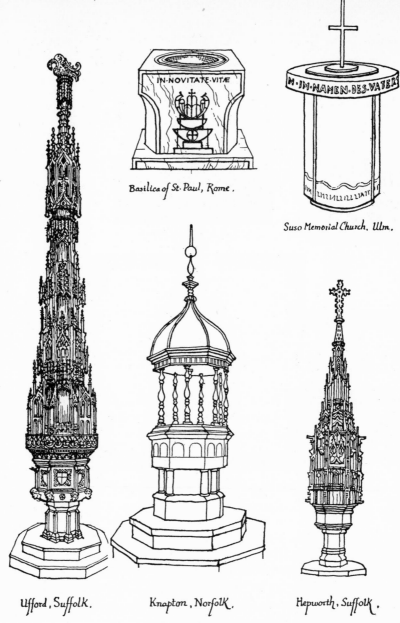

Basilica of St. Paul, Rome.

Suso Memorial Church, Ulm.

Ufford, Suffolk.   Knapton, Norfolk.   Hepworth, Suffolk.

Font covers — mediaeval and modern.

separate from the church, in a chapel within the church, or at the back of the church, close to the main entrance. All that is insisted on in the *Roman Ritual* is that "the place of Baptism is to be properly situated, of becoming shape

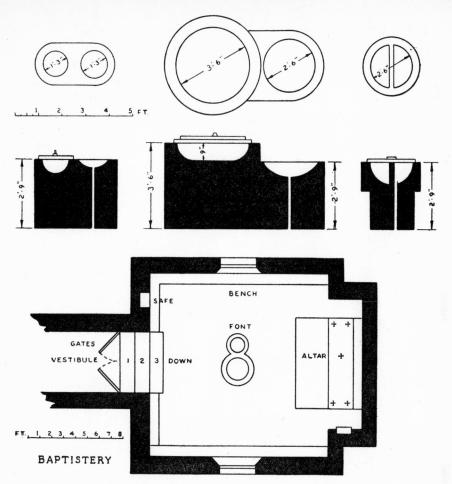

Plans and sections of fonts, and plan of baptistery.

and of solid material, and one which is well adapted to hold water, becomingly ornamented, and surrounded by a railing, closed with lock and key, and so well covered that dust and dirt will not enter, and on it, where such decoration is feasible, there should be a picture or statue of St. John the Baptist baptising Christ."[3]

The Sacred Congregation of Rites has declared that the sacristy should not be used for the administration of Baptism, except in cases of grave necessity.

Where the church is too small to permit the erection of a separate baptistery, which in any case should be near the main entrance, the best place for the font is at the west end of the church. There are practical reasons for this position, for it is sometimes forgotten that the rubrics order that the preliminary ceremonies of Baptism are to be performed *"ad limen ecclesiae"* (the threshold of the church), otherwise the port or narthex.[4] The second part of the rite takes place in the nave of the church;

PLAN

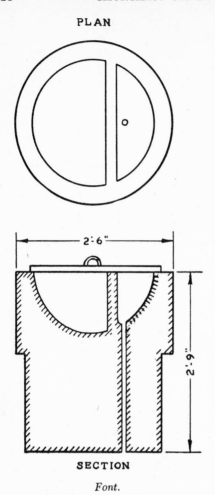

SECTION

Font.

A convenient height is about 2 ft. 9 in. from the ground. Many liturgical authorities recommend that the font, or at least the baptistery, should be one step or more *below* the level of the floor of the nave or narthex, a requirement based on an old tradition. Modern fonts have been evolved from the mediaeval arrangement of having two distinct receptacles, one that contained the blessed water, and was protected by a wooden or metal cover, the other, much smaller, which was placed at the side to receive the water which was poured over the head of the person baptised.[5] To-day these two receptacles or basins are generally fitted into the top level of the font and both covered when not in use.

In most modern fonts the basin containing the baptismal water is the larger.[6] In a large church it should be about 3 ft. in diameter and about 9 in. in depth. It is easier to keep clean if it is made with concave sides, not right-angled at the bottom. It is difficult to keep any kind of font clean owing to the mixture of the holy oils with the water when the font is blessed at Easter and Pentecost. It is sometimes recommended that the oil that gathers round the edge of the font can be absorbed with cotton wool, the latter being dried and afterwards burnt, the ashes being thrown into the piscina or sacrarium (see p. 135).

The second basin, to receive the water that flows from the head of the person baptised, should be not less than 1 ft. 3 in. in diameter, even 1 ft. 9 in. in a large church. It can be about 9 in. in depth, with a pipe at the bottom, draining into the ground or into a movable container beneath the font, the contents of which

the actual enclosure of the baptistery or font only being entered when the priest has changed his purple stole for a white one. No matter where the font is situated it is quite wrong to carry out the entire ceremony in one place.

MATERIAL, SIZE, AND DESIGN

A font may be constructed of impermeable stone or marble, or of metal. Wood may be used, provided that the actual basins are of some nonporous material (e.g., silver, bronze, or lead).

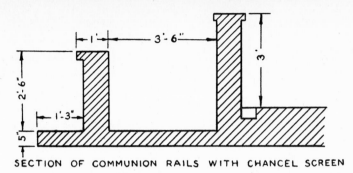

SECTION OF COMMUNION RAILS WITH CHANCEL SCREEN

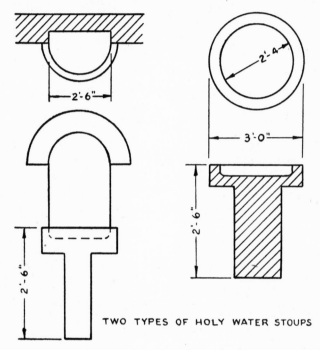

TWO TYPES OF HOLY WATER STOUPS

should be emptied into the piscina or sacrarium after the ceremony.[7]

There should be a fairly broad edge round the top of the font — about 4 in. upon which the holy oils, etc., can be placed.[8]

It has been stated already that every font must be fitted with a cover, and closed with lock and key when not in use. If the font is small the cover can be made to lift off, or it can be fitted with hinges.[9] An even better method is to have the cover suspended from the ceiling or from the baldaquin over the font, should there be one. A chain with a counterweight attached can be used for this purpose.

OTHER DETAILS OF A BAPTISTERY

1. It is recommended that the oil of the catechumens and the sacred chrism which are used in Baptism, should be

kept in a cupboard or aumbry, either fixed to the wall or built into it. The aumbry should be marked *Olea Sacra* or *Olea Bapt.* It is permissible to hang a white veil in front of it.

2. A second cupboard (with a good lock) should be provided to hold all the other requisites for Baptism: (*a*) a shell, or small silver vessel to pour the water on the person baptised;[10] (*b*) a wax candle;[11] (*c*) salt, blessed according to the proper form, in the *Rituale*,[12] which is best kept dry in a small glass-covered vessel; (*d*) cotton-wool — also kept in a tin or glass vessel;[13] (*e*) a white cloth to be placed on the head of the candidate;[14] (*f*) two clean towels; (*g*) two stoles — white and purple; (*h*) blank forms on which the names of the godparents and the baptised person can be written down; (*i*) a copy of the *Rituale Romanum*, or rather the particular edition authorized for the country.[15]

3. A small table on which the above

articles can be laid out during the ceremony.

4. One or two chairs or a bench, either within the enclosure of the baptistery or just outside.

If the font stands in the nave or anywhere else in the open church, the railed-in space round it should be sufficiently large to contain the priest and the godparents. In conclusion, it should never be forgotten that the baptistery is the most sacred part of a church next to the altar, for which reason it must be kept scrupulously clean and tidy. It should never be turned into an altar of repose during Holy Week, or the font hidden away behind the crib at Christmas as is sometimes done. After all, Baptism is the "doorway to all the other sacraments" — *janua ac fundamentum*, the gateway and foundation — as it is described in Canon Law. In view of the dignity of this sacrament the Catholic Church has always insisted on the provision of fitting surroundings for conferring it.[16]

NOTES

1. C.J.C. 774, § 1.
2. C.J.C. 1191, § 2.
3. *Rit. Rom.*, II, i, 46.
4. *Ibid.*, ii, 17.
5. No matter how beautiful mediaeval fonts may be, it is unsuitable to reproduce them in a present-day Catholic church, for they are not adapted to the existing rite of Baptism as laid down in the *Roman Ritual*.
6. The top of a font should project a few inches over the bottom, otherwise the priest will knock his feet against the lower edge.
7. *Rit. Rom.*, II, i, 60; *Mem. Rit.*, VI, II, para. V, 9. It is a convenience to have a small sacrarium fitted into the wall of the baptistery, as well as another in the sacristy or sanctuary.
8. St. Charles' dimensions for a baptistery of the Roman pattern, as opposed to that used in the Ambrosian rite, are as follows: (*a*) the railings to be fixed at a distance of at least 1 ft.

4½ in. from the font; (*b*) the font (shape 1); lower vase to be a void 4 ft. 1½ in. wide, 2 ft. 9 in. deep, and made of stone or marble 5½ in. thick; upper vase (font proper) to be 2 ft. 9 in. wide, about 8¼ in. deep, and placed about 11 in. higher than the "lower vase." Shape II: lower vase about 3 ft. 5¼ in. in diameter, 5½ in. to 6 in. deep, and placed on a base not higher than 2 ft. 9 in. from the pavement to the vase brim. Upper vase to have a diameter of 1 to 10 in. inclusive of its thickness. Shape III: to be made of an oval block 3 ft. 3½ in. long by 2 ft. ¾ in. broad, to contain two basins cut out with about 2 in. between them, and made of the same depth and diameter. The accompanying diagrams illustrate these three forms of fonts.

It is curious that while St. Charles Borromeo makes no mention of tabernacle veils, he orders that the font cover (which he calls a *ciborium*) should be covered with a canopy of silk, or of "half-silk of a white colour" so as to correspond with the ritual colour of this sacrament. A "decent linen cloth" is also mentioned as sufficient.

9. A font cover should be constructed in such a way that it can be easily removed or raised up. But all that is really needed is something that will keep out dust and dirt.

10. *Rit. Rom.*, II, i, 59.

11. *Ibid.*, i, 65.

12. *Ibid.*, 2, 6.

13. *Ibid.*, i, 61.

14. *Ibid.*, i, 64.

15. *Ibid.*, i, 66.

16. If a proof of the honour and respect which the Church orders to be paid to the baptismal font is needed, what more can be asked than the injunction that the space round it should be kept *locked* when not in use? Even altars are not obliged to be enclosed by rails and secured from irreverence by locked gates.

CHAPTER XII

THE PORCH AND MAIN ENTRANCE

HISTORICAL NOTES

A porch is primarily a covered approach to the entrance of a building. In the first six centuries of Christianity these covered approaches were put to a very practical use. More often than not there was a court-yard with open cloisters round it. In the centre of the court-yard (known as an *atrium*) was a well or fountain[1] where the worshippers washed their hands before entering the building — a relic of which still survives in our holy-water stoups.

Large porches or court-yards were necessary in primitive times, for there were classes of people who were not allowed to enter the church proper. They were known as *penitents*. They stood in the open court-yard or porch and asked the prayers of the faithful. Sometimes there was a porch known as a *narthex*. This arrangement is merely the survival of the planning of a typical Roman house which the first Christians used as a church. It can be seen at S. Ambrogio, Milan; S. Clemente, Rome, and in many other churches in Southern Europe and the Near East.

When the outer court-yard was done away with, churches still retained a large open porch. There are examples of this in many of the Roman basilicas. By the time Christianity reached Britain there was no longer any need for an atrium,

or narthex. The strictly penitential discipline of the first centuries had been greatly modified, and Baptism was not put off so long as was the custom in earlier ages. So the penitents disappeared, also the *catechumens*. The porch became smaller and had little liturgical significance.[2]

PRACTICAL NECESSITY

Nowadays, porches are often regarded as almost a luxury, and in many churches they are dispensed with from motives of economy. But they can still serve a useful purpose during the procession on Palm Sunday, or for the first part of the ceremonies on Holy Saturday — especially if the weather happens to be rainy or windy.*

NARTHEX OR VESTIBULE

When a church does not possess a porch to the main entrance there is an even greater need for a narthex or vestibule, i.e., a reasonably large space at the back of the church, shut off from the nave by doors, preferably with glass in the upper panels. If a church cannot be kept open all day for any good reason, at least the narthex can remain

---

* We should therefore strive, not only to provide porches, but a true and fully developed *atrium,* surrounded by colonnades, to offer shelter for processions and a transition from the noise of the city to the quiet of the church. — H. A. R.

open, and kneeling desks can be placed close up to the doors so that visitors can make a visit to the Blessed Sacrament.[3] "Churches in which the Blessed Sacrament is reserved, especially parish churches, should be open at least a few hours daily for the people."[4] Another practical reason for having a narthex is to prevent draughts. Even the side entrances to a church ought to be fitted with *inside* porches, for the same reason. Perhaps it is superfluous to mention that all church doors should be made to open outwards.

BULLETIN BOARDS

There should be a notice board outside every church as well as a bulletin board inside the porch or narthex. The list of services should be given in full, at least on the board inside the church, as well as the name of the parish priest. A notice board painted white, with black lettering — broad and simple in character — is much easier to read than gold lettering on brown or black, which are used so often.

Bulletin boards inside a church should be covered with serge or baize. A weekly list of services as well as other parochial notices should be fixed on with drawing pins or thumb-tacks. An alternative position for the chief bulletin board, especially in large churches, is set right back from the wall of the narthex or vestibule, and resting on a movable base. In this case the notices can be pinned up on both sides. No matter how or where the bulletin boards are placed, care should be taken that they are in a good light, so that people can read what is displayed on them.

BOOK RACK

Every church, no matter how small, should have a case or rack for pamphlets placed in the porch or narthex. There should also be a table upon which Catholic papers can be laid out for sale on Sunday mornings.

In addition to a rack for pamphlets, every large church should have an open box for parish and missionary magazines and leaflets, with a money-box underneath or inserted into the wall above.

ALMS BOXES

There should be several alms boxes placed near the entrance of a church, and clearly marked with the objects for which they are intended. More often than not these boxes are made of wood and screwed onto the wall, so that they can easily be removed by any thief. It should be obvious that boxes containing money in a public place should be made as strongly as possible. It is much better to have small iron boxes cemented into the walls, which can be bought from any manufacturer of safes. Some of the more recent types are fitted with automatic burglar alarms. Where a church has a basement, a good plan is to place the actual receptacle into which the money drops in the basement.

In large churches it is a good idea to have all the alms boxes side by side at the top of a square or hexagonal column, which can be firmly fixed into the floor near the main entrance. Each box should be clearly marked with the object for which it is intended, e.g., "Church," "Holy Souls," "Poor," "Peter's Pence," "Propagation of the Faith," etc.

HOLY-WATER STOUPS

Historical Notes

There are three kinds of holy-water stoups: (1) stationary stoups, placed at the entrance of a church; (2) portable stoups, used for sacramental rites and aspersions; and (3) private stoups, in which holy water is kept in houses.

Originally the holy-water stoup was the fountain for ablutions which stood in the centre of the atrium or court-yard of the primitive Christian churches. When the atrium ceased to be an essential part of a church, the fountain (*cantharus* or *phiala*) was reduced to a smaller vessel for holding blessed water, and placed within the church or in the porch or narthex. It would seem that there were no stationary holy-water stoups in Western Europe until the eleventh century. The existing examples of early holy-water stoups vary considerably in size and shape, some being as large as baptismal fonts, but usually much smaller. At first they were often placed against a column near the entrance of a church, or else stood on a stone base, either circular or hexagonal in shape. From about the fourteenth century holy-water stoups began to be set in the wall, and surmounted with a carved canopy. Many of these can still be seen in English pre-Reformation churches. Strange as it may appear it was not uncommon during the Middle Ages to have special stoups reserved for certain classes of the faithful. For instance, there might be three holy-water stoups at the entrance of a church: for clerics, nobility, and poorer folk. The niche-shaped holy-water stoup sunk into the wall gave place after the sixteenth century to large or small basins, generally set on a pedestal, and resembling a baptismal font in shape. Very often these holy-water "fonts" are as large as those used for baptisms, especially in Italy, where they are richly decorated with carvings. During the seventeenth century large shells became very popular, and they are still used in some countries.

Size, Shape, and Material

St. Charles Borromeo lays down the following rules regarding the shape, size, and material of holy-water stoups: "The vessel intended for holy water shall be of marble or of solid stone, neither porous nor with cracks. It shall rest upon a handsomely wrought column and shall not be placed outside of the church but within it and, in so far as possible, to the right of those who enter. There shall be one at the door which the men enter and one at the women's door. They shall not be fastened to the wall but removed from it as far as convenient. A column or base will support them and it must represent nothing profane. A sprinkler (terminating with bristles and not a sponge) shall be attached by a chain to the basin, the latter to be of brass, ivory, or some other suitable material artistically wrought."[5]

In large churches it is much more convenient to have the holy-water stoups set well away from the walls, otherwise it is awkward for people to get near them, should there be a crowd. But in small churches it saves space to have them projecting from or set back into the walls. A block of stone can be hollowed out to contain a porcelain basin, which should be cemented into the stone. Large holy-water stoups, set on pedestals, should be about 3 ft. 6 in. from the ground; 3 ft. in diameter across the top; the basin about 2 ft. 4 in. diameter and about 3 in. in depth. Smaller stoups, jutting out from or set back into the wall, should be about 2 ft. in width, with a depth of about 3 in. If there is a niche it should be about 1 ft. in height, or more, according to the width at the base.

The material can be marble, stone, or concrete, but it must be nonporous. The shape should always be concave, otherwise it is difficult to keep the font clean. Shells are not recommended. They collect dirt and their sharp edges may scratch the fingers. The water should be changed at least once a week and the inside of the stoup cleaned out, otherwise a sediment will gather at the bottom and round the edges.

Small holy-water stoups, such as are sold by Catholic repositories, should never be hung up in a church. They are only suitable for domestic use. A holy*-water stoup is an obligatory piece

* A new appreciation of "holy" water is badly needed, lest secondary notions get the

of church furniture, and for this reason should form part of the essential fittings, and not be a merely temporary ornament which has little or no relation to the rest of the building.

best of this beautiful sacramental. Its origin seems to be the *cantharus*, a running-water fountain in the atrium of the basilica which was set up for lustral purposes, i.e., to cleanse face, hands, and feet before entering the church. A Greek stone cantharus found in Sicily contains the admonition, not only to wash our faces, but to cleanse our souls at the same time. From the running fountain to the stoup of our day is a big step in every way. The lustral character seems to have vanished from the mind of the laity who thinks more of the incidentals than the primary purpose, otherwise they would sense that it is not exactly logical to take the sacred lustral water that should renew our baptismal spirit (when sprinkling ourselves we make an act of contrition pronouncing the sacred words also used at baptism: in the name of the Father, etc. (a) before Sunday High Mass, when it is the priests duty to sprinkle us (*Asperges, Vidi Aquam*), (b) after Mass, when we leave the church (reason: we need cleansing from the dust of venial sin, before we participate in the Great Mysteries, but after participation we are, or at least ought to be, clean). If it is not a purely mechanical habit that makes us do so many things, it is probably the thought of gaining the indulgence which induces us to repeat a less sensible rite. We may, however, gain as much of the indulgence promised, if we do the rite once in its right place and with greater devotion. — H. A. R.

NOTES

1. The cantharus.
2. But in some places it afforded sanctuary to criminals who were fleeing from justice. You can still see the great sanctuary knocker in a porch at Durham Cathedral. There are instances of a room over the porch being used by hermits or anchorites during the Middle Ages.
3. There should be one or more holy-water stoups at each door normally used by worshippers. It is useful to have a few benches or chairs in the narthex of a church. In country places an open wire door to let in air is useful in summer, for it prevents birds from flying into the church.
4. Canon 1266.
5. *Instructions,* Chap. XXI.

CHAPTER XIII

THE PULPIT

HISTORICAL NOTES

The word *pulpit* is derived from the Latin *pulpitum,* which means a stage or scaffold. In the earlier ages of Christianity no special place for preaching was provided. The homily after the Lessons in the Mass of the Catechumens, which was always an essential part of the Liturgy, was delivered from the *ambo,* i.e., a sort of raised desk on the side of the chancel from which the deacon sang the Gospel. In some churches there was a second ambo on the opposite side of the chancel for the chanting of the Epistle. Many of these *ambones* can still be seen in the older basilicas in Rome and in other parts of Southern Europe. The ambo did not always stand in the chancel. For instance, it was under the great dome at Santa Sophia, Constantinople, and in the midst of the nave at Ravenna — to mention but two examples. As time went on, pulpits began to be erected on one or other side of the nave, or less frequently as part of the rood-loft. Ambones disappeared with the development of Gothic architecture, and the Epistle and Gospel were usually sung *"in plano,"* i.e., in the sanctuary below and away from the altar steps, as is prescribed by the rubrics of the modern Roman rite.[1]

Fine examples of mediaeval pulpits are to be found all over Europe. Many of them are constructed of wood, and as a rule they are much smaller than those erected to-day. Some are elaborately decorated with carving, others have sounding boards or testers. On the panels one often finds carved images of saints or painted figures, although many of the latter have long since been destroyed. The woodwork of the pulpit itself was often enriched with gold and colour. In Continental countries there are wonderful pulpits in the Renaissance and Baroque styles. The marble pulpits in Italy, designed by Donatello and other sculptors of the early Renaissance period, are famous; so, too, the riotously ornate Baroque pulpits in Belgium, or that unique pulpit at Cracow in Poland, built in the form of a ship, with sails, masts, and rigging, held up by sea monsters. At the present time, especially on the continent of Europe, there is a tendency to revive the older type of ambo at the entrance to the sanctuary in preference to the usual nave pulpit.

POSITION, MATERIAL, AND DESIGN

No definite rules are laid down as to the position, material, or design of pulpits. But it is advisable not to erect a permanent pulpit in a large church until its acoustics have been tested. It is suggested that a temporary wooden pulpit should be made, and moved about until the best position has been found. In

1. Rome. S. Lorenzo
2. Rome. S. Cesareo
3. Venice. S. Marco
4. Sefton, Lancs. England
5. Abbey Dore, Hereford „
6. Burnham Norton, Norfolk.
7. Worle, Somerset . . .

Pre-Reformation pulpits.

cathedral churches the pulpit should be on the Epistle side, so that the preacher can see the bishop seated on his throne in the sanctuary. In an ordinary parish church it is more convenient for the pulpit to be on the Gospel side, so that the sacred ministers at High Mass can see and hear the preacher when they are sitting down. On the other hand, since most men are right-handed, the average preacher will feel more at his ease if his right arm is not up against a wall or a column, and able to gesticulate freely. So for this reason the Epistle side of a church may be preferred as the position for a pulpit. It should not be too far down the nave, otherwise many of the congregation will be behind it.

If the pulpit stands in the nave, it should not be pushed too far back under an arch, or too close to the side wall. Otherwise the preacher has to strain his voice to be heard. The ideal spot for a pulpit is where the voice rings true and clear; where gesture is easiest and unrestrained; and where the preacher can be best seen by the congregation.

In a large church the top of the pulpit should be about twice as high as the shoulders of people who are sitting down; in small churches, about the same level as the shoulders of the listeners.[2]

Pulpits as a general rule, in stone or marble, are not so satisfactory as those carried out in wood. It looks warmer and gives more colour to a church, and at the same time it is more pleasant to hold on to than stone or marble which are the coldest of materials. An open-work metal pulpit is not to be recommended; it is distracting to see the preacher's cassock and feet.

There should be a door at the top of the pulpit steps. Many an eloquent preacher would feel far more at his ease if he knew there was no danger of falling backwards. Thirty-eight to forty inches is a convenient height for the sides of a pulpit. Most modern pulpits are too low and wide. Where a pulpit is too low a preacher is often at a loss to know what to do with his hands. The ledge at the top should be at least 5 in. broad to allow books to rest on it. It should be made quite flat. A small shelf for books with a little ledge is a convenience, and also prevents the preacher from leaning too far over the edge. There should likewise be a desk, strongly made with rounded edges that will not cut the hands. It should be fixed in firmly, but be readily adjustable, both as to the slope and the height. Some preachers object to pulpit desks, therefore it should be made in such a way that it can be removed if not wanted. Should a church happen to possess a metal pulpit-desk, the best thing to do is to cover it with a cloth of some rich material — not necessarily of the liturgical colour of the Sunday or feast day. Incidentally it may be well to point out that the desk should look diagonally across the church, not due west. An alternative to a pulpit-desk is a large cushion, covered with some rich fabric and adorned with tassels.

It is useful to have a small clock fitted into the top of the pulpit in case the preacher has not a watch with him. But should there be a west gallery a large clock can be placed thereon on the end wall. Another alternative is to make a round hole in the pulpit ledge to hold a watch.

1. *Batschums (Voralburg, Austria)*, H. C. Baurat and Clemens Holzmeister.
2. *Fonteiais (Switzerland)*, F. Dumas. 3. *Bléharies (France)*, H. Lacoste.
4. *St. Jacques, Ypres (Belgium)*, Ateliers d'Art de l'abbaye de Maredsous.

Some preachers would welcome a small fixed seat in a pulpit. It can be made with a hinge so as to be out of the way when not required. In Italy preachers often sit down between sections of their discourses.

The lighting is an important detail often forgotten. An electric light should be fixed so that it shines down on the preacher without casting shadows on his face. It should be well shaded, and at a reasonable height above the head. The switch should be within easy reach of the preacher — in the pulpit, not below. A hassock or kneeler should be remembered. A crucifix is not obligatory but is customary in many countries.

The *Caeremoniale Episcoporum*[3] states that on greater feasts the pulpit may be adorned with silk coverings of the liturgical colour — a custom which is observed far more by Protestant sects than by Catholics! At pontifical requiem Masses the pulpit may be covered with a black cloth.[4] All draperies must be removed from a pulpit after Mass on Maundy Thursday and on Good Friday, also when sermons on the Passion are preached.[5]

NOTES

1. *Ritus Servandus in Celeb. Miss.*, VI, 5.
2. A sounding board is essential in very large churches, and there is a good deal to be said in favour of a microphone with loud speakers.
3. *Caer. Ep.*, L. I, c. XII, n. 18.
4. *Ibid.*, L. II, c. II, n. 18.
5. S.R.C. 2891, ad 3.

CHAPTER XIV

CONFESSIONALS

HISTORICAL NOTES

Confessional boxes are comparatively recent additions to the accessories of worship. They were unknown in the earlier ages of Christianity. It is doubtful if any special piece of church furniture for the administration of the sacrament of Penance made its appearance before the fifteenth century. During the Middle Ages, when the majority of lay folk seldom went to the sacraments more than two or three times a year, confessions were usually heard by a priest sitting in the chancel; the penitent kneeling at his side without any sort of screen between them. Sometimes a choir-stall may have served as a confessional. The evolution of the confessional box is interesting. The primitive idea was that sacramental confession should be made in the open church without any attempt at hiding either the confessor or penitent. The modern idea, at least in English-speaking countries, is to ensure the greatest privacy for both parties.

ST. CHARLES BORROMEO'S INSTRUCTIONS[1]

St. Charles Borromeo, when drawing up his *Instructions on the Fabric of the Church* at the close of the sixteenth century, insisted that confessionals should be placed at the sides of the church in some open and clear space, partly on the south side and partly on the north. He states that "with the bishop's leave" it is permissable to place them sometimes also in other parts of the church, according to its size and plan, as, for instance, within certain chapels which are of ample size, or at the entrance or threshold, in such a manner that the confessor be within the enclosure of the railings, but the penitent outside. "By this arrangement, the chapel railings may be made to keep off such persons as would rush up without order to the sacred tribunal and place themselves too close to the person who is engaged in making his confession, to the probable disturbance either of the penitent himself or of the confessor." It is worth noting that St. Charles orders that the penitent should always be turned towards the high altar in the case of confessionals erected on the sides of churches. He recommends that every parish church should have at least two confessionals: one for women, the other for men.

Regarding the form, it is stated that it should be entirely made of boards, either of walnut or other kind of wood; that it should be enclosed on both sides and at the back, as well as covered at the top; but that it should be entirely open in front, and not in any way closed in. "Nevertheless, and especially in more frequented churches, it should have a door of lattice work, or of wooden bars

159

placed about 2¾ in. apart from each other with a lock and bolt, to prevent laymen, vagrants, or dirty people from sitting and idly sleeping in it, when the confessor does not happen to occupy it, to the great irreverence of the sacred above the pavement of the church, and it should be about 5 ft. 6 in. long by 2 ft. 9 in. broad. The seat for the confessor should be about 1 ft. 6 in. high above the base; about 2 ft. long, and about 1 ft. 4½ in. deep. The total height of the

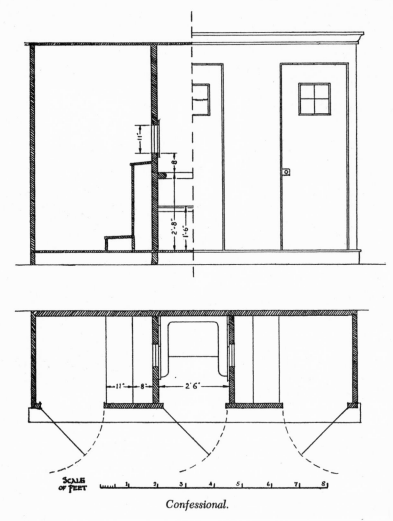

Confessional.

ministry which is exercised therein" (par. 3).

The base of the confessional, on which rest the feet of both the confessor and penitent, should be raised 5½ in. at most confessional should be about 5 ft. 6 in. St. Charles orders a small wooden rail for the confessor to rest his arm on, to be raised or lowered at will.

The penitent's "pew," i.e., the kneeling

desk, should be about 9 in. deep at the bottom, rising in a slope to about 2 ft. 6 in. from the base, with a length of 2 ft. ¾ in., having at the top a slightly inclined

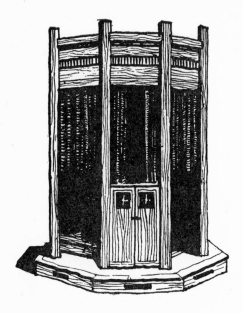

board 2 ft. long by 8½ in. broad. A kneeler is attached at the bottom, 5½ in. high, 11 in. broad, and as long as the "pew." The opening for confession is to be boarded in between the confessor and penitent, to be made at a height of 1 ft. 10 in. from the confessor's seat up to its lowest side, and to be 11 in. high by 8¼ in. wide. "To this opening should be fixed, on the side of the penitent, an iron plate full of holes, each as small as a pea. Moreover, on the confessor's side should be attached to the opening a light serge cloth or muslin, such as is called *bunting*" (par. 10).

St. Charles orders a crucifix to be placed on the penitent's side; also two boards on the confessor's side on which are printed certain prayers and formulas of absolution, lists of reserved cases, etc. He states that no alms boxes are to be placed in or near confessionals. No instructions are given for double confessionals such as are more common to-day in town churches.

CANONICAL LEGISLATION

Neither Canon Law nor any other liturgical authority has much to say about the design and construction of

Types of confessionals.

confessionals. The only points that are insisted on are:

1. "The confessional seat where women's confessions are heard must be situated in an *open and conspicuous* place, normally in a church, or public or semipublic oratory, set apart for women."[2]

2. "The confessional must be provided with an immovable screen of

fine mesh between the penitent and the confessor."[3]

Nothing more is *necessary* for a confessional: merely a seat for the confessor, situated in a part of the church where it is visible to the majority of the congregation, and a screen fitted with a small grating, covered with wire mesh or a piece of metal, pierced with small holes.

Despite the perfectly clear rules laid down in Canon Law concerning the position of confessionals in churches, public and semipublic oratories, it is very common to find them hidden away at the back of a church or in a chapel, so that they are as inconspicuous as possible.[*] In some churches it is impossible for the congregation to see the confessionals

unless they turn right round in their seats. For they are poked away in the narthex or vestibule or in the baptistery. Should a church be provided with confessionals at the back of the nave where they are not in "an open and conspicuous place," the best thing to do is to install something on the lines of red and green

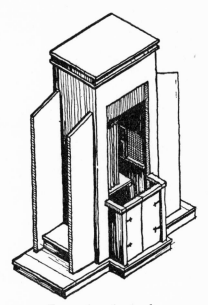

Types of confessionals.

"traffic lights" on the columns of the nave or on the walls of the aisles. They can be made to work automatically when the penitent kneels down or gets up from the prie-dieu or bench, thus showing when it is "all clear" for someone else to follow, or when the confessional is occupied.

The best place for confessionals is at the side of a church, either against the walls of the nave or in the aisles, with plenty of space between them, so that the different "queues" do not get mixed up in the entrances and exits.

---

[*] This does not contradict the establishment of chapels for the purpose of confession and nothing but confessions away from the eucharistic "body" of the church building. Our churches may gain a great deal by a clearer architectural separation of the various functions for which they have been built. The law of the Church already requires a separate baptistery, close to the gate, as the sacrament of Baptism is the gate to all other sacraments. A corresponding "Confessional Chapel" — the second gate to the sacraments of the living and a rebaptism, if I may call it thus — built and furnished in the spirit of penance and hope with a calvary, the Stations of the Cross and a Pieta would certainly functionalize our present all-purpose churches. There are many reasons for doing this, two practical ones: greater privacy for those who receive the sacrament of Penance, while services are held in the main body of the church and the possibility of leaving the main part unheated, while confessions are being heard. It should have easy access from the street and rectory, etc. By bringing the stations into this chapel we also solve the problem of the present "clash" in mood and "level" between the meditated "presence" of the stations and the sacramental "presence" of our Lord's *Passio beata* on the altar. A purer version of the eucharistic banquet hall and the sacrificial space, as set apart from other rites, can only help us to enter more profoundly into the mysteries. — *H. A. R.*

DESIGN AND CONSTRUCTION

The plan and construction of confessionals must largely depend on the size of the church and the number of confessions normally heard there.

1. In a small chapel or semiprivate oratory a movable wooden screen, standing on a firm base, will suffice.

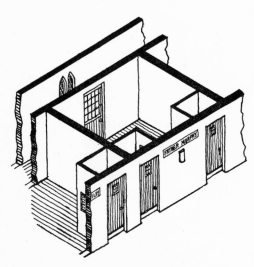

Sectional diagram showing arrangement of elaborate Anglo-American confessionals.

2. In a small parish church, served by one priest, there is a choice between a wooden confessional box, with one compartment for the penitent, standing against the wall or a more solid structure built into the wall and projecting outside. It can be provided with two small windows, one in each compartment.

3. In a large church, served by two or more priests, there should be a confessional for each of them. The name of each priest should be clearly marked above the door. If there is sufficient space, double-boxes should be erected, i.e., with places for penitents on either side of the priest. This arrangement saves time and is less physical strain on the confessor. But it is very important that the compartments should be soundproof so that the waiting penitent cannot hear the other penitent or priest. Here, again, the confessionals can be movable wooden structures, standing in the aisles or transepts, or else built into the outside walls of the aisles, which is really more convenient, as it saves space.

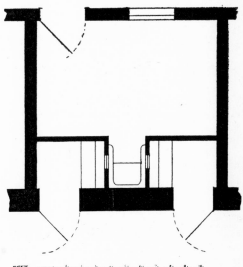

FEET

Plan of double confessional, with room attached.

4. In a very large church, particularly one served by a religious community, where the priests may have to spend many hours on end in hearing confessions, yet with intervals between penitents, by far the most convenient plan is to have the confessionals built as small rooms, opening into a cloister or passage, leading to the presbytery. In

this system there is no need to provide entrances for the priests into the church — merely one or two compartments for the penitents, with the confessor's seat fitted in between them, with its back against the wall of the church (see plan, p. 163). An electric light over the penitent's door, where the name of each confessor should also be shown, indicates

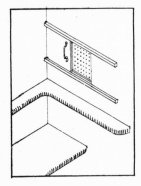

Detail of a sliding panel in confessional.

if the priest is within. Should the light be switched off, the penitent can summon the priest by pressing an electric bell. It is also advisable that there should be another board outside the box intimating if a particular priest is "at home" or "out."

The room inside should be provided with a table, chairs, book shelf, clock, and some system for heating, either a gas stove or an electric heater. Should there be a passage or cloister outside, a window can be inserted to give light, which should be made to open, but for the sake of privacy a skylight in the roof is more convenient. Or else glass panels can be fitted into the upper panels of the door giving access to the passage.

PRACTICAL DETAILS

An ordinary confessional should be at least 5 ft. 9 in. high, preferably over 6 ft. Both the priest's and penitent's compartments should be at least 2 ft. wide, and about 3 ft. 6 in. deep, to allow the penitent to kneel down.

The seat* for the confessor should be about 18 in. off the ground, and not less than 2 ft. in length, and about 17 in. deep. The seat should be made with a slightly sloping back and arm rests on a level with the bottom of the screen at which the penitent leans. There should be an electric light fitted on the left side so that the priest can read, should he wish to do so. The front part of the confessor's compartment can be filled in with a door (better fitted with glass panels), or with a heavy curtain hung over its entire length. In Italy most confessionals have a low door which only comes up about half the height of the box. Some have plain or folding doors across the upper part of the front which can be kept open when the priest is not actually hearing a confession.

Careful attention should be paid to the ventilation of a confessional, especially in a town church where priests have to remain in the boxes for several hours continuously.

It is important that the priest should be able to see out of the confessional,

---

* There seems to be no reason why the seat of the confessional could not be an armchair of good and conservative design, of course not an easy chair, as this would contradict the instructions of the Congregation of Rites and also not convey the idea of the judicial chair — the sacrament is judgment of mercy, the seated priest the judging Christ, the whole an "anticipated Parousia." — *H. A. R.*

especially when hearing childrens' confessions. They may need keeping in order. Hence the advantage of having a half-door with a curtain in front of the box. Otherwise curtains are not to be recommended. They collect dust and are unsanitary.

should be 6 in. off the ground and at least 11 in. broad.

The screened window between the priest and penitent should be about 11 in. high and not less than 8 in. wide. It should be inserted into the wall at a level of about 2 ft. above the confessor's

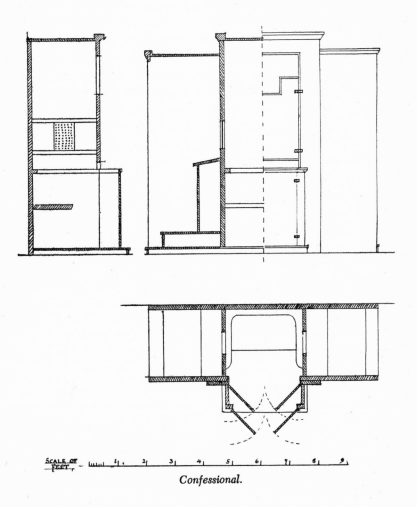

SCALE OF FEET

Confessional.

In the penitent's compartment there should be a projecting board against which he can lean: about 2 ft. 6 in. long, about 8 or 9 in. in breadth, with a slight slope towards the top. The kneeler

seat. Should there be two places for penitents it is necessary to have a sliding panel fixed to both gratings which can be opened or closed by the priest. The grating can be filled in with fine wire mesh or with a sheet of metal pierced with small holes. On the other hand it is often useful to have a small orifice through which the priest can pass leaflets or pictures or a note to a deaf penitent.

It is a general custom to hang up a small crucifix where the penitent can see it.

The entrance can be closed with an ordinary wooden door opening outwards — preferably self-closing — or with a heavy curtain suspended on a rod.

In the *Rituale Romanum*[4] it is stated that there should be a purple stole and a surplice, if it be the custom of the place to wear one, in every confessional.

NOTE. There exists such a great diversity both in the method of administering the sacrament of Penance and in the type of confessionals, that it can be understood why Canon Law only insists on a minimum of requirements. "In Spain it is the custom for men to stand up face to face with the priest sitting down in the confessional, kneeling down afterwards to receive absolution. The same practice may be found in Naples. But in most country places in Italy the confessions of men are always heard in the sacristy; the boxes in the church being reserved for women. In Milan Cathedral the confessionals stand all round the back of the high altar in the apse; in St. Peter's, Rome, they occupy both transepts. Spanish confessionals often look like large wardrobes when they are not in use. Sometimes they are placed in a room off the church. The room-type of confessional is to be found in many of the new churches in Holland, where in some of them the penitent's grille is fitted with a "capacious slit like that of a letter box, through which books and papers can be passed from priest to penitent or vice versa."[5]

Some of the modern churches in France and Belgium have very solid confessionals of brick, concrete, or stone, but unlike those commonly found in Britain, the penitent's compartments are nearly always quite open, either with or without a curtain. It is more usual for the priest's compartment to be closed with a low gate or wooden door (with a curtain inside) than to have a door completely closing the entrance.

NOTES

1. *Instructions,* Chap. XXIII.
2. C.J.C. 909, § 1.
3. *Ibid.,* § 2.

4. *Rom. Rit.,* III, c. I, n. 10.
5. Forse, E. J. G., *Ceremonial Curiosities* (1938), p. 68.

CHAPTER XV

SEATING ACCOMMODATION

PRACTICAL NECESSITY

In Southern Europe, and indeed in most parts of the world except countries north of the Alps and in North America, fixed seating accommodation filling up the whole or the greater part of a church, would be regarded as almost superfluous. But in Anglo-Saxon lands, no church, whether Catholic or Protestant, is looked upon as complete until the entire floor space apart from the sanctuary, has been filled up with benches, pews, or chairs.

HISTORICAL NOTES

During the early ages of Christianity it is highly improbable that permanent seats were ever contemplated. It was usual for the men and women to be separated.[1] Penitents stood in the narthex, catechumens occupied the rear of the nave, the rest of the faithful, according to their social status, stood in the front part of the nave or in the aisles. Wooden benches found their way into English parish churches about the thirteenth century, and then were only used at first by the more wealthy members of the congregation or by women. Previous to this date the only permanent seats were stone benches against the side walls or around the piers of the nave. The early wooden benches in England were very plain and solid structures, and not in the least luxurious. Certain antiquarians are of the opinion that the mediaeval custom of vergers with wands or staves leading processions, arose from the difficulty of forcing a way through the standing or kneeling congregations. In Italy there is still always someone to clear the way at the head of a procession.

As time went on pews and benches became much more ornate. Some of the surviving examples of mediaeval benches have elaborately carved ends. But the Gothic revivalists of the past century were responsible for the destruction of thousands of old pews and benches all over England. The only excuse for this vandalism is that most of the early benches and pews did not conform to modern ideas of comfort. They were far too narrow and too low in the backs. In some of the old Catholic chapels in Scotland, erected in the penal times, one can still find long, narrow benches with no backs — mere forms, which are more than penitential during a long sermon! Even before the Reformation pews began to be appropriated by families or individuals, despite the disapproval of the ecclesiastical authorities. The now almost universal custom in some countries of "pew rents" would have scandalized our Catholic forefathers.

CANONICAL REQUIREMENTS

Canon Law has not much to say about seating accommodation in churches, and even the few regulations that are laid down are seldom observed, owing to the difficulty of changing local customs, most of which have either been approved or tolerated by the ecclesiastical authorities.

Canon 1262 states that "conformable to ancient discipline it is desirable that the women should be separated from the men in church." This custom is still observed in country places in Italy, France, and elsewhere on the continent of Europe, but is seldom — if ever — found in English-speaking countries. In ancient times, as has been mentioned already, the men used to stand on the right side of the entrance, the women on the left. And it is worth mentioning that social prestige was not forgotten, for widows and virgins, as well as the nobility of both sexes, were expected to take their place near the sanctuary. Fr. Augustine, O.S.B., remarks: "In this country (United States) it will, we fear, be difficult to carry out this 'desire' of the Church, on account of our custom of having family pews."[2] And the same is equally true in Great Britain.

Canon 1263 tells us that "a distinguished place or seat in the church may be reserved for civil magistrates, according to their dignity and rank, but the liturgical laws must be observed." In the *Caeremoniale Episcoporum*[3] it is explained that the seats reserved for distinguished laymen—princes, magistrates, etc. — should be placed outside the sanctuary. They may occupy an ordinary bench or a prie-dieu, which may be covered with some rich fabric, but no canopy is allowed.[4] Only with a special papal indult may magistrates occupy a place within the sanctuary or choir.[5] It is an abuse for laymen to occupy the choir-stalls in a collegiate, conventual, or parish church during services,[6] although the custom is tolerated in some countries.

Canon 1263, § 2, lays down that "no Catholic may have a seat reserved for himself and his family in church, without the express permission of the Ordinary, and that the Ordinary shall not give his consent until he is satisfied that the rest of the faithful can be conveniently seated." According to Canon 1181, "admission to the church for divine service must be entirely free, and every contrary custom is hereby reprobated." It would therefore appear quite clear that it is a grave abuse to have men stand in the porch of a church to collect money from the faithful who wish to assist at Mass or any other service. On the other hand, the wording of Canon 1263 implies that, given the permission of the bishop, seat rents are permissible even if not altogether desirable. What really matters is that there should be sufficient accommodation in church for everybody — rich and poor.

What is more, the wording of the whole of Canon 1263 makes it quite clear that a bishop may revoke any concessions should he feel there is sufficient reason to do so. The Sacred Congregation of Rites has laid down that laymen acquire no personal right to pews and sittings, even by paying rents for them for a number of years.[7]

IMPORTANCE OF RIGHT SEATING IN A CHURCH

Owing to the fact that the seating accommodation of a modern church takes up practically all the floor space, thus distracting the eye from the rest of the building, even the most beautiful church can be ruined by the insertion of the wrong type of pews, benches, or chairs. Many priests and architects fail to realize this. A proof that some architects do realize that a church may be spoilt by seating accommodation is to be found in the fact that a perspective drawing of the interior of a new church often shows no seats in the nave! After all, a church is nothing more than a big furnished room, and no matter how good its proportions and details of the architecture may be when empty, the *furniture* will make or mar it when in place. The seats are the most conspicuous furniture when one enters a church.

CHAIRS OR PEWS?

Chairs have the advantage of being cheaper than either benches or pews, but unless they are of good workmanship they can be uncomfortable as well as ugly. Perhaps the most satisfactory type of modern seatings are the benches found in some Scandinavian churches. They are generally made of pine, stained or painted in bright colours, a pleasing contrast to the oak or varnished wood of English churches. Painted pews give a note of warmth and brightness, and form a suitable background to the rest of the colour scheme.

On the other hand, there is much to be said in favour of the Roman method of seating — loose chairs which each individual may place where he likes! When not in use the chairs can be piled up against a wall or columns, thus leaving the nave empty.

In small churches the solid, yet easily moved type of bench found in certain parts of Italy, might well be imitated. These benches are ideal for kneeling upright in a reverent position, and yet equally convenient when sitting. Where fixed rows of chairs have to be provided, tip-up kneelers, covered with rubber, are recommended instead of dust-collecting hassocks.[8] Lastly, why are so few modern churches fitted with tip-up chairs, similar to those found in theatres? They cost more, it is true, but they are infinitely practical rather than a long bench, and allow late-comers to pass between those who are already in their places.

LIMITATION OF FIXED SEATS; AISLES

In conclusion it may be said that far too many fixed seats are provided in most churches. The value of open spaces is forgotten, also the greater ease in keeping a church clean if not crowded up with benches and pews. There should always be wide gangways round the entrance doors, and plenty of space in the aisles. In a small church a width of 6 ft. is convenient for the centre aisle,[9] and not less than 3 ft. for side aisles. In cathedrals and large churches the centre aisles should be at least 6 ft. wide. Again, there is a curious psychological effect of drawing the congregation nearer together and concentrating them in one part of the building. But, of course, this does not apply to the big churches in large towns, which are often far too small for the accommodation of the crowds that flock to the various Sunday Masses. However in places where the congregation fluctuates according to the seasons of the year, i.e., in holiday resorts — there is much to be said in favour of only providing permanent seating accommodation in part of the church, adding chairs when needed, and keeping them stored away at other times. There should always be a central aisle in the nave, not only for practical reasons, but also because nothing looks so bad* as an unbroken mass of pews extending right across the centre of a church.

SIZE AND SPACING OF PEWS AND CHAIRS

The space between the back of one pew or row of chairs and another should be not less than 3 ft.; and the seating space in each pew or chair not less than 20 in. Thus a pew 6 ft. 8 in. long will accommodate four persons. Pews should

---

* To add an "impractical" idea: pews in themselves are a necessary evil. How would St. Peter's in Rome or Santa Sabina look, if their beautiful space were cluttered with pews? Aren't pews one of the main reasons why our congregations have been immobilized, refuse to take part in processions, feel like an "audience," stay put in "their places," are lined up in a sort of schoolroom or drill fashion? Take your pews out of your church and you will experience a new architectural beauty; the columns and pillars will "rise," the sanctuary will assume new and more majestic proportions, the light will diffuse in a different way, and the shrines will stand out in new significance. Such a space clamors for processions and close participation of the "con-gregation" in the liturgy. Alas! There is little hope that we will be able to relegate the pews to the side aisles for the aged, the infirm, and the mothers with children, while the strong and healthy stand and kneel in the open space of the center. If a modern designer turned out lightweight, backless stools at a low price we might find a solution in the middle of the two extremes! — *H. A. R.*

not be made too high: 2 ft. 8 in. is a convenient height. The backs should not slope more than 1 in. from the seat to the top of the rail. The kneeling bench, if there is one attached to the back of a pew, should be 6 to 7 in. off the ground, and a depth of 9 in. will provide comfort for the worshipper. It should be noted that this distance is measured, not from the base of the front pew, but from a perpendicular dropped from the back edge of this pew to the floor. A space should be left beneath the seats so that a brush may be passed under. If fixed kneelers are not provided, *thick* kneeling pads should be hung on hooks opposite each seat.

If benches or chairs are put too close together, it is impossible to kneel upright. Should a church be fitted with chairs the line of each row may be marked on the floor by brass-headed nails at either end of the row. A convenient spacing for chairs is 2 ft. 10 in. by 1 ft. 8 in. No bench or pew should be more than 15 ft. long, and if over 10 ft., should be open at both ends.

There should not be more than one ledge for books.

MATERIAL FOR FLOORS

It is always a problem to decide which is the best material for the floor of a church, above all that part of the building which is given up to the congregation. In cold countries it is wiser to have wooden flooring for the space which is occupied by seats, preferably wood blocks, set on a solid concrete foundation. The blocks should be of oak or pine. Boards nailed to joists are not so satisfactory though cheaper.

The aisles or alleys can be paved with stone or marble if expense is no object, but there is much to be said in favour of rubber, which is easier to keep clean and is silent.

Terrazzo mosaic, i.e., small bits of crushed marble set in cement and polished, is warmer than marble slabs. It makes a good surface for aisles, and is easily washed.

Stone paving looks well in the sanctuary, but it shows up spots of grease and wax from the acolytes' candles. Highly polished marble has the disadvantage of being easily scratched, and there is always the danger of slipping on it. So in most cases it is better to avoid it in any part of a church, certainly in northern countries.

NOTES

1. St. Charles' *Instructions* indicate that men and women were still separated during the sixteenth century. He allows *"predelle"* or kneeling desks for women, but strange to say, states that "there should be no benches for men to kneel upon" (Chap. XXVI).

2. *Commentary on the New Code of Canon Law*, Vol. VI, p. 205.

3. *Caer. Ep.*, c. XIII, n. 13.

4. S.C.R. 680, 726.

5. S.C.R. 959 f.

6. S.C.R. 157.

7. S.R.C., Nov. 22, 1642, n. 816.

8. It is a good method to have six chairs joined together by a wooden bar, fixed below the seats. This prevents them slipping about.

An alternative is to have the row of seats joined together, and the two outside legs of those at the end of the row fixed into slots on the floor. In this way the chairs are bound to remain in position, no matter how much people may lean on them.

9. The benches nearest the communion rails should be movable, so as to allow free passage for priest and servers during the absolutions after a requiem Mass. It is often difficult to get around the catafalque or coffin. Care should also be given to leave sufficient space at corners during the carrying of coffins in and out of a church, especially where there is no central passage. Most of our American churches provide for sufficient space for the coffin, by shortening the first three or four pews.

CHAPTER XVI

THE SACRISTY

HISTORICAL NOTES

Until the later Middle Ages, parish churches seldom possessed sacristies or vestries. It seems to have been an almost universal custom to keep vestments and sacred vessels in aumbries or cupboards in the church. In cathedrals and large churches each altar had its lockers or aumbries. Copes were kept in large semi-circular chests, some of which still survive in English cathedrals. There are exceptions to this general rule, especially in France, where many mediaeval cathedrals have large sacristies. In England a general place for the vestry was between the high altar and the east wall. There are some fine sacristies in Italy of the early Renaissance period. The modern type of sacristy is largely based on these Italian examples, where everything is arranged for convenience and efficiency.

St. Charles Borromeo laid down detailed instructions for sacristy construction which may well be studied by present-day priests and architects.[1] He insists that it must be an adjunct of all churches, according to the dignity of the church and its practical needs, with ample room for the storing of vestments and vessels.

POSITION AND PLAN

It is difficult to determine the best position for a sacristy or sacristies without reference to the nature of the site and available space. It may be at the side of the sanctuary or behind it. It is practical to have the priest's sacristy on one side of the high altar and the working sacristy on the other, connected by a passage behind the east wall. The two can also be joined under one roof, behind, or at the side of, the church. There should, if possible, be two doors, one opening onto the sanctuary, the other into the body of the church. The latter should be wide enough to allow three persons to walk side by side. Width should range from 3 ft. 4 in. to 3 ft. 6 in., with sufficient height to clear the processional crucifix when held aloft. It is wise to have iron bars across the sacristy windows.

One rule should never be forgotten: a sacristy should be too large rather than too small! If practical, a rectangular shape is more convenient than square. Light, ventilation, and heating must be remembered. Roof lighting is convenient in a large sacristy. St. Charles wisely recommends that there should be two or more windows, if possible opposite to each other in the same relative position, "so that, with this provision for a current of air, the place may not be damp or moist."[2] In fact, as much care should be put into its planning and arrangement as in any other part of a church.

Even in a small church or mission chapel served by one priest, it is recommended that the sacristy should not be less than 15 ft. in length and about the same width, preferably larger. Where there is only one sacristy more has to be kept in it.

1. *Vestment Chest*

This, the chief article of furniture, can be made of any hardwood. It should stand on a low base, about 4 in. off the ground, and measure 3 ft. 3 in. to not more than 3 ft. 6 in. in height, 4 ft. 9 in. long, and 2 ft. 9 in. deep. It is better to have six narrow drawers on one side, and twelve or more long shallow drawers on the other, the latter having double doors,* or roll panels (like the cover of a roll-topped desk), in front. The length of these drawers should not be less than 3 ft. 8 in., so as to give sufficient room for a normal-sized chasuble to be placed on it lengthways. It is more convenient to have shallow drawers, about 2 or 3 in. deep, so that only one set of vestments can be kept in each drawer. To preserve vestments the trays are covered with soft woolen material. The front edges, which should not be more than

---

* Doors or roll panels can be dispensed with if the individual drawer is well sealed against dust. Very shallow drawers accommodating only one set of vestments have the advantage of cutting down the labor and inconvenience of removing several sets of vestments to get to the desired one. This will be appreciated by the country pastor who is his own sacristan. Instead of a wool bottom a smooth and glazed fiber board bottom will be preferable in dusty climates. — *H. A. R.*

1¼ in. high, are better rounded off. Cedar wood, if it can be afforded, is an ideal lining, for it keeps out moths. Heavily embroidered vestments require cotton-wool under the folds, and a piece of white linen or calico should be laid over the vestments to keep out dust. Chasubles can also be kept hanging each on its own yoke, with a small piece of wood sticking out (under chasuble) on which to hang the stole and maniple.

Side drawers can hold amices, purificators, corporals, cinctures, palls, towels, tabernacle veils, altar breads, etc. Lavender bags may be put among linen.

When vestments are laid out it is convenient to spread a baize or woolen mat over the top of the chest, kept in place by hooks affixed to the back, to avoid slipping. It may be attached to a roller, and turned back when not in use.

2. *Cope Chest*

Copes should be kept in a closet on a stand. The latter can be made with a wooden upright, about 5 ft. 6 in. high, with a firm base, and a round yoke at the top. Copes should be hung on separate yokes, and covered with a dust cloth.

3. *Cupboard for Candlesticks, Vases, Etc.*

A special cupboard with two deep drawers should hold candle-ends, dusters, polishing cloths, etc., and storing candles; and another drawer for cruets, etc.

Shelves should be provided for Benediction candlesticks, holy-water vessel, bottle of altar wine, reliquaries, etc.

The censer can be hung from an iron bracket, about 6 in. long, fixed into a wall, or from a shelf on which the incense tin and charcoal jar may be placed, together with the incense boat.

Tongs and wire spoons for heating charcoal can hang on pegs or screw-hooks. Incense and charcoal can be kept at the bottom of a cupboard; the former in tins, the latter in an earthenware jar rather than in boxes.

Charcoal is conveniently heated over a gas jet, or electric heater, but a candle will suffice.

4. Cupboard for Albs, Surplices, and Cottas

It is convenient to have a cupboard where albs, surplices, and cottas can be hung rather than folded in drawers, where they get crushed. But the hanging of albs and cottas is a somewhat controversial matter; with the Roman "crimped" variety hanging is out of the question!

5. Safe

A steel, fire-proof safe, should hold the sacred vessels, monstrance, and parish registers.

6. Lavabo

A tap and basin should be provided in a convenient place,[3] with a towel hanging from a wooden roller at hand.

To save space it is a good plan to recess the basin into a wall. There should be a rack to dry purificators and to drain cruets. It is convenient to have running water. Over the Lavabo a card should give the prayer said by the priest when washing his hands before vesting.

7. Prie-Dieu

Provision should be made for a prie-dieu where the priest can make his preparation for Mass and thanksgiving afterwards. A large framed copy of the prescribed prayers should be hung facing the prie-dieu.

8. Sink

A washing-up sink and drainer covered with a board is useful, even in a small sacristy, to arrange flowers, etc.

9. Crucifix

A crucifix or picture of the crucifixion should hang over the vestment chest.

10. Holy-Water Stoup and Vessel

There should be a holy-water stoup on the right-hand side of the door leading into the sanctuary or church. Holy water should be kept in a special vessel, provided with a tap, in a position where it is accessible to the faithful.

11. Bell

It is the custom in Italy and other Catholic countries to have a bell, just inside the church, near the door leading into the sanctuary, which is sounded when the priest enters for Mass or other functions. This is not obligatory.

12. Chairs and Other Furniture

Provision should be made for a bench or one or two chairs, a reliable clock, one or two full-sized mirrors. (If only some celebrants could see themselves fully before appearing in public!) Cork-carpet, rubber, or linoleum are the best materials for floor covering. An electric radiator or gas fire is essential.

The switchboard for electric light in the church should be handy in the sacristy.

13. *Other Requirements*

a) Two wood or preferably metal *boxes* for altar breads. The cover should fit tightly, to prevent dampness.

b) *Cards* giving the following titles and proper names:
   (1) *Nomen Pontificis*
   (2) *Nomen Ordinarii*
   (3) *Titulus Ecclesiae*
   (4) *Oratio Imperata.*

c) A copy of the *Ordo* in a frame, with two pages open.

d) *Books.* Even a small church will require the following books which should be kept in a cupboard when not in use:
   (1) *Missale Romanum,* with Masses proper to the province and diocese
   (2) *Missale Defunctorum*
   (3) *Liber Epistolarum et Evangeliorum.* This is only used where there is High Mass.
   (4) *Rituale Romanum*
   (5) *Register for Visiting Priests*
   (6) *Epistles and Gospels in English*
   (7) *Notice Book*
   (8) *Ritus Servandus*
   (9) *Anniversaries of Departed Members* of the congregation and benefactors.

e) *Official Documents.* It is the custom in many places to have certain documents framed and hung up, e.g.:
   (1) List of days on which Benediction and solemn exposition is allowed by the Ordinary;
   (2) The testimony of the valid erection of the Stations of the Cross;
   (3) Relics that may be exposed on certain days.

f) The vesting prayers for Mass.

14. *Racks for Torches and Processional Cross*

There should be two or more torches for Benediction and processions and, if possible, glass lanterns for use out of doors. Torches and the processional cross may be kept in a rack with slots, lined with rubber.

SACRISTY REQUIREMENTS FOR A LARGE CHURCH

In a church, i.e., served by three or more priests, the following additional requirements will be needed.

Vestment Chest

This should be long enough to allow three priests to vest side by side, i.e., about 9 ft. in length, 3 ft. 3 in. high, and at least 2 ft. 9 in. deep. There should be two sets of twelve shallow drawers, with double doors in front, or roll shutters, which are more practical and convenient. At one side there can be a set of narrow drawers for corporals, purificators, veils, amices, etc. Above the top of the chest there can be another row of six cupboards, about 18 in. high, in which the priests keep their own birettas, amices, purificators, etc. — in one of them the altar-bread boxes can be placed.

At either end of the chest or elsewhere should be two cupboards for copes and albs. On each cupboard door a card should indicate its contents. To prevent vestments, particularly lace albs, etc., from getting torn, it is prudent to have handles with ball catches.

Many prefer to hang chasubles and dalmatics as well as copes from yokes on extending rods in large cupboards. St. Charles recommends this method for "more precious vestments."[4] There should be a separate cupboard for cassocks, surplices, and cottas.

Frontals will need a special case. If of the "Roman" type, i.e., stretched on a wooden frame, the best plan is to have a chest open at the top. It should be wide enough to contain twice the number of frontals generally used. If frontals can be folded, they should be kept in a cupboard with shallow shelves, wide enough to allow each one to be folded in four, with frontlets or superfrontals if they are used.

Work Sacristy

Every church, if possible, should have a separate work sacristy. The servers' cassocks, surplices, etc., should be kept there, with thuribles, incense, candles, candlesticks, torches, flower vases — everything not directly connected with the celebration of Mass.

There should be a cupboard for banners, and another for the altar wine and cruets. A sink with a board, covered with lead is useful for cleaning brasswork and arranging flower vases. There should be cupboards for brooms, mops, polishers, and pails. There can hardly be too many cupboards and drawers in a work sacristy.

Here, or in a store-room adjacent, space must be provided for keeping the following ceremonial accessories: (1) holy-water vessel and sprinkler; (2) processional crucifixes; (3) processional canopy; (4) *ombrellino;* (5) paschal candlestick; (6) triple candlestick and candle; (10) Tenebrae candlestick; (11) funeral candlesticks — four or six; (12) catafalque; (13) crib figures; (14)

carpets; (15) processional statues; (16) banner poles.

In a well-appointed church there should be a lavatory.

Sacristy Confessional

It may be useful to have a confessional screen in the priest's sacristy for the convenience of deaf persons.

On the other hand, it is not advisable to have a confessional in the doorway leading from the church to the sacristy as is sometimes done in small churches for the sake of saving space. Should anyone wish to go to confession before Mass, the servers have to be turned out of the sacristy! Should confessions be heard at any other time it is impossible for anyone else to work in the sacristy. There may, however, be churches where this is the only way that a confessional can be inserted.

In large town parishes it is convenient to have a confessional bell fitted outside the sacristy door so that a priest can be called without ringing the presbytery bell.

Business Sacristy

An almost essential feature of a large church is an office where parish business is done. In big towns there are innumerable calls upon the clergy. Parish registers have to be consulted frequently for records of baptisms and marriages, certificates of all kinds have to be provided and attested, stipends for Masses received, and the distribution of monies collected for the various needs of a large parish. It is often inconvenient for priests — not to mention his housekeepers — to receive callers at the presbytery, especially if it does not adjoin the church. It is more convenient both for priests and people if business can be transacted at church.[5]

The room should have a knee-hole desk, chairs, cupboards, shelves, and be well heated. There should be a steel safe for registers and notice books and where the collection monies can be deposited. A cupboard for objects left in church, such as handbags, prayer-books, handkerchiefs, and rosaries, should not be forgotten!

Old registers may thus be consulted at any moment. A shelf with standard reference books, Catholic and local directories, is useful. On the wall there may be a framed large-scale map of the parish, and photographs of parochial interest.

Should a town church not have its parish hall or schools adjacent, then it is essential that there should be a large room, well lighted and heated, for meetings of guilds and confraternities, e.g., Children of Mary, St. Vincent de Paul, Altar Society, etc. Such a room will provide a meeting-place for all parochial organizations, and as their meetings usually take place before or after services, it is far more convenient if such meetings can be held at the church. The room should be furnished with rows of chairs with a gangway in the centre, possibly with a low platform with a table and chairs at one end. Cupboards for books, etc., should be provided. A piano to accompany singing is useful. A few good pictures on the walls will make the room homelike.

NOTES

1. *Instructions*, Chap. XXVIII.
2. *Op. cit.*, Chap. XVIII, par. 2.
3. *Rit. Cel. Miss.*, Tit. I, n. 1.
4. *Op. cit.*, Chap. XXVIII, par. 12.

5. In Rome the "business sacristy" invariably consists of a large writing table in the ordinary sacristy. A separate room is not provided.

CHAPTER XVII

THE SACRED VESSELS

"Sacred vessels" are those used for the celebration of Mass, or to contain the Blessed Sacrament. They comprise: *chalice* and *paten, ciborium, pyx,* and *lunette.* "Non-sacred vessels" include the *monstrance* and *communion plate.*

Chalices and patens must be consecrated by a bishop or dignitary authorized to perform this function.[1] The ciborium, pyx, and lunette must be blessed by a priest having faculties — other sacred vessels *may* be blessed. All sacred vessels lose blessing or consecration if:

1. They have been so badly damaged or changed in form that they are unfit for their purpose;

2. They have been used for unsuitable purposes or exposed for public sale.[2]

Chalices and patens do not lose their consecration by regilding. There is a grave obligation to have them regilt if the surface gold has worn away.[3]

THE CHALICE AND PATEN

Historical Notes

The chalice is the most important of all sacred vessels. It is not known what type of cup was used at the Last Supper, and none of the legendary cups can be regarded as authentic. The earliest chalices were often made of glass, although metal was also used, and even wood. Some of these primitive chalices were large and had two handles, for the

laity were communicated under both kinds until the fourteenth and fifteenth century. A small pipe, or reed, was used in some places for communicating clergy and people. This practice has survived in a papal High Mass, when the pope and the deacon receive the Precious Blood through separate gold tubes. The subdeacon drinks directly from the chalice. It is doubtful if there are any chalices in existence which date from before the eighth century. They are usually two-handled cups, with large bowls and low bases. After the twelfth century the chalice became smaller as it was no longer needed to communicate the laity. The typical mediaeval chalice has a shallow cup, a broad base, and a round knob. As time went on the chalice grew taller, until by the end of the eighteenth century, it had become almost top heavy, the cup often being larger than the base, and the tapering stem very narrow.

Material, Size, and Style

According to modern present legislation, the chalice cup must be of gold or silver — if of the latter, the inside surface must be gilt.[4] The base and stem may be of any metal.

No definite shape is prescribed by the rubrics, but a good chalice should not be too large, and should be evenly balanced, with a heavy base. The knob or ball beneath the cup, which has to be held

178

Greek

St Godregand (8th cent)

St. Bathilde (7th cent.)

Antioch (6th cent.)

Ardagh (8th cent.)

English (14th cent.)

French (18th cent.)

German (17th cent)

Typical chalices.

Modern chalices.

1. Abbaye de Saint-Wandrille, France.
2. Abbaye de Mont-César, Louvain, Belgium.

3. Abbaye de Saint-Wandrille, France.
4. M. l'abbé Jadot ("La Croix Latine").

between the first and second fingers at certain places in the Canon of the Mass, ought to be easy to grip, and without sharp projections. There should be no projecting ornamentation round the edge of the cup, making it difficult to drink out of. The bowl should be neither too narrow nor too deep, nor yet too saucer shaped. If the base is encrusted with large jewels there is a danger that the edge of a lace alb may catch in it. According to instructions issued during a visitation of the churches of Rome in 1904, it is recommended that chalices should not be more than 28 centimetres high (just over 11 in.) and not less than 16 centimetres broad (about 6¼ in.).

Most authorities give 8 in. as a minimum height, though some modern examples are a good deal less than this.

The Paten

This should be slightly larger in circumference than the top of the chalice bowl. It must be concave, so that it rests securely on the chalice, and not too heavily. The edges must be thin so that fragments of the Sacred Host may be gathered up from the corporal. The underneath part may be engraved, but the top must be quite plain. A small incised cross near the edge of the outer surface is often inserted, although this is not usual in Rome. Like the chalice, the paten must be made of gold or silver, with at least the upper surface silver gilt. Patens with a depressed centre, and a surrounding flat edge — like a plate — are generally regarded as inconvenient, but some priests like them.

THE PYX AND CIBORIUM

In these days of frequent Communion with the reserved Sacrament, a large vessel, in shape not unlike a covered chalice, known as a ciborium, is used to hold the Sacred Particles consecrated at Mass and reserved in the tabernacle. In mediaeval times, as has already been explained, the pyx was often suspended above the altar and covered with a white veil. A survival of this custom is to be found in the white silk veil which must cover the ciborium when it contains the Blessed Sacrament.[5] No rules are laid down as to the material

15ᵀᴴ CENTURY   18ᵀᴴ CENTURY   16ᵀᴴ CENTURY.

LA CROIX LATINE (BELGIUM)   JEAN HESSE (FRANCE)   PRINKNASH ABBEY.

Monstrances.

of the ciborium, other than that it must be solid and suitable, and well closed.[6] The inside of the cup must be gilt, as the Blessed Sacrament must rest only on gold or linen. Usually the shape is broader than a chalice, and the curved sides are not so round. Sometimes the bottom of the cup is made convex, with a slight elevation which makes it easier to lift out the small Hosts. The lid is surmounted by a small cross or emblem.

The size of a ciborium is determined by the number of particles needed for Communion. In a large parish the ciboria may be as wide as 7 in.; the normal diameter is about 4 in.

The Pyx

When the Blessed Sacrament is taken to the sick it is put into a small, round box, usually of silver, about 1½ to 2 in. in diameter, and less than 1 in. deep. In parishes where sick calls are numerous there should be a pyx large enough to hold ten or twelve small Hosts. The bottom is generally slightly convex. It is convenient for the cover to be hinged, with a spring catch. The inside should be gilt. The priest carrying the Blessed Sacrament in the pyx places it in a small silk bag, hung round his neck by a silk cord.

THE MONSTRANCE

The monstrance, or *ostensorium,* is a special vessel for "showing" the Sacred Host to the people, i.e., a shrine for public exposition of the Blessed Sacrament.

Historical Notes

Vessels for carrying the Blessed Sacrament in processions seem to have been introduced as early as the eleventh century, but they were more like portable shrines or closed-in reliquaries. It is doubtful if the Sacred Host was exposed to view before the thirteenth century, and this practice did not become general until about two hundred years later, except on the feast and during the Octave of Corpus Christi. The earliest monstrances preserved are in the form of a cylindrical tower, made of crystal, and covered with a metal spire, supported by flying buttresses. The Sacred Host — then as now — was placed in a *lunette,* or lunula, i.e., a crescent-shaped clip, or a small circle of metal inserted in the monstrance. By the sixteenth century the monstrance had assumed the shape of a sun, surrounded by rays. Since then this form has been the most usual.

Material and Form

It can be made of any metal. Gold or silver are usual, though brass or copper gilt are also used.[7] Although Pope Clement XI recommended that monstrances should be made in the form of a sun with rays, any other reasonable shape is lawful. The only detail that is obligatory is a small cross on the top.[8] The monstrance should not be adorned with small statues of saints, for it is forbidden to place these even on the altar during exposition (see p. 127).

A monstrance can be of any size — there is one at Toledo more than 12 ft. high! As the monstrance has to be carried in processions, it is obvious that it must not be too heavy — or that the central part is separate from the base.

When standing on the altar, and not in use, the monstrance should be covered with a silk veil, which may hang loosely or be shaped to fit over the monstrance.[9]

No vessel used in connection with ecclesiastical functions lends itself so readily to freedom in design than the monstrance, as much liberty in shape and material is allowed by rubrics.

THE LUNETTE

The lunette in its earliest form consisted of two crescents, on either side of the consecrated Host. It must be of gold or of silver gilt.[10] It may have two round glasses, surrounded by a rim, in which case the Host rests on the bottom of the rim and is enclosed by the glasses; though it must not touch them.[11]

If the lunette is without glass, it must be placed in a small metal box called *custodia* (silver gilt or gilded inside), when in the tabernacle. If the Host is enclosed with glass, the lunette may be placed in the tabernacle without the custodia.[12] The custodia may hold the lunette vertically or horizontally. The lunette is fitted into the monstrance or custodia with a slot or groove.

THE COMMUNION PLATE

On March 29, 1929, the Congregation of the Sacraments ordered that a small metal plate, gilt on the inner surface, must be held beneath the chin of persons receiving Holy Communion. No shape was prescribed, but for convenience it is better that there are two small handles at each side. Should it be the custom for the server to hold the plate, one long handle is more convenient. The plate should be about the size of an ordinary paten used at Mass, and without a rim, so that it can be purified easily. When not in use, the communion plate can be kept in a bag or case on the credence table. As it is handled by large numbers of people it should be cleaned and polished frequently.

NOTE. Chalices and patens (after consecration), as well as purificators, palls, and corporals which have been used at Mass, may be handled only by tonsured clerics, or lay folk who have charge of them, e.g., sacristans.[13] Other persons may touch them only with special permission of the Holy See.[14]

Purificators, palls, and corporals, which have been used may not be washed by lay folk, until they have been thoroughly rinsed by a cleric in major orders. The water after use must be emptied into the sacrarium, or if there should not be one in the church or sacristy, thrown into the fire.[15]

NOTES

1. *Rit. Cel. Miss.*, I, n. 1.
2. C.J.C. 1305, § 1, 1°, 2.
3. *Ibid.*, § 2.
4. *Rit. Cel. Miss.*, VII, n. 4.
5. Canon 1270; *Rit. Rom.*, IV, c. 1, n. 5.
6. Canon 1270.
7. S.R.C. 3162, ad 6.
8. S.R.C. 2957.
9. S.R.C. 4268, ad 7.
10. S.R.C. 3162, ad 6.
11. S.R.C. 3234, ad 4; 3974.
12. S.R.C. 3947.
13. Canon 1306, § 1.
14. S.R.C. 4198, ad 15.
15. Canon 1306, § 2.

CHAPTER XVIII

SACRED VESTMENTS

HISTORICAL NOTES

It is an instinct of humanity to wear special clothes for ceremonial occasions, especially for religious ceremonies. Nearly every one of the great world religions has evolved a uniform to be worn by its officiating priests. The Christian Church has been no exception to this general rule.[1]

During the first centuries of Christianity there was no distinction between civil and ecclesiastical dress. The first Christian presbyters and deacons wore the same garments during the celebration of the Eucharist as during their ordinary avocations. From motives of respect for the sacredness of the function, it may be presumed that the clergy would set aside their best and cleanest garments. Then came the barbarian invasions of the Huns, Goths, and Vandals, which led to a change of fashion in men's clothing as well as in the way of life of the Mediterranean peoples. The barbarian dress, leaving the legs free and unencumbered with flowing draperies, may have been more practical and convenient, but it was not considered suitable for Christian worship, at least so far as the officiating clergy were concerned. So, when Sundays and feast days arrived, old garments which had been carefully preserved would be brought out, even though the style and cut were no longer

"up to date." And in this way a special priestly costume was gradually evolved — the liturgical vestments with which we are familiar. Few realize that these strange-looking garments are really nothing more than a modification of the ordinary everyday clothes once worn by Roman citizens.

The Eucharist vestments were not an "invention" of the Church. They were not derived from the splendid vestments worn by Jewish priests. They have only become "sacrificial" because they were the clothes worn by priests and laymen in the days of persecution, and which have been retained from motives of reverence and conservative instincts. They are a constant reminder of the sufferings of the early Christians and the martyrs; garments hallowed by the traditions of many centuries and which have become part and parcel of Catholic worship, although not necessarily essential to it. The time may come when a new and fierce persecution may make it necessary for priests to say Mass in trousers and a short jacket![2]

During the Middle Ages, long after the number of liturgical vestments had been fixed definitely, there was a tendency to "decorate" them, and to cut down their size. Some of them ceased to have any practical or functional purpose, and became mere ornaments, retained from conservative instincts. So to-day, except in places where there has been a revival of the earlier types of vestments, it is almost impossible to detect any relationship between the original secular garments of the first ages of Christianity and the purely decorative "Gothic" vestments evolved in the later Middle Ages and copied by "Gothic" revivalists of the nineteenth century.

LITURGICAL REQUIREMENTS

There are two kinds of vestments used in the celebration of Mass: (a) the outer vestments of silk (chasuble, dalmatic, tunicle, stole, and maniple); (b) the inner vestments of linen (amice, alb, and cincture). The rubrics of the Missal lay down no definite rules concerning the shape, material, or decoration of vestments, merely that they are to be intact, clean, and *beautiful,* also that they must be blessed.[3] Canon Law lays down that the liturgical laws and ecclesiastical tradition, must in the best possible way, as also the laws of Sacred Art, be observed as to the form and material of vestments.[4]

It should be noted that it is not permissible when making vestments to depart from the recognised usage of the Church in Rome and to introduce another style and shape of vestment, even an old one, without consulting the Apostolic See. There is a difference of opinion as to the precise meaning of this rescript of the Sacred Congregation of Rites.[5] However, most authorities seem to be agreed that it rules out all forms of vestments which are not based on those *actually* worn in Rome — unless previous permission has been obtained to reintroduce vestments of an earlier

shape. On the other hand, as Father O'Connell points out, "some writers, however, think that [the primitive or mediaeval type of vestment, or the Gothic Revival shape] is permitted, despite the clear terms of decree 4398." And he adds: "It seems to be the unanimous wish, not only of the lovers of sacred art, but also of rubricians, that the Holy See may in the future permit, or at least tolerate, the restoration of the more ample mediaeval form of the chasuble."[6]

It may be noted: (1) Exhibitions of full-shaped vestments have been held in Rome and not condemned; (2) It may be presumed that there is permission to use full vestments in the United States, Great Britain, Belgium, Holland, Switzerland, Austria, Germany, and France, since they are found in all these countries. It is the business of the local bishop to establish facts and interpret the law. The Sacred Congregation of Rites wishes to prevent scandal which might occur in places where the faithful are accustomed to a particular shape of vestment. (3) As St. Charles' vestments have approbation, it can be presumed that this full shape can be used in any country where the Roman rite is followed.

Soft, pliable materials are better than stiff brocades. Incidentally, a lightweight vestment is more comfortable! Hard-woven silk cannot be recommended too highly. Hard and stiff metal braids are not desirable. An argument in favour of full vestments is that their revival might help to draw East and West together; their outward forms of vesture would then be the same at rock bottom.

LITURGICAL COLOURS

During the early ages of the Christian Church, secular clothes were usually white. On occasions of mourning the toga of the Roman citizen, otherwise always white, was grey or some dark colour — the emperor alone wore a toga of purple — i.e., a rich red, not violet. Other forms of cloak were usually of a dark colour, but the prevailing note of everyday dress was white. Thus the vestments used in the early Church, except the chasuble, would also have been white.

It was not until the Middle Ages that colour sequences for vestments were drawn up, and there was a great variety of practice before the Reformation. Except in cathedrals and large churches, the best vestments, regardless of colour, were used for the highest feasts. Certain dioceses, particularly in France and Spain, evolved colour sequences of great elaboration. In some of the English cathedrals, e.g., Lichfield and Exeter, there were rather vaguely defined sequences. As a general rule plain, unbleached linen, rather like sackcloth, marked with crosses and other devices in red, was used in Lent. White, too, was often used at Pentecost as well as during Paschaltide. Red was the usual colour for Passiontide, and blue was common for Advent. The Sarum Missal, on the other hand, orders red for all Sundays out of Lent, and in some churches it was used during Advent and Lent. So great was the diversity of practice in England alone before the Reformation!

The modern Roman colour sequence, now obligatory wherever the Roman rite is followed, consists of five colours — white, red, green, violet, and black.[7] Any *shade* of these colours is allowed. It is worth noting that the Roman violet is the same colour as the reddish purple used in the ceremonial robes of prelates, not the blue-violet of the flower, nor the crude purple so often seen. Yellow vestments are not permitted, even as a substitute for cloth of gold, which may replace white, red, or green on great feasts.[8] Neither is blue allowed except by special permission, although it is permitted in Spain and in the Spanish colonies of Latin America on the Feast of the Immaculate Conception. Real cloth of silver may be used instead of white.[9] Mixtures of colours — except in the ornaments and linings — is forbidden.[10] Rose vestments may be worn on the fourth Sunday of Lent and the third Sunday of Advent.[11] The decoration and lining of vestments may be any suitable colour.[12]

THE STOLE[*]

The stole was originally a large linen handkerchief thrown over the left shoulder by the deacon at Mass — rather in the same manner as a waiter carries a napkin when serving a meal. It was used to cleanse the sacred vessels. As time went on, linen cloths — now reduced in size and known as purificators — came into use, the deacon's stole ceased to have any practical purpose and became a mere ornament. It was folded into a

[*] According to other authorities, especially the recent research by Joseph Braun, S.J., the history of this vestment is quite uncertain. The word *stola*, from the Greek στόλη, was first used in Gaul, whence it migrated to Rome and superseded the word *Orarium*. — H. A. R.

narrow strip and eventually became a flat band of silk or other rich stuff and not of linen. Yet the deacon still continued to wear his stole over his left shoulder, but now *under* his dalmatic. When bishops and priests adopted the stole as a vestment (which at Rome did not take place till as late as the twelfth century), it was worn round the neck with both ends hanging down in front. About the sixth century, priests in Gaul crossed the two ends on the breast, keeping them in place by the girdle, and this custom was adopted everywhere in Western Europe during the Middle Ages.

Both the deacon's and the priest's stole are derived from the linen cloth called *orarium,* which name has nothing to do with the word *orare* — to pray — but comes from *os–oris,* a mouth. The orarium was a face-cloth, and could be used both as a kind of muffler round the neck or over the head, or as we have seen, as a napkin. The name *stole* is derived from the Latin *stola,*[13] which originally meant the long robe worn by Roman ladies, but which was later applied to any garment of state, and even to mere badges of office, such as the stole, which ceased to be a garment. The amice also seems to have been derived from the orarium, and took its place as a neckcloth or head covering when the *orarium* became the stole. Mediaeval stoles were very long and narrow. Broad stoles with spade-shaped ends came into fashion during the eighteenth century.

For the sake of convenience a stole should not be less than 9 ft. in length, exclusive of the fringe. The width should be about 2½ in. at the neck, broadening to about 3½ in. and not more than 5 in. at the ends. The stole may be quite straight, or made in two pieces, joined at the neck. This latter form helps to make it lie more smoothly on the shoulders under the chasuble. But this is not needed when the stole is made of very soft material and kept quite narrow. It is unnecessary to sew on a piece of linen (the linen is a relic of the times when priests wore their hair long), or lace in the middle, as the stole should be worn, not close up to the neck, but between the shoulders. Only one cross is required, i.e., in the middle.[14] The ends may be adorned with a silk fringe or tassels, not stiff gold braid. Three crosses on the stole and maniple are invariable at Rome. Gold fringes are much used.

THE MANIPLE

The maniple, or *fanon* (this word is derived from the Latin *pannus,* meaning a piece of cloth; the letters *p* and *f* being interchangeable) started by being a napkin or handkerchief, rather like the stole, and it was also used by deacons and acolytes to cleanse the sacred vessels, to wipe the celebrant's mouth or eyes, etc. It was carried in the left hand, and lingered on as a practical necessity much longer than the stole. The maniple did not become a mere ornament until the twelfth century. But for more than a hundred years before this it had been suspended from the left wrist as it is to-day.

Many maniples are made far too short and tend to sweep the altar when the priest raises his left arm. A maniple should never be less than 2 ft. in length, and as much as 3 ft. 6 in. is still more

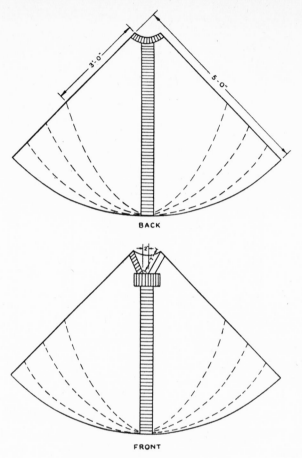

BACK

FRONT

Ancient Roman chasuble showing
gradual cutting away at sides.

convenient for the wearer. It should not be stiffened, but hang loose. If it is made to fit closely round the arm, at both sides, an elastic band or two tapes are not necessary to keep it in position. The usual Roman maniple has wide ends, and is shorter than those recommended. Like the stole, only one cross is needed on the maniple – in the centre, although in Rome three crosses are the rule. An interesting relic of the practical origin of the maniple has survived in the custom of discarding it whenever the priest, deacon, or subdeacon, are not actually fulfilling some function directly connected with the Mass – e.g., at solemn Benediction. The maniple should be retained if a sermon is preached at Mass by one of the sacred ministers. Bishops, abbots, and other prelates having the use of *pontificalia,* do not put on the maniple until after the *Indulgentiam,* etc., after the *Confiteor* at the beginning of a Mass of the living.

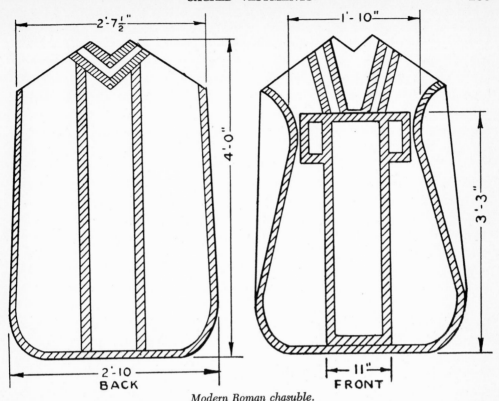

Modern Roman chasuble.

THE CHASUBLE

Historical Notes

It is not easy to realize when looking at a typical modern chasuble — i.e., the vestment worn by priests or bishops over all the other garments when celebrating Mass — that in its original form it was nothing more than a large semicircular cloak, covering the whole body, with a hole in the top for the head to pass through. The primitive chasuble was not unlike one of those waterproof capes now worn by soldiers and cyclists.

Cloaks of this type were worn by the middle and poorer classes who were not legally Roman citizens, and who were not entitled to the toga. It was known as *phenolion* in Greek and *paenula*, or *planeta*, in Latin. "The cloak that I left at Troas," mentioned by St. Paul in the second Epistle to Timothy (4:13) was perhaps a primitive chasuble, but the apostle may have worn it as a rain coat as well as when celebrating the Divine Mysteries! Some time or other this garment was given the nickname of *casula* — meaning a little house or tent — and no better word could have been chosen, for the cloak offered a place of refuge from wind, rain, or storm.

It has been stated already that the presbyters and bishops of the early Church wore no distinctive uniform when celebrating sacred functions. But when secular fashions changed, the Church retained clothes of an earlier period, using them for religious purposes only. The *paenula*, or *planeta*, had become a garment of dignity worn by state officials and even taking the place of the toga. So it became the sacrificial vestment of the Christian priesthood.

At one time it was supposed that the primitive chasuble was completely round, so that, if laid flat on the ground it would form a circular disk. Subsequent research has made it clear that the original "little house" was invariably bell-shaped, i.e., rather like a cope with the front edges joined. In fact, the two garments were in origin the same. The open form of (the cope) was found more convenient as a rain cloak! The chasuble would have been made out of a semicircle of cloth with the straight edge folded over in the middle and the two borders sewn together. Should the garment have been made of any heavy material it would have been awkward because of the weight on the arms.

During the Middle Ages when heavier fabrics became more common and embroidery more elaborate, it was almost impossible for the priest to raise his hands or arms unless the deacon or subdeacon were at his side to roll back the chasuble. So, by degrees the chasuble was lightened by cutting it away on the arms; the length in front and behind remaining practically unaltered for many centuries. This process of shortening and cutting away the sides to secure greater freedom of movement went on from the thirteenth to the seventeenth century, until the chasuble lost all trace of its original cloak form and assumed the appearance of two stiffened panels joined by shoulder straps, rather like a modern "sandwich man's" boards. It is

worth mentioning that the rubrics of the Roman Missal, which date from 1570, presume that the priest will be wearing a full and ample chasuble, such as was still almost universal at that date. Otherwise there would be no practical reason for the directions to the deacon at High Mass to lift up the edges of the chasuble at the Elevation:[15] "the minister with his left hand raises the edge of the hinder portion of the chasuble *lest it should impede the celebrant* in the raising of his arms. . . ."

There are several types of the post-Reformation chasubles which were evolved during the seventeenth and eighteenth centuries — Italian, French, German, and Spanish. The Italian (usually called "Roman") is rectangular shaped at the back, extending just beyond the edge of the shoulders and cut away in front, rather like a fiddle. The back is ornamented with a broad orphrey in the shape of a pillar. There is a broad T-shaped cross in front, while the opening for the neck is long and has a square end. The opening at the back is slightly pointed and not nearly so deep. The typical French chasuble is shorter and stiffer and has a Latin cross at the back and a pillar in front. The Italian model usually hangs quite loosely from the shoulders, the Spanish type is longer than either the French or Italian, but is more cut away on the shoulders, so that, from behind, the bottom appears to be wider than the top.

The orphreys were originally nothing more than strips of material covering the principal seams back and front. They served a purely practical purpose of hiding and strengthening seams, and were for ornament or to rouse pious thoughts in the worshippers.

The so-called "Gothic" chasuble should really be called "Gothic Revival," for it has little in common with any known mediaeval vestment, being cut out with a front and back shape complete, joined along the shoulders and decorated with a Y-shaped cross, leaving the seams uncovered. The correct way to construct a real conical-shaped chasuble is to cut out two pieces of material and have two seams down the back and front. To ease the set of the shoulders a narrow yoke can be inserted, thus making a wider shoulder angle, and providing scope for an extra orphrey in conjunction with the upright pillar on the main seam. What must be remembered is that the logical framework for decoration on a chasuble is its constructional seams. Should it be possible to obtain wide enough material there is no reason why there should be any seam down the back of a chasuble or any orphrey. Conical or semicircular chasubles look better and are easier to wear if made without lining, in which case the edge can be turned inwards and hidden with a narrow braid.

No particular shape of chasuble is prescribed by the rubrics of the Missal, its form being determined by the general law that governs all vestments (see page 185).[16]

The modern division of chasubles, according to shape alone, into Gothic, semi-Gothic, and Roman is both false and unreal. Renaissance architecture did not affect the *shape* of vestments, only the style of decoration was changed. . . . "All vestments in *lawful* use in countries following the Roman rite are 'Roman,' though they may be decorated in accordance with any national or individual taste or standards provided these be worthy."[17] Full and flowing chasubles were being worn in Rome long after the Basilica of St. Peter had been built and, as has already been pointed out, were envisaged by the compilers of the present *Roman Missal, Ritus Servandus in Celebratione Missae,*[18] and *Caeremoniale Episcoporum.*[19] After the sixteenth century the cutting down of vestments proceeded much more rapidly in countries north of the Alps than around the Mediterranean. As a matter of fact the modern Italian chasuble is, in its decorative elements, much nearer the original garment than the so-called Gothic one.

Practical Details

The following measurements are suggested for a Roman chasuble of ample size:

Length: 42 in. (minimum)
Width at back (across shoulders): 30 or 31 in.
Width in front (across chest): 21 in.
Width in front (at bottom): 27 in.
Breadth of pillar and cross: 8 to 12 in.
    (Including the braid which is generally about an inch wide).[20]

A full, cone-shaped chasuble is made up semicircular with a radius of 62 in., slightly shorter in front, about 2 in. less. They may be mitigated to taste by cutting away the sides.

The Roman chasubles that were being worn when the *Roman Missal* was drawn up at the close of the sixteenth century were very long and reached down to the heels. St. Charles Borromeo laid down that for the province of Milan the chasuble was never to be less than 54 in. across the widest part — i.e., 27 in. at each side of the neck. St. Charles directs that the chasuble should be wide enough "to make a fold at the elbows," i.e., it should lie on the forearm and so reach midway between elbow and wrist. What is more, the Borromean legislation obtained the formal approval of the Holy See.[21] So, as we are recommended in Canon Law to bear in mind "ecclesiastical tradition" as well as "liturgical laws" so far as the form and material of vestments are concerned, this genuinely Roman form of chasuble, such as is envisaged in the *Roman Missal* and *Caeremoniale* might well be revived more often, provided that no lawful objections are offered.

The Broad Stole and Folded Chasuble

The so-called "broad stole," worn by the deacon over his left shoulder from the Gospel till after the Communion on certain days when folded chasubles are used at High Mass instead of a dalmatic and tunicle, e.g., in Lent, is really nothing more than a substitute for a chasuble folded into a long strip, which was the primitive practice, and which is still provided for in the rubrics. To do this the chasuble must be folded lengthways before being put over the shoulder and then fastened under into the girdle at the right arm. The custom of using a broad band of violet or black silk came in during the eighteenth century when chasubles had become so stiff that they could not be folded. If a broad stole is

worn it should be made about 42 in. long and from 10 to 12 in. wide. There should be no cross on it, and it should be quite plain.[22]

In these days chasubles are folded about half-way up in front as is ordered in the rubrics of the Missal.[23] Originally they were folded up at the sides, leaving the arms free, thus having much the same appearance as the ordinary Italian chasuble.

THE COPE

The Latin word for cope is *pluviale*, which might be translated "rain-coat." The word cope is derived from *cappa*, which was the name for this garment in Gaul. The word *cappa*, again, is derived from *caput* — the head — and refers to the hood which was always attached to the cope. This vestment, as the name *pluviale* implies, was originally used for purely utilitarian purposes, and was not reserved for clerics. It was merely a semicircular cloak made of wool and sewn together on the breast, being thence open to the feet. Except that it was open in front, there was little to distinguish the cope from the chasuble.

During the Middle Ages, the cope developed into a purely ceremonial garment and the hood degenerated into a flat, shield-shaped appendage at the back. The older utilitarian form, made of black woolen stuff, was still worn closed in front like a chasuble for outdoor use (the closed cope or *cappa clausa*). The *cappa choralis* or choir cope, open in front, was worn in church over the surplice by canons during cold weather.

The vestment cope is used for services other than the Mass itself. It is also a kind of "state robe" for bishops and other prelates, worn with the mitre on certain occasions. But it is not, like the chasuble, the special vestment of a priest and may also be worn by any cleric. In some countries copes are worn by lay cantors in choir functions, but this is an abuse.

Copes being semicircular in form are usually made with a perfectly straight upper edge, but they hang far better if shaped round the shoulders. This prevents the overlapping of the lower edges in front, and the awkward appearance of the back of the neck sticking up in a point. Although a semicircular cope, made of rich embroidered velvet or brocade with a stiff lining, does possess a certain dignity, it must be admitted that a thin cope with graceful folds, well shaped on the shoulders, is more in keeping with the original purpose of this vestment — i.e., a cloak. What is more, such a cope is far more comfortable to wear, although it may not appeal to priests who prefer to follow Roman fashions! It would seem that it is obligatory to have a hood or flat shield on the back of a cope if we conform to Roman fashions. The hood may be round or pointed, and a real hood of soft material looks best of all. As the "accepted usage of the Church in Rome" does not include copes of unusual shape, it is doubtful if any of these alternative designs is rubrically correct at the present time. The orphreys, i.e., bands of embroidery made of different stuff from the ground of the vestment, should not be made too broad. The clasp, or morse (from *morsus,* "bite"), can be of the same material as the cope itself or of metal. However, metal clasps are not worn in Rome. Only a prelate may wear a jewelled morse.[24]

THE DALMATIC

The dalmatic is a robe with wide sleeves, reaching to or below the knees. It is so called because it was originally a tunic of Dalmatian wool, introduced into Rome in the fourth century as an outer garment for deacons. It was also worn by the pope beneath his chasuble, but for a long time bishops did not adopt it, and then only with special permission from the pope. It was not until the ninth century that the dalmatic became the recognised vestment for deacons throughout Western Europe, even in Gaul and Spain, where hitherto deacons had worn only albs. Gradually the right to wear dalmatics was extended to abbots and other priests outside Rome, but only on special occasions.

From the earliest representations of dalmatics in frescoes and mosaics at Rome and Ravenna, one realizes that the shape of this vestment has undergone considerable changes since the fourth century. Originally it was a long, wide tunic reaching to the feet, with very wide sleeves. It was made of linen or wool. Silk dalmatics do not seem to have become general until about the twelfth century. Until the tenth century, dalmatics were white, and it was only in countries outside Italy that coloured dalmatics were first introduced. Eventually they were made to conform to the colour of the chasuble worn by the priest at High Mass.

The earliest dalmatics were adorned with two vertical stripes of purple or red material, known as *clavi,* and with a band round the hem of the sleeves. As far back as the seventh century a fringe was sometimes added on the sleeves or along the side slits, which had already become common so as to make it easier to put on the vestment. At the close of times tassels were added to represent the tufts of wool and fringes which were originally on the ends of the *clavi.*

There are no definite rules concerning the precise shape or size of dalmatics. Whether the primitive, mediaeval, or seventeenth-century French style is

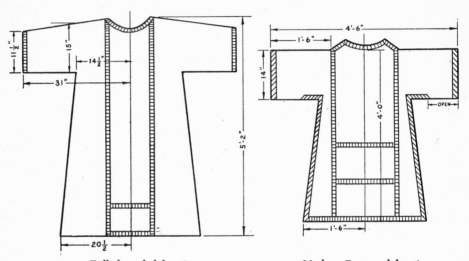

Full-shaped dalmatic.   Modern Roman dalmatic.

the Middle Ages the sides of the dalmatic were often open right up to the sleeves. In some countries, especially in France, the sleeves were slit open so that they hung over the shoulders like wings or epaulettes. But this fashion did not appear before the seventh century, and in Rome dalmatics have nearly always retained the closed sleeves. There has always been a great diversity in the ornamentation of this vestment since the early part of the Middle Ages. Sometimes the dalmatic was quite plain, with no decoration. More often than not there were two narrow strips of richer fabric (the former *clavi*), running from the shoulder to the hem and united at the bottom by two narrow cross strips. Some-

adopted is largely a matter of taste, though it may be more in accordance with the prevailing mentality to conform to the traditional modern Roman form.[25] On the other hand, a long vestment, reaching well below the knees, with ample sleeves coming below the elbow or even to the wrists is in keeping with ecclesiastical tradition,[26] and is probably the most satisfactory kind of dalmatic. In order that it should hang gracefully, it is better not to have a stiff lining. There is no reason to have any lining, for that matter.

The dimensions for a dalmatic of the Roman shape are:[27]

Length: 48 in. (at least)

Breadth under the arms: 24 in.

Breadth at the bottom: 38 in.

Width of sleeves: 14 in.

Length of sleeves: 18 in.

A dalmatic of the "primitive" shape should be at least 50 in. from neck to bottom hem, with a width of 50 in. at the bottom. The sleeves should extend to the wrists, or at least half-way between the elbow and wrists of a normal-sized man.

THE TUNICLE

The tunic, or tunicle, is a vestment worn by the subdeacon at High Mass and at other functions. Originally the subdeacon wore an alb, but at one time or other a simpler form of over-tunic was adopted which came to be hardly distinguishable from a dalmatic, except that the sleeves were generally longer and narrower, and there was less ornamentation. The early history of the subdeacon's tunicle is somewhat obscure, and there was a great diversity of usage before the ninth century. The tunicle is worn by bishops under the dalmatic when celebrating pontifical Mass. In this instance, both dalmatic and tunicle are made of very thin, unlined silk for greater convenience. The tunicles worn in the Roman basilicas are usually almost identical with the dalmatics; in fact, interchangeable. However, in some churches one finds tunicles with longer and narrower sleeves and no ornamental bands between the *clavi*. In pre-Reformation times it was very common for the clerk who carried the cross to wear a tunicle, and this vestment was also worn by servers and thurifers.

The following are the dimensions for a tunicle of the traditional Roman shape:[28]

Length: 42 in. (at least)

Breadth under arms: 24 in.

Breadth at bottom: 36 in.

Sleeves perhaps 2 in. shorter and narrower than those in dalmatic.

THE AMICE

The amice is a square or oblong piece of linen, and is the first vestment to be put on by the priest when vesting for Mass. Some liturgists are of the opinion that the amice used to be a large handkerchief, worn to protect the richer vestments from the perspiration which in hot countries may stream from the face and neck. Others say that it was a sort of muffler which could be drawn up over the head to form a kind of hood, as a protection either against the cold or against the sun. The truth seems to consist in the combination of both theories. The amice (from *amictus* — a loose wrap or scarf) could be used for either purpose — as a neckcloth or a head-covering.

Nowadays the amice merely lies over the neck and upper part of the shoulders. But there is a rubric in the Roman Missal that orders the priest to lay the amice *on* his head for a moment, before tucking it round his neck. This proves that this vestment was originally, at least in some cases, a head-covering. Many of the older religious orders, too, including most Benedictine congregations, still put the amice over the hood of their habit, and in some cases, it is made to fit the hood.[29]

The size of an amice should be about 36 by 24 in., not less, to allow for the double fold when worn. Tapes should be attached to the two uppermost cor-

Mediaeval vestments (from A. W. Pugin's *Glossary of Ecclesiastical Ornament and Costume*, London, 1846).

Modern "full-shaped" vestments (Prinknash Abbey, England).

Modern Roman dalmatic and chasuble.

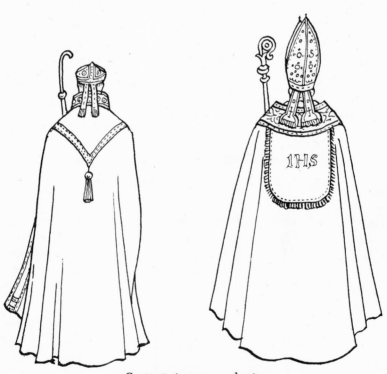

Contrasts in copes and mitres.

Alb.

Folded chasuble.

Mediaeval
chasuble.

Broad stole.

Surplice.

French chasuble.

Dalmatic.

Modern French
dalmatic.

Gothic-Revival
chasuble.

Modern Roman
chasuble.

Primitive
mitre.

19th century
French mitre.

Cotta.

Mediaeval
mitre.

Primitive
chasuble.

ners, in order to tie it round the body, and these tapes should be at least 4 ft. long, even 6 ft. is quite convenient. The amice may be of plain linen or embroidered.[30]

THE ALB

The alb is a white linen garment with close-fitting sleeves. It reaches to the feet. The name "alb" is a contraction of the Latin name *tunica alba* — a white tunic — and the garment is derived from the white tunic (at first made of wool, later of linen) that was part of the ordinary secular attire among the Greeks and Romans during the first centuries of Christianity. Until the middle of the eleventh century, the alb was worn by all grades of clerics when taking part in ecclesiastical functions. It was also worn by monks in choir on great festivals. During the Middle Ages albs were frequently made of silk or cloth of gold, and seem to have been of any colour, in spite of the name "alb" (white) and were regarded as a sort of under-tunic. As time went on the surplice or rochet took the place of the alb for choir functions, the latter being chiefly worn at Mass.

There are two shapes of albs in use at the present time. In the one (the sack shape), the width is the same at the top and bottom; in the other, the top part above the waist is narrower and made with gussets and the lower part is made wide. The former is perhaps the most convenient as it can be worn by any priest, no matter what may be his build. An alb is more practical if fastened at the neck with a button; tapes have a way of getting into a knot. Again, the alb

may have a round neck opening without either button or tapes, sufficiently large for the alb to be passed over the head. The rubrics of the Roman Missal[31] as well as those of the *Caeremoniale Episcoporum*[32] emphasize that the alb should be made long enough, presuming that it will be raised up round the waist when girded.

Albs may be ornamented in three ways, although the rubrics do not imply that this is necessary:[33] (1) by lace sewn onto the cuffs and lower part of the skirt; (2) by coloured embroidery round the cuffs and lower part; (3) apparels — like those described in connection with the amice. The same objection to putting apparels on amices applies to albs: i.e., they are no longer the "accepted usage of the Church in Rome."[34] Some authorities maintain that apparelled albs should not be introduced "without consulting the Apostolic See." But here again, this form of *decoration* of an alb *may* be a matter of individual preference. It is not specifically mentioned by the Sacred Congregation of Rites.

If lace is used it is better to have a foundation of silk or stuff which should be of the same colour as that of the cassock of the wearer.[35] A simple priest ought not to be mistaken for a prelate by patches of purple showing through his alb! Still, a coloured foundation is tolerated. Open-work lace albs are often dangerous garments, especially if too long for the wearer, for it is easy for him to put his foot through the lace. Moreover, lace on vestments is a sign of rank, for which reason it is used by prelates on their rochets.[36] So it is not really suitable for ordinary priests. At

Surplices.

girdle may be made of any material, but silk is reserved for prelates.[38] It is usually white, but it should be of the same colour as the vestments.[39] The length may vary from 12 to 14 ft. Tassels of any size can be worn, according to individual preference!

THE SURPLICE

The surplice is a form of the alb and is a large-sleeved linen garment reaching to well below the knee. It was worn in England and France as early as the eleventh century. The name is derived from the two Latin words *super* (above) and *pellicea* (fur-clothing), since it was worn over the fur-lined tunics which were a practical necessity in the days when churches were not heated in winter. Its loose shape and large sleeves are probably accounted for by its use, for a narrow-sleeved, fitted garment would not have gone over a heavy fur-lined coat. The surplice does not appear to have been worn in Rome until the thirteenth century, and the cotta is now worn in most Roman churches.

Rome ordinary priests usually have a very narrow border of lace on their albs. Embroidery can be made to look very effective if the right sort of design is used. It can be of any colour, not necessarily in red or blue thread. Apparels can be tacked onto the sleeves and on the front and back of the lower part of the skirt, immediately along the hem. They should be about 8 by 10 or 12 in. in size, or longer, if preferred, and should be of the same material and colour as on the apparel of the amice.

THE GIRDLE OR CINCTURE

The alb, like the old Roman tunic, is girded with a cincture which is now usually made in the form of a cord with tassels or fringes at each end. Formerly it was often a flat band of embroidered silk, and secured with a clasp or buckle. A sash is no longer tolerated by the Sacred Congregation of Rites.[37] The

The early surplices came down to the feet, and up to the time of the Reformation always reached well below the knee and hung in very loose folds. By the end of the eighteenth century this once flowing garment had shrunk to such an extent that it hardly reached to the hips. In some places the sleeves disappeared altogether; elsewhere they were slit up the sides. Or again there were sleeveless surplices, open right up the side, rather like scapulars. Lastly there was a curious form without any sleeves, rather like a very full chasuble, which was worn in Italy during the sixteenth and seven-

teenth centuries. The sudden development of the lace industry all over Europe
in the sixteenth century led to the sleeves
and hem of the surplices being adorned
with this new and fashionable material.
In later years it was not uncommon to
find more lace than linen in a surplice.

A well-cut surplice should reach to
about 6 in. above the feet. Even in its
most abbreviated form it looks better if
it extends several inches below the knees.

It should be made very full, having
a circumference of about 4½ yd. at the
bottom. The sleeves should be almost the
same length as the hem of the skirt.
Smocking round the opening adds to the
effect, but is not essential. There should
not be any slit in front, but the opening
should be made large enough to come
about half-way down the shoulders of
the wearer.

Roman cottas.

THE COTTA

The Roman cotta is a later development of the mediaeval surplice — much
shorter and less ample. The sleeves only
reach to the elbow. Both sleeves and
hem are often decorated with lace.
Roman cottas are usually slightly
starched and then compressed into narrow folds, i.e., goffered. Lawn is sometimes used instead of linen and it is
common to have an opening in front
with tapes or ribbons. The reason why
the cotta should be worn in preference
to a surplice is that it happens to be
"the recognised usage of the Church in
Rome." It certainly costs less than a full
surplice, unless it is adorned with expensive lace, and there are those who
prefer its abbreviated shape to that of
the full surplice.[40] On the other hand,
it is the surplice which is invariably
ordered by the rubrics which do not
mention the cotta. So it would seem that
the former may be the more "correct"
vestment! A Roman cotta is T shaped,
about 24 in. in length, exclusive of lace
about 1 in. wide. The sleeves are 17 in.
long, exclusive of lace, and about 32 in.
in circumference. The shoulder pieces
are about 4¼ in. square, edged with
narrow lace; the circumference of the
body, about 8 ft. 8 in.

THE ROCHET

The rochet (from the German *rock* —
a tunic or coat), like the surplice, is an
adaptation of the alb, but while shorter
than the latter it has tight-fitting sleeves.
In the Middle Ages these were made
very tight, and so long that they had
to be wrinkled up the arm. The rochet

is worn by the pope, cardinals, bishops, other prelates and canons, and also now by abbots. Formerly religious bishops and abbots did not wear the rochet. It is usually adorned with lace on the cuffs and the lower edge, the depth of the lace depending on the dignity of the wearer. As in the case of the surplice, a rochet of plain linen is a more dignified garment, especially if it is made long enough to fall below the knees. The same rules as to a coloured foundation for lace on the alb apply to the rochet.

THE BIRETTA

The biretta is a square cap with three or four ridges or peaks on its upper surface, generally surmounted with a silk tuft. During earlier ages clerics used to wear a hood as well as a cap. This hood was a separate article of dress in itself, and consisted of the part covering the head, to which was attached a short cape covering the shoulders. The headpiece of the hood was peaked at the back to make it easier to pull it off the head. This peak was lengthened during the fourteenth century and became the long tail-like appendage called the "liripipe." In the sixteenth century, the liripipe was separated from the hood and was worn round the neck, like a scarf which, in fact, it became.[41]

When the hood ceased to be a head-covering and became a mark of distinction, the cap took its place as part of the choir habit of the secular clergy. In the twelfth and up to the fifteenth century this cap was round, rather like an old-fashioned "smoking cap." In the sixteenth century it became square and was made with two or three folds on the top, to make it easier to take off. It also had a small button or tuft for the same reason. Finally, the square cap developed into the modern biretta. It is interesting to note that the "mortar-board" cap, worn by university students, is really nothing more than the mediaeval form of biretta, flattened out, with a skull-cap (often worn as well as the square cap or biretta) sewn onto it.

Cardinals wear red birettas; bishops violet. Domestic prelates have a violet tuft on their black birettas. Certain canons regular, Cistercian abbots, and the Benedictine abbot of Prinknash, wear white birettas. The colour for ordinary priests is black.

A four-pointed, crown-like biretta is used by the Spanish and German clergy and by some teaching brothers.

NOTE. It might be a good thing if modern churches were provided with iron pegs to hang up the birettas, as prescribed by St. Charles, for every altar (*Instructions*, Chap. XV, par. 3). He says that these pegs should be on the Epistle side, near the "cruet niche," about 2 ft. 9 in. from the pavement, and recommends that they should be ornamented in some way "especially in brass," at the point where they are fixed in the wall. Such pegs would prevent the risk of the servers stepping on them when they are left on the floor of the sanctuary!

THE HUMERAL VEIL

The humeral veil is a long scarf, measuring about 8 to 9 ft. long by 20 to 36 in. wide. It is worn by the priest at Benediction and by the subdeacon at High Mass. The ends are used to hold either the paten or monstrance. The humeral veil also covers the sacred vessels, etc., which are laid out on the credence table during the first part of High Mass. It should be made of silk, though originally it was linen.[42] Neither ornamentation nor clasp is necessary, though both are usually added. A clasp helps the subdeacon to keep the veil on his shoulders.

It would seem that the humeral veil did not make its appearance in the Roman Ritual before the latter part of the Middle Ages, although it was used in other parts of Europe as early as the eighth century. It was mentioned, under the name of *sindon,* in the oldest Roman Ordo, when it was worn not by the subdeacon, but by acolytes who had charge of the sacred vessels. The *vimpa* — another form of humeral veil, now worn by clerks of the mitre and crozier at pontifical ceremonies, is the survival of the veil worn by acolytes from about the eighth century. Vimpas are usually made of silk and should always be white, although it is fairly common to make them correspond to the colours of the vestments. It is believed that the extremities of the surplice were formerly used to hold the crozier and mitre, and that the present vimpa only came into existence when the surplice was reduced in size.

CHALICE VEIL AND BURSE

The chalice veil and burse did not become general until the sixteenth century. Until that time the chalice was often brought to the altar in a bag. A chalice veil should be large enough to cover an average-sized chalice, i.e., from 22 to 30 in. square. It may be adorned with a cross, but this is not recommended. It necessitates always folding the veil in the same direction, hence it wears out quicker.

The burse, known in mediaeval England as a "corporal case," is a case or purse in which the folded corporal is carried to and from the altar. It is not definitely known when it first came into use, but it was not until the seventeenth century that it became obligatory.

A burse of average size should be about 9 to 12 in. square. It is usually made of two pieces of cardboard, fixed together on three sides. The outer sides are covered with silk of the same material and colour of the vestments; the inner part with linen. It can be made with or without gussets, and may have a cross on one of the outer sides. Roman burses never have gussets.

PONTIFICAL VESTMENTS AND INSIGNIA

In addition to the ordinary vestments worn by a priest, a bishop when celebrating pontifical High Mass wears buskins, sandals, pectoral cross, tunicle, dalmatic, mitre, gloves, and ring. Should the bishop be the Ordinary of the diocese he also carries a crozier. When sitting down his knees are covered with a gremial veil. When entering or leaving the church the Ordinary wears a *mozzetta,* a *cappa magna,* rochet, cassock, and biretta. Any other bishop wears a mantelletta and has not the privilege of a *cappa magna.*

1. *Buskins* are really ceremonial stockings reaching to the knees and put on over the ordinary, violet, silk stockings. They are made of silk, often richly em-

broidered. At one time they were worn by ordinary priests, but since the eighth century have been exclusive to bishops and more recently to certain minor prelates. The buskins usually conform to the colour of the vestments worn at Mass, but they are not worn when black vestments are used.

2. *Sandals,* such as are now worn by bishops, are really low shoes, with leather soles and upper parts of silk or velvet, usually embroidered. Like buskins the colour of the sandals conforms to that of the vestments. A bishop does not wear sandals either at requiem Masses or on Good Friday. Both sandals and buskins seem to be very ancient vestments, and appear in mosaics of the fifth and sixth centuries. Originally the footgear were real sandals, i.e., covering only the tip of the foot and the heel, being fastened with straps. Sandals became part of the special pontifical vestments about the tenth century, and in the twelfth century their use was also granted to abbots. The present shape dates from the sixteenth century.

3. So far as is known the *pectoral cross* did not become an official ornament for bishops until the seventeenth century. Crosses were worn by every Christian man and woman in very early days, but out of private devotion and hidden under the upper garments. The original private character of the pectoral cross is still shown by the fact that the pope, when wearing his red mozzetta over the rochet, never uses the pectoral cross. The latter is only worn by him over the white cassock of everyday life. Again, bishops, when pontificating at Mass, wear the cross under their upper vestments. Be-

sides cardinals, bishops, abbots, and abbesses, certain other prelates now wear this cross. There are definite rules as to the metal of which the cross is made, and as to the cord or chain from which it is hung round the neck. But in practice these rules are not observed very carefully. A bishop's pectoral cross usually contains relics of martyrs.

4. Special *rings* seem to have been worn by bishops as part of their insignia from about the seventh century. These rings have been worn on the fourth finger of the right hand since the ninth century. The ring is worn outside the gloves when a bishop is pontificating, for which reason a special ring of larger size than normally worn is sometimes used. Many other prelates besides bishops are now permitted to wear a ring, e.g., cardinals who are not bishops, abbots, and protonotaries, as well as canons in some dioceses. Protonotaries can only wear rings out of Rome. Mediaeval bishops often wore other rings in addition to their episcopal one, and it is interesting to note that the *Caeremoniale Episcoporum* makes provision for this practice.

5. *Gloves* are worn by a bishop when celebrating pontifical High Mass, up to the Offertory. They are made of silk, and are generally embroidered on the back and on the wrists. The colour of the gloves must correspond with the liturgical colour of the vestments. They are not worn for requiem Masses or on Good Friday. Episcopal gloves were first worn at Rome during the tenth century, but were used earlier in France. The probable reason for their introduction is likely to have been ceremonial rather than

Pontifical vestments.

practical. Until the latter part of the Middle Ages episcopal gloves were white in colour and generally knitted. The privilege of wearing gloves began to be granted to abbots and other prelates during the eleventh century.

6. The *mitre* is a kind of folding cap. It is made up of two parts of equal shape, each stiffened by a lining and rising to a peak. The two parts are sewn together at the sides, but joined above by thin material that can fold together. There are two lappets (*infulae*) hanging down from the back, usually with fringed ends. Much has been written concerning the history and antiquity of the mitre. It is enough to say that this episcopal head-dress is derived from a soft, round cap with a circular band tied round the base with pendent ends at the back, worn by bishops from about the close of the eleventh century. This cap was itself derived from a non-liturgical head-

covering worn by the popes as early as the eighth century which, later, developed into the tiara or triple crown. So great has been the transformation of the mitre during the past eight hundred years that it is almost impossible to realize that there can be any connection between the original round cap and the tower-like mitres of the eighteenth century. First came a dent in the middle of the soft cap, just like the dent made in the crown of a modern felt hat; then the dents and puffs on each side became permanent features without which no self-respecting bishop would have dreamed of wearing his mitre any more than a modern male would dream of wearing a Trilby hat without a dent in the crown, unless he wished to be eccentric. Sometime during the twelfth century a bishop must have had a brain wave and turned his mitre round, so that the puffs came at the front and back, instead of at the sides. From now onwards the evolution was rapid, although not consistent in every part of Western Europe. The puffs became horns, ending in points, stiffened with parchment, making an ideal surface to be covered with embroidery and jewels. Higher and higher grew the mitres until by the seventeenth century they arrived at the shape of a "bishop" in a set of chess-men or a British guardsman's "bearskin" — with diagonal sides and curved horns.

The earliest mitres were always white, but during the Middle Ages mitres were made in all colours, the more ornate being decorated with precious stones and metal as well as embroidery. The *Caeremoniale* distinguishes three grades of mitres: (1) the *precious* — made of cloth of gold or white silk, and adorned with jewels; (2) the *gold* — made of plain cloth of gold — originally white silk with gold bands (orphreys); (3) the *simple* — made of white silk or linen and with lappets fringed with red. The use of these three mitres is determined by the rubrics. Cardinals, bishops, abbots, and certain other dignitaries — e.g., protonotaries apostolic — have the right to wear mitres, but only out of Rome in the latter instance.

There is no definite legislation about the size and shape of mitres. Some bishops prefer the tall mitre on account of its imposing appearance; others like a soft squat one because it is more comfortable and easier to keep on. Some say this episcopal head-dress cannot be too low; others say it can hardly be tall enough! So there we must leave the matter.

NOTES

1. At one time it was supposed that there was a definite connection between the vestments worn by Jewish priests under the Old Covenant and Christian priestly vestments. But there is no evidence to prove this theory, which was only put forth in the Middle Ages by ecclesiastical writers. For a short time and only in certain places, an ornament directly copied from the Jewish high priest's breast-plate was worn by bishops, on the chasuble.

2. During the past war, French chaplains often said Mass in the trenches, wearing their uniform and only a stole over their shoulders.

3. *Rit. Cel. Miss.*, I, n. 2.

4. C.J.C. 1297, § 3.

5. S.R.C. 4398. See O'Connell, *The Celebration of Mass*, Bk. I, pp. 259, 265, 266.

6. O'Connell, *op. cit.*, p. 268, n. 34.

7. The first Roman colour sequence was drawn up by Pope Innocent III (1198–1216). It was printed in Burckard's *Ordo Missae* in 1502, and was made obligatory in the General Rubrics of the Missal of 1570.

8. S.R.C. 2704, ad 4; 2769, ad 5; 2986, ad 5; 3191, ad 4.

9. Cf. Stercky, *Manuel de Liturgie*, I, p. 78, note.

10. S.R.C. 3145; 3191, ad 4; 3646, ad 2 and 3.

11. S.R.C. 4084, ad 3.

12. S.R.C. 2675; 2682, ad 50; 2799, ad 5.

13. Which in turn goes back to στόλη.

14. *Rit. Cel. Miss.*, I, 3.

15. *Rub. Cel. Miss.*, c. VIII, 8.

16. Cf. O'Connell, *The Celebration of Mass*, Bk. I, p. 265. Nothing could be more foreign to the mind of the Church than a rigid pinning down of the whole Catholic world to a national or "period" style which, even though Roman, is local, and especially in these days when the Holy See is so strongly urging, not only a native clergy, but also a native art in missionary countries. As Father Martindale, S.J., has pointed out, a stiff garment without folds is entirely foreign to the mind of an African native. So it is more than likely that sooner or later the present legislation may be modified in favour of full vestments. The attitude of the authorities of the Sacred Congregation of Rites towards the whole matter may be understood from the following incident related by the rector of one of the national colleges in Rome. He was presented with a full chasuble, but before he ventured to wear it, went to the S.R.C. to obtain

permission. "Had you asked permission *before* the chasuble had been made, perhaps we should have refused it," was the reply, "but as you have actually been given such a vestment we cannot very well forbid you to wear it or to have it altered!"

17. James, Raymond, *Origin and Development of Roman Liturgical Vestments*, p. 19.

18. VIII, 6, 8.

19. L. II, c. VIII, n. 19.

20. *Directions for Altar Societies*, 4 ed., p. 58.

21. Cf. James, *op. cit.*, p. 20.

22. S.R.C. 3006, ad 7.

23. *Rub. Cel. Miss.*, XIX, 6.

24. *Caer. Ep.*

25. S.R.C. 4398.

26. C.J.C. 1296, § 2.

27. *Directions for Altar Societies*, 4 ed., p. 60.

28. *Ibid.*

29. When this hood-form of the amice is worn, it takes the place of a biretta.

30. Apparels, i.e., pieces of coloured brocade or other rich material tacked lightly to the linen, so that they can be taken off when the amice is sent to the wash — are an effective decoration. But it is doubtful if apparels can be made to square with the Decree 4398 which forbids the revival of an old type of vestment, without consulting the Apostolic See (see p. 185). They are not "the recognised usage of the Church in Rome," although still worn at Milan, Lyons, and in Spain. On the other hand, since apparels are a decoration and not a vestment, does this decree affect them?

Apparels were very popular in the Middle Ages and seem to have originated in France, but gave way to lace in the sixteenth century. The dimensions of an amice apparel should be about 29 in. by 3 in. It should lie close up to the edge of the amice, equidistant from the tapes. There should be an interlining of canvas and a lining of linen, also a cord or braid round the outside edges. There is no reason why the apparel should conform to the liturgical colour of the vestment worn, for it is merely a decoration. Any colour that looks well with the particular vestment will serve, and bits of brocade or gold tissue with a bold pattern are as good as anything. When the apparelled amice has been arranged round the neck, it must be kept on the head until the chasuble or other upper vestment has been put on. The apparel forms a collar, hiding the white linen entirely, except in front. As the amice has to be kissed before it is put on, a small cross is sometimes embroidered in the middle of the top between the tapes. *Rit. Serv. Miss.*, I, 3; *Caer. Ep.*, L. I, c. IX, n. 1.

31. *Rub. Cel. Miss.*, i, 3.

32. *Caer. Ep.*, c. VIII, n. 13.

33. S.R.C. 3191, ad 5; 3780, ad 5; 3804, ad 12.

34. S.R.C. 4398.

35. S.R.C. 3780, ad 5; 4048, ad 7; 4186, ad 3.

36. S.R.C. 4154.

37. S.R.C. 4048, ad 6.

38. S.R.C. 2067, ad 7; 3118.

39. S.R.C. 2194, ad 3.

40. S.R.C. 4398.

41. It is still thus worn by the Anglican clergy.

42. *Caer. Ep.*, L. I, c. X, n. 5; L. II, c. XXIII, n. 3; c. XXXIII, n. 14.

CHAPTER XIX

OTHER CEREMONIAL ACCESSORIES

The following ceremonial accessories are required by churches where the normal functions of the liturgy are carried out in full: thurible and incense boat; holy-water vat and sprinkler; acolytes' candlesticks and torches; processional cross; canopy for the Blessed Sacrament and simple canopy (*ombrellino*); paschal candle and candlestick; triple candle and candlestick; funeral candlesticks; funeral pall or hearse-cloth; bier or hearse; Tenebrae candlestick; urn for altar of repose; Gospel lectern; banners; faldstool. In a small church only the first four are really *essential*, unless the ceremonies of Holy Week are carried out.

THURIBLE AND INCENSE BOAT

Historical Notes

Although the first Christians used incense for embalming the dead and for other purposes, it seems that it was not employed as a ceremonial accessory of worship until the third or fourth century. Incense was first burned at Christian funerals, and is thus mentioned by St. John Chrysostom,[1] and St. Hilary of Arles.[2] But the first reference to incense being used in connection with the Eucharist is in Origen[3] (d. *c.* 254), although some critics maintain that the reference is purely metaphorical. "At first incense was used only in processions. Incense carried before some great person as a sign of honour was a familiar idea in the first centuries. It was carried be-

fore consuls; so Christians, with the development of the idea of ritual splendour, carried it before their bishop. From that to incensing persons is but a step. As it was swung before a bishop in procession, so it would naturally be waved before him at his throne. Then, accepted as a sign of respect like bowing and kneeling, it would be applied symbolically to things, especially to the altar throne as type of Christ."[4]

By the seventh century we come across references to incense being burned in churches on saints' days, of special censers being made and offered to churches.

The earliest type of censers were shaped like urns or vases, and often stood on the ground. Then a handle was added, next a perforated cover, and finally chains were introduced about the eleventh century for obvious reasons of convenience. Since then there has been little change in the shape of censers.

Shape, Size, and Material

Neither the rubrics of the Missal and *Caeremoniale Episcoporum* nor the decrees of the Sacred Congregation of Rites have anything to say about the form and material of the censer and incense boat.

A censer consists of a cup and bowl, supported on a base. Into the cup is fitted a hollow, movable pan for holding the lighted charcoal, onto which the grains of incense are sprinkled. Fitting onto the cup is a perforated lid. Rings are fixed to both the cup and the lid, and through them are inserted three chains, about three feet long, which are attached to a convex disk, in the top of which is a large ring which serves as a handle for the thurifer by which to hold it. A fourth chain, with a ring at the upper end, is attached to the top of the cover, and made fast to the disk through a hole, so that the cover can be lifted to put in the incense.

In the French type of thurible, generally used in Great Britain, the four chains are encircled by a movable ring to keep them together. In the Roman type there is no ring, and the chains are loose. Censers can be of any size, but small ones are much more convenient to handle, especially for small servers![5]

Incense is usually kept in a small, boat-shaped metal vessel, fitted with a lid. If the spoon is like an ordinary dessert spoon there is less likelihood that the incense will be spilt than when a flat spoon is used.

A pair of small tongs, kept in the sacristy, will prevent the thurifer from soiling his hands when lighting the charcoal, which is best heated in a small wire basket with a handle, held over a candle, electric stove, or gas jet.

There has always been a great variety in the material of which censers are made. Gold, silver, copper, brass, and even iron have been used.

Incense

Incense is an aromatic gum or sap, obtained from certain resinous trees.

In Rome nothing else but gum *olibanum* — pure incense — is used in churches. It has the advantage of being cheaper than any mixed form, and is less stuffy and sickly than fancy mixtures. Other ingredients used are gum benzoin, myrrh, cascarilla bark, red sandalwood, Chinese cinnamon, and rosin. Benzoin should be avoided as its fumes sometimes affect certain people.

For the ceremony of the consecration of bells, the rubrics of the *Pontificale* order "tiniana" and myrrh to be burnt. A special thurible, without chains and with a hinged cover, should be used at this function.

HOLY-WATER VAT AND SPRINKLER

It is ordered in the Roman Missal (*Ordo ad faciendam aquam benedictam*) that, on Sunday, salt and water shall be blessed in the sacristy, and that the celebrant of the principal Mass shall sprinkle the congregation with the blessed water before Mass, according to the rite in the Missal. A holy-water vessel and sprinkler are needed for this function as for many other ceremonies, e.g., the blessing of the ashes on Ash Wednesday, of candles on the Feast of the Purification, and for use at funerals and solemn Requiems.

This ceremony goes back to at least the tenth century, and should never be omitted without proper authority, except before pontifical Mass.[6] When the Blessed Sacrament is exposed the altar is not sprinkled.

The vessel for the holy water should be a small metal pail with a handle — silver, bronze, brass, or copper. The inside surface should be of material that will not corrode easily. The Roman form of vat (*secchiello*) is generally low and broad; the French type is deeper.

In earlier ages branches of hyssop, palm, and boxwood, wisps of straw, and even the tail of a fox were used as *aspersoria*. About the thirteenth century a rod surmounted with bristles was introduced, some of the handles being richly ornamented. The usual modern form of sprinkler consists of a short handle with a round metal knob, pierced with holes, containing a sponge. It can be unscrewed. Sometimes a brush on a metal handle is used.

THE PROCESSIONAL CROSS

Each church should possess at least one processional crucifix. The inclusive length of the staff and cross should be about 6 ft. 8 in. It is more convenient to have the staff made of wood, metal being heavier and more costly. There is no reason why the whole should not be made of wood and painted, for a cheap brass crucifix can look very shoddy.

The cross should be made to take off the staff, for it is carried without it at the burial of an infant (*Rit. Rom.*). If the top of the cross is made of metal it should be kept covered when not in use, to keep off dust and to prevent tarnishing.

It is a pity that the combination of altar and processional cross which was very common in the Middle Ages is nowadays rubrically incorrect, for the crucifix now placed on the altar is derived from the cross carried at the head of the procession during the singing of the Introit at Mass. This cross, on the arrival of the sacred ministers in the sanctuary, was placed behind or at one side of the altar. Even to-day in the basilicas of Rome the cross carried before the Chapter going processionally from the sacristy to the choir is always placed near the altar (usually by the credence) during the celebration of Mass.

THE CANOPY FOR THE BLESSED SACRAMENT

For processions of the Blessed Sacrament a canopy of silk or other rich material, and supported by at least four poles at each corner (there may be six or eight if the canopy is very large) is essential. In Rome it is known as a *baldaquin*. The colour should be gold or white, so far as the groundwork is concerned, but it can be adorned with any kind of embroidery or decoration. In some places in Italy it is customary to use a purple canopy for the procession on Good Friday, and a red one for processions with a relic of the true cross or other relics of the Passion. But the use of a purple canopy is quite incorrect.

Simple Canopy (*Ombrellino*)

When the Blessed Sacrament is carried from one part of the church to another a special kind of umbrella (*ombrellino*) made of white silk and ornamented with a deep gold fringe is used. The handle is much longer than that of an ordinary umbrella, and the top is flat, not conical, for the ribs are not flexible.

ACOLYTES' CANDLESTICKS AND TORCHES

Acolytes' candlesticks may be of any size or material so long as they are convenient to hold. In Rome it is the custom for the acolytes at High Mass to carry candlesticks similar in design to those on the altar, and when not in use they stand on the credence table. This is historically correct, for, as explained (page 106), the altar candlesticks are really acolytes' candlesticks placed on the altar. Now they are the *double* of the latter.

The best material for processional torches is gilded or painted wood. They should be about 3 ft. 9 in. high. Bases, if used, should be made separate and well weighted. This enables the shafts of the torches to be dropped into the bases and lifted out. Strictly speaking, a torch should not resemble a candlestick. In Rome a torch usually consists of four candles stuck together, with four wicks making a large flame. They are carried in before the Consecration at High Mass, eight being used on great festivals.

For outdoor processions and funerals, swinging glass lanterns, fixed to staves by means of U-shaped brackets, are useful.

THE PASCHAL CANDLE AND CANDLESTICK

The paschal candle, blessed at the solemn service on Easter eve and lighted at High Mass and vespers until Ascension Day, is a most ancient accessory of worship. There is a reference to a form of blessing of a candle, suggestive of the *Exsultet* in the Roman liturgy, in one of the letters of St. Jerome,[7] and it is mentioned again and again by the early Fathers of the Church. The Venerable Bede tells us that in 701 it was the custom in Rome to inscribe the date and other particulars of the calendar, either on a parchment affixed to the

candle or painted on the surface of the wax. This is still done in the Cistercian rite.

In many churches in Italy the paschal candlestick is a permanent structure of marble, erected in the sanctuary. During the Middle Ages the candlestick increased in size, and was known as the "paschal post." At Salisbury Cathedral (1517) it was 36 ft. in height, and at Westminster Abbey in 1558, during the reign of Queen Mary, more than three hundredweight of wax was used for the candle.

Few churches are able to afford an elaborate paschal candlestick, and there is something undignified in the typical lacquered brass of commerce. The best plan is to have one made of wood, painted, and gilded. It should not be less than 6 ft. in height.

The material of the candle must be bees-wax, according to the percentage determined by the bishop of each diocese.[8] It is important to make sure that grains of incense have been inserted into the small disks sometimes used. (The disks are quite unnecessary as small "blobs" of incense will readily adhere when heated.) It is not obligatory to use a new paschal candle every year.[9] Five new grains of incense must be inserted each Easter eve. At Rome five "pinecones" are stuck or screwed into the paschal candle: the centre one painted gold, the other four silver. Grains of incense are stuck onto these.

TRIPLE CANDLE AND CANDLESTICK

A triple candlestick is needed during the ceremonies on Holy Saturday, although the wording of the rubrics of the *Caeremoniale Episcoporum* and the Missal imply that all that is needed is a rod with three candles temporarily fastened together at the top: *"Praeparetur arundo cum tribus candelis in summitate positis."*[10] It is less trouble to use a special candlestick and the triple candles obtained from church furnishers.

The triple candle seems to have been first used about the twelfth century. Before that date two candles were common. The use of two or three candles seems to have been a purely practical precaution against the light of the newly blessed fire going out — as might easily happen in a draughty church. Both in the Ambrosian and Mozarabic rites only one candle is used, as in the pre-Reformation Sarum rite.

FUNERAL CANDLESTICKS

Special candlesticks are required for funerals and solemn requiem Masses. They are best made of wood or iron, about 4 ft. high, and painted — not necessarily black, although this is traditional, but any colour that will go with the decorations on the pall, e.g., red or dark blue, also with the unbleached wax candles used on such occasions. Four is the minimum needed, but it is better to have eight, i.e., three to stand at each side, and one at each end of the bier.

TENEBRAE CANDLESTICK OR HEARSE[11]

Should the office of Tenebrae be sung during Holy Week, a triangle, fitted with fifteen spikes or sockets for candles — seven on each side and one on the top — will be needed. The triangle itself can be made of wood or iron and rest on a post or rod, about 4 ft. from the ground, or higher if preferred.

FUNERAL PALL OR HEARSE-CLOTH

It is desirable that every parish church should possess a funeral pall or hearse-cloth. When the coffin rests upon the bier or hearse during a requiem Mass, or when it is being carried to and from the church or through the streets, it is only decent that it should be covered. The typical coffin supplied by an undertaker is not a beautiful object. The comparatively modern custom of covering a coffin with flowers, except in the case of baptised children,[12] is probably due to the instinctive feeling that it ought to be hidden. It is quite incorrect for adults, although it is the usual custom in most English-speaking countries.

The mediaeval palls were often gorgeous affairs, decorated with badges of the deceased person or benefactors, and not always black. A black pall can have ornamentation of any other colour — white, red, blue, or purple being appropriate. Although such crude allegories of death, as skulls, cross-bones, tears, or "gouttes," are forbidden on vestments, they are permitted on palls.[13] A national flag may be used for members of the navy, army, and air force.

Where a church does not possess a catafalque or bier, the absolutions at a Requiem where the corpse is not present may be given over a pall spread on the floor of the sanctuary.[14]

URN FOR THE ALTAR OF REPOSE

It is the custom in Rome to reserve the Blessed Sacrament on the altar of repose in a box or a small urn-shaped vessel. In appearance it resembles a sarcophagus. It is not covered with a veil. The tabernacle of a side altar may be used. In this case it should be veiled in the usual manner.[15]

LECTERN

A folding lectern is useful in churches where High Mass is sung regularly. It can be made of wood or metal, with the desk itself of leather so that it can be folded up easily and not be too heavy to carry about. When open, the bottom should be about 5 ft. from the ground.

At Rome the lectern — *leggio* — is either of elaborately carved wood gilded, or else of plain wood entirely covered in silk of the colour of the day. St. Peter's possesses about a dozen carved lecterns.

BANNERS

It is certain that banners in connection with Christian worship have been carried in processions from the time of Constantine, and there are constant references to their use right through the Middle Ages — a reminder of which can be seen in the banners of the Knights of the Garter and of the Bath which hang above the choir-stalls in St. George's Chapel, Windsor, and in Henry VII's Chapel in Westminster Abbey.

The usual type of banner carried in processions nowadays is a poor sort of thing, not so much because it is cheap — rather contrary — but because those who were responsible for the design have not realized that a strong, bold colour scheme is essential in a banner, which has to be seen at a distance, not closely. Some of the most effective banners are often made up of odd bits of silk or velvet that produce the effect of a patchwork quilt or old-fashioned tea cosy. The use of expensive materials is to be discour-

aged on banners intended for outdoor use. A shower of rain can ruin them forever! Processional banners are viewed from the back as well as from the front, so both sides should be ornamented to some degree. It is not expensive materials that matter so much in a banner as design. That is a reason for having recourse to experts when possible.

FALDSTOOL

It is useful for a church where Confirmation is held quite frequently to possess a wood or metal faldstool, i.e., a folding chair without a back, used in pontifical functions by a bishop. In shape it is like the letter X. The seat is generally made of cloth or leather. Cushions will be needed of the various liturgical colours. In Rome faldstools are covered with silk of the colour of the day.

KNEELING DESK

A wooden kneeling desk (*prie-dieu*) is also required for pontifical functions and for other occasions, e.g., a nuptial Mass, when two are necessary for the bride and bridegroom. When a bishop pontificates the desk is covered with silk or woolen material and provided with two cushions — red for a cardinal, green for a bishop, except in penitential seasons when violet vestments are worn, or at requiem functions.

THE STATIONS OF THE CROSS

Historical Notes

The origin of the devotion known as the Stations, or Way of the Cross, may be traced to the Holy Land. Pilgrims who returned from Palestine wished to reproduce the holy places in their own countries in the form of small chapels. As early as the fifth century a group of such chapels was built at the Monastery of S. Stefano, Bologna. They represented — miniature — the more famous shrines in Jerusalem. It was not until the fifteenth century that anything like the modern devotion made its appearance. The earliest use of the word "stations" as applied to halting places in the Via Dolorosa at Jerusalem is found in the writings of an English pilgrim, William Wey, who visited the Holy Land in 1458 and 1462. During the fifteenth and sixteenth centuries many reproductions of the holy places were erected in France, Italy, Spain, and Germany. Most of them were situated outside churches. A few were on a very ambitious scale, like the famous Via Crucis on the Sacro Monte at Milan, erected in 1481 by the Franciscans, where forty-three chapels and over nine hundred statues were scattered over the mountainside!

At first there was no uniformity in number, and it is not definitely known how it came to be fixed. Some of the earlier books of devotion used by pilgrims at Jerusalem give nineteen, twenty-five, or fifty-seven stations. In the latter part of the sixteenth century the fourteen stations first appeared in the Netherlands, but, even then, the number was not adopted everywhere.

Canonical Requirements

To facilitate the erection of Stations of the Cross, hitherto a somewhat complicated process, the Sacred Penitentiary decreed in March, 1938, that all that is now necessary is for a priest to obtain the faculty of erection which some ecclesiastics possess by common law and others by delegation, e.g., all cardinals, bishops, including titular bishops, the major and local superiors of the Friars Minor. Other priests must obtain the faculty from the Holy See. The rector of a secular church may therefore seek the faculty from the Holy See, through the Ordinary, or permit the act of erection to be carried out by a Franciscan friar delegated by his superiors. Nothing more is required for valid erection, though the permission of the Ordinary should be obtained, with a written document recording the permission for and fact of the erection for the parochial archives.

Apart from this the only essential feature to gain the indulgences, are fourteen crosses, which must be of wood. The crosses may be attached to pictures or images, or separate. As they are kissed during the erection they should be removable should the picture or sculpture of the station be above the head of the priest officiating.

There is no need to have either pictures or sculpture, and in a small church it is better to be content with the crosses alone, and the subject of each station painted beneath it in good lettering.

Size, Style, and Material

The size, style, and position of a set of stations is an important matter, and it is wise to leave the choice or design to the architect, or at any rate not to disfigure his building with a set of stations out of keeping with it. Stations may be hung on the walls or on the columns of the nave, but it is better to keep them out of the line of direct vision of the sanctuary and high altar.

At the present time when a set of Stations of the Cross is regarded as an almost essential feature in the furniture of a church, chapel, or oratory, it is well to recall the fact that this particular devotion is no more than a *supplementary accessory of piety,* and is not obligatory. There are no Stations of the Cross in the patriarchal basilicas of Rome.

If lack of means makes it impossible for a church to buy a good set of stations, it is much better to be content with the fourteen wooden crosses, rather than put up, even temporarily, a set of cheap oleographs. The crosses themselves can be of any shape or size or colour. Bright red crosses look well on a white or cream wall surface. The lettering of the inscriptions, if done by a capable sign writer, can be made quite decorative as well as legible.

As to the material for stations, no general principles can be given. There is an immense choice — paintings, wood or stone carvings in low or high relief, mosaic "opus sectile," enamel, terra cotta, bronze, or silver. In a small chapel or oratory framed wood engravings look well. It should not be forgotten that the purpose of these representations of incidents in the Passion is to arouse greater devotion in those who are "making the Stations." It is therefore important that in style and treatment they should be intelligible to simple folk who know nothing about art. It should be remembered that Canon 1279 forbids exhibiting an "unusual image" — *imaginem insolitam* — in churches, and that Stations are not carried out to prove the technical capabilities of an artist, but for a very definite function.

MEMORIAL TABLETS

The erection of tablets with inscriptions and the names of the faithful departed whose bodies are not buried in the church, has been forbidden by several decrees of the S.R.C. and Canon Law.[16] This legislation is principally directed against an abuse of the rights claimed by founders and patrons of churches. However, like every other ecclesiastical law it may be dispensed providing that a proper authorization is obtained. It should be noted that the latest decree[17] does not enjoin the removal of tablets already in existence, lest offence should be given to relatives. The law is a salutary check on a practice which, if unrestricted, would convert a parish church into a mausoleum.[18] Brass or white marble tablets are seldom satisfactory and generally an eyesore. Painted wood tablets have the advantage of costing less, and if the lettering is done by a capable sign writer, are an effective decoration. They can be adorned with gold and colours.

MURAL HANGINGS

In some churches textile hangings add to the appearance of the sanctuary. In fact, they are much better than the marble decoration that is now so popular; the colours of the marble usually being far too pale. What is more, marble, except in rare cases, is unsuited to a northern climate. It suggests coolness, and what is needed is warmth. Wooden panelling round the lower part of the sanctuary walls is strongly recommended in preference to marble. Hangings achieve the same result, i.e., to concentrate the main attention on the altar. For this reason it is better to make them of some fairly simple material without a strong pattern, unless the altar, reredos, etc., are of elaborate design, when a rich tapestry can be used. Casement cloth or linen are better than serge, for the latter collects dust. Hangings should be made very full with deep folds. About half as much again of the total length of the wall should be allowed. Hangings may be suspended from hooks or passed through iron rods by means of wide hems. The rods should not be more than 6 ft. long for convenience.

PICTURES[19], *

What has already been said about statues in church applies equally to pictures. Unless they are appropriate to the surroundings, a church is better without pictures. They serve two purposes — decoration and devotion. Where original paintings are beyond the means of a particular congregation there is no reason why colour reproductions should not be used. They are infinitely better than most commercial plaster statues.

---

* The very vocabulary of the instructions in note 19, if not the ideas expressed indicate that St. Charles, as is to be expected, subscribes to the art theories of his own time which are those of Raphael, da Vinci, and, perhaps to a much lesser degree, of Michaelangelo. For our days we have to allow certain changes and we have to make due allowance for the ways of expression of modern men. What we must preserve from these directions are the warnings against extremes, subjectivism, secularism, and profane tendencies. What is beautiful has been answered differently by the mosaicists of Ravenna, the Carolingian and Ottonian painters, by Duccio, Giotto, and Leonardo, by Poussin and by Rouault. To harness our church art in such definitely "period" canons of beauty as that of the Renaissance has produced sad results. — H. A. R.

In Italy it is common for the picture of the Madonna to be fitted with branch candlesticks attached to either side of the frame, each branch holding one or two candles, which are lit during special devotions to our Lady.

HYMN BOARDS

In most churches it is the custom to have hymn boards hanging or affixed to the walls or columns. Usually they are an eyesore, both as regards design and figures. Since they have to be displayed in a prominent place, great care should be given to the design. The cards should be black with white lettering. The frames can be decorated with gold and colours.

ALMS BAGS AND PLATES

If alms bags are used, they should be made of some hard-wearing material, e.g., leather, not silk, and are best fitted with metal or wooden handles. Bags are more convenient and safer than plates, or baskets lined with green baize, and are more easily passed along the pews or benches. Perhaps the ideal form is a wooden or metal box fitted with a lock and handle, the top being provided with a narrow slit into which the coins can be dropped. The opening should be made diagonally, in such a way that the coins will fall into the box at once.

FLAGS FOR OUTDOOR USE*

In Great Britain and its dominions, it is not permissible for a church to fly the

---

* We in America have been very liberal in our use of the national flag inside and outside of our churches. By this time practically every church has the star spangled banner in the sanctuary next to the papal flag. You will never see a national flag inside a church in Italy, Austria, Poland, Germany, or any other

Union Jack; the only flags that are appropriate being the banners of the patron saints of the country: e.g., St. George, St. Andrew, St. David, or St. Patrick. Most Catholic churches hoist the papal flag when they possess a flag staff. There is no reason why a special flag with the ecclesiastical emblem of the saint to whom the church is dedicated should not be flown if there is room for it.

European country with the possible exception of France and perhaps Belgium. The reason is understandable, as on that narrow continent national flags are symbols of strife and antagonism and often the symbol of a state in opposition to the Church, as, e.g., in Cavour's Italy or Bismarck's Germany, not to speak of the ill-famed swastika of Hitler. In countries like Austria and Switzerland the old tradition of serene supranationalism stood in the way of a development as the one we have seen. The American flag, before becoming a possible standard of nationalism and aggressiveness is above all a symbol of freedom, brotherhood, and equal rights and ought therefore to be regarded differently. — *H. A. R.*

NOTES

1. Migne, *P. L.*, LXI, 560.
2. Migne, *P. L.*, L, 1269.
3. Migne, *P. G.*, XIII, 965 a.
4. Fortescue, *The Mass*, p. 228.
5. In convent chapels, where a priest may have to give benediction with only one server or with none, a thurible stand, fitted with a crook on top, is almost essential. It should be about 4 ft. high, but need *not* be made of lacquered brass.
6. Fortescue-O'Connell, *Ceremonies of the Roman Rite*, 7 ed., p. 95.
7. Migne, *P. L.*, XXX, 188.
8. S.R.C. 4147.
9. S.R.C. 3895, ad 1.
10. *Caer. Ep.*, L. II, c. XXVII, n. 1.
11. So called because it resembles a harrow, i.e., a triangle with spikes.
12. *Rit. Rom.*, Tit. VI, c. VII, par. 1.
13. *Caer. Ep.*, L. I, c. XI, n. 1; S.R.C. 4174, ad 1.
14. S.R.C. 2525, ad 5.
15. See Fortescue-O'Connell, *op. cit.*, p. 307.
16. 1450 § 2, ad 1.
17. S.R.C. 4376
18. Cf. *The Clergy Review*, Vol. III, p. 143.
19. It may be of interest to give some of the directions on holy images and pictures published by St. Charles Borromeo (*Instructions*, Chap. XVII), although they are hardly likely to appeal to the more "modern" school of artists and sculptors! In general, these instructions conform to those found in the Code of Canon Law. "As to the sculptured figures and paintings of saints, it is decreed by the Council of Trent that the bishop must watch vigilantly that these decrees are observed; moreover, heavy punishment is meted out to those painters and sculptors who depart from the prescribed rules (Concil. Trent, sess. 25). . . . Whatever is profane, immodest, or obscene or provocative of temptation shall be absolutely avoided; again, what is merely curious and does not lend itself to devotion, or by which the minds and eyes of the faithful may be offended, shall be shunned completely. In such works the true likeness of the saint whose image is to be represented should, as far as possible, be reproduced and care must be taken that the image of no other man, whether living or dead, shall be purposely represented. Moreover, the effigies of beasts of burden, dogs, fishes, or others of the brute creation ought not to be made in a church or other sacred place, unless in the presentation of scenes from sacred history, or the custom of holy Mother Church require otherwise. The whole expression of holy images should aptly and decorously correspond to the dignity and sanctity of their prototype, from the demeanour, the position, and the adornment of the body."

A practical point is that the names of the saints should be inscribed under the images less known. St. Charles strictly forbids "borders, such as for the sake of ornamentation painters and sculptors are wont to add to images . . . for example, they should not contain human heads portrayed with deformity, such as are commonly called *mascheroni* (large masks); nor little birds, nor the sea, nor verdent meadows, nor such like things which are represented for the sake of pleasure or of wanton prospect and adornment; unless such things agree truly with the sacred subject which is represented, or in the case of votive tablets whereon are painted both heads and such other things as are mentioned above, in explanation of vows."

CHAPTER XX

THE ORGAN AND CHOIR

HISTORICAL NOTES

An organ of some kind seems to have been used as a means of accompaniment to vocal music in churches from a very remote period. There are references to organs as far back as the sixth century, but they appear to have been of a primitive kind, without stops and a number of bellows worked by relays of men. The mediaeval organs which came into use about the twelfth century varied considerably in size; some were portable and could be moved about, others were "positive," i.e., stationary. Sometimes a large church had several organs. Stops did not come into general use until the fifteenth century, although they were a much earlier invention. The mediaeval organ — often referred to as "a pair of organs," as we speak of a pair of bellows, generally seems to have stood in the rood-loft, which was a very favourite place for the choir. In fact it was the musicians' gallery. When the rood-lofts were pulled down in so many English parish churches at the Reformation, the singers, too, had to find accommodation on the floor, unless a gallery was erected for them at the west end of the church, which unfortunately in other parts of Europe, was and still remained, the normal position for the choir.

Other instruments besides the organ were used in church services during the Middle Ages, even more so after the sixteenth century when small or large orchestras became very common, especially in France, Italy, and Germany. Again and again regulations have been made to control the use of instruments in church, beginning with Benedict XIII, and re-enforced by later pontiffs. In 1903, Pius X, in his *Motu Proprio* on church music, stated that "although the music proper to the Church is purely vocal music, music with the accompaniment of the organ is also permitted. In some special cases, within due limits and with proper regards, other instruments may be allowed, but never without the special license of the Ordinary, according to the prescription of the *Caeremoniale Episcoporum.*"

This same idea is expressed in Canon 1264 which says: "All kinds of lascivious music, whether accompanied by the organ or other instruments, or rendered vocally, must be entirely eliminated from churches; and the liturgical laws concerning sacred music must be obeyed."

The points to be made clear are: (1) *that an organ is not an essential piece of furniture in a church or an obligatory accessory of worship,* despite the fact that this particular instrument has been generally used to accompany vocal music from the twelfth century;

219

(2) that "other instruments" are not prohibited as an accompaniment to singing.

The use of the organ is limited to certain definite occasions.[1]

POSITION OF ORGAN

No rules are laid down as to the position of the organ in a church. Its position should be determined by the position of the choir or main body of singers, should there be no choir in the liturgical sense.

Mr. F. C. Eden writes that "there is no liturgical or theological reason why [the organ] should be in one part of the church rather than in another, as there is in the case of the altar, rood-screen, and font. . . . Convenience alone dictates its position, and the most convenient place to one who takes a broad view of all the conditions, ceremonial, aesthetic, and so forth, may not necessarily be the best place in the purely musical sense. A balance must be struck. Musical considerations will be allowed great weight, but after all a church is not a concert-room, where acoustics and accommodation alone govern planning and arrangements."[2]

This same writer goes on to say that in small churches the only possible places for the organ are the west gallery, the rood-loft, and behind the altar. He sums up his conclusions as follows:

"1) In churches of the first magnitude there should be two organs, a small one to accompany the singers, in a raised position about twenty feet away, and a large one at the west* end, or in what-

ever part of the church musical and structural considerations may suggest as the most suitable.

"2) In medium-size churches the organ and singers should be in a gallery, raised some twelve feet above the floor, and preferable at the west end.

"3) In smaller churches it is advisable to substitute for the organ or harmonium a small orchestra, the performers being seated in a gallery and subjected to proper discipline and control."

But, as has been stated already, musical instruments other than the organ may not be used in Catholic churches without the special consent of the Ordinary.[3] It is definitely forbidden to use pianos or what are termed "noisy instruments" (*instrumentorum majorem vel minorem strepitum edentium*), which include drums, castanets, cymbals, etc. Violins, violas, violincellos, and double basses are allowed: *"Propter sinum gravem ac continuum, quem in similitudinem organi edere possunt,"* but carillons, harps, xylophones, triangles, and so on, are prohibited because of "frivolous associations" (*propter levitatem*).[4] At the same time it is permitted to employ flutes, clarinets, oboes, and bassoons, with the consent of the Ordinary.[5] But trombones are banned.[6] Lastly, gramophones may not be used in any public service, not

---

* The east-west orientation of churches, one of the oldest Church traditions, is not always observed in our large cities where sites have to

be taken as they are available. Let us remember that in Rome the orientation (derived from the word *orient*) is in practically all cases, with the exception of St. Paul-outside-the-Walls, really an "occidentation," i.e., the altar is in the west apse and the gate at the east end. However, the priest looks toward the east, since he faces the congregation in all these old basilicas. The *"Oremus"* of the liturgical prayers at Mass and vespers were a signal for the faithful to turn around, eastward. — H. A. R.

even if strictly liturgical music, e.g., plain-chant records, is put on.[7]

ORGAN CASES

A badly designed organ case can be a great eyesore. F. C. Eden reminds us that the following points should be observed in their design:

1. That the case should impede the egress of sound as little as possible;

2. That there must be plenty of speaking room about the mouths of the pipes, especially the loud ones;

3. That access must be provided for tuning and repairs.

He reminds us that in old organs the exposed metal pipes were never treated decoratively,* but left plain, except when gilded. Only the wooden pipes were painted and decorated.

He lays down the following hints for the design of organ pipes:

1. The pipe ends should be concealed by carved shades and that no pipes should stick up above the cornice;

2. The woodwork and not the pipe should be painted;

3. No ironwork should be used about the case;

4. The feet of the pipes should be tall;

5. Important pipes may be embossed;

6. Shutters and projecting reeds are both sensible and ornamental;

7. In simpler cases the uprights dividing the different compartments of pipes should be narrow on the face.

---

* Great artistic effect has been achieved in modern European churches, especially in Switzerland, Germany, and Italy by reducing all woodwork to a necessary minimum. The decorative effect can be achieved solely by a careful visual arrangement of the "speaking" pipes, eliminating sham mute pipes altogether. — H. A. R.

If many modern organ cases are compared with some of those erected during the eighteenth century it will soon be realized how much more beautiful are the latter than the former.

The dark woodwork and gilt pipes produce a dignified effect.

The console should be placed in such a position that the organist can observe clearly the sacred functions.

THE CHOIR

The average modern church choir is a very differently constituted body to what it was in the earlier ages of Christianity, when the choir was always composed of clerics. During the Middle Ages many large churches had their own choir schools, where orphan boys and others received a general as well as a musical education. It was not until the Renaissance period that church choirs became laicized. But in many places the laymen and boys continued to occupy seats in the chancel or sanctuary. They not only took possession of the seats of the minor clergy, but also adopted their special dress — the surplice or cotta.

Women were forbidden to take any part in church music, except in the case of nuns in their own chapels, or in public churches where they were at liberty to join with the rest of the congregation in the Common of the Mass, where both the words and the music were so familiar and often repeated that they could be sung from memory. The idea that a choir is a picked body of male or female singers, whose job it is to render appropriate (or inappropriate) pieces of some kind of sacred music during the celebration of Mass and Benediction, is utterly foreign to Catholic tradition. The main purpose of a choir is to chant those portions of the liturgy that vary with the seasons and which cannot be sung by the congregation.

The *Motu Proprio* of Pius X makes it quite clear that wherever possible the liturgical chant should be rendered by men and boys, who are really taking the place of the ecclesiastical choir and a substitute for the once universal *chorus cantorum* composed of clerics. Thus, the presence of women in a strictly liturgical choir is impossible, for its place must be in the chancel or sanctuary behind the altar. But in parish churches where there is a body of singers composed of women and girls as well as men and boys, it is prescribed that they occupy distinct places, so far as possible.[8]

Unless the local Ordinary should consider it inevitable in certain places, what is known as a "mixed choir" is no longer tolerated.[9]

As one of the chief aims of the *Motu*

Proprio of Pius X was to encourage the laity to take their part in liturgical music, which belongs to them by right, perhaps the best way to achieve this ideal in small parishes, is to do away with a special place for the choir altogether and scatter a trained group of singers in the congregation, so that they can lead the main body of worshippers. When building a new church or remodelling an old one, both priest and architect should consider this plan, even if it may seem revolutionary at first.

There should be congregational music practices — the singing of the hymns and the chanting of the Common of the Mass being led by four or even two cantors — women, if no men are available. Only in this way will the laity learn to "pray the Mass," and they must be helped to do so even by the planning of a church which will necessitate the abolition of the favourite choir gallery, and probably the resignation of the local *prima donna!*

NOTES

1. Cf. *Caer. Ep.*, L. I, c. 28, nn. 1, 3, 4, 5; c. 28, n. 2.
2. F. C. Eden, "The Organ," p. 2. (Incorporated Church Building Society pamphlet).
3. *Motu Proprio* of Pius X, 1903, n. 15 b.
4. S.R.C. 4156, ad 1.
5. *Ibid.*

6. S.R.C. 4226, ad 1.
7. S.R.C. 4247. For further detail governing the use of musical instruments in Catholic churches, see Fiorenzo Romita, *Jus Musicae Liturgicae* (1936), pp. 238–242.
8. S.R.C. 4216, 4231.
9. S.R.C. 4231.

CHAPTER XXI

BELLS AND BELFRIES

Canon Law declares that "it is proper for churches to be provided with bells, to call the faithful to divine service and other religious functions."[1]

HISTORICAL NOTES

Bells, or more correctly a "signal" (*signum*), for calling the faithful to take part in worship, are first mentioned in the sixth century. They served not only to call the laity to church, but, in the cases of monasteries, to rouse the community from their beds to take part in the night office of Matins. Very little is known about bells until the seventh and eighth centuries. The word *campana* — bells, first appears in the *Liber Pontificalis* of Pope Stephen II, 752–757. There are references to church bells being used by the Celtic monks at Iona and elsewhere, also to belfries being erected in Italy. Small hand bells were very popular in Ireland and several of these early Christian bells have been preserved. They were regarded with great veneration. Oaths were taken on them, and they were carried into battle. In later times foreign missionaries, such as St. Francis Xavier, made use of small bells when preaching to the heathen.

During the Middle Ages every church, large and small, was almost invariably provided with one or more bells. In fact, the idea grew up that no religious service could take place without the ringing of a bell. One of the earliest examples of church bells dates from the eleventh century. Some of the later mediaeval bells were very large. There was one at Canterbury that needed twenty-four men to ring it. Sixty-three men were required for the whole peal of five bells. Mediaeval Canon Law in England laid down that a cathedral have five or more bells, a parish church two or three. Churches of the mendicant orders and public oratories were restricted to one bell. In earlier times complaints were often made by religious orders that bishops refused to allow them to ring bells in their churches. This grievance was settled by Pope Gregory IX (1227–1241).

After the Reformation and until the past century it was forbidden to ring bells in any places of worship in Great Britain except those belonging to the Established Churches, so, even to-day, bells are often regarded as a luxury and not an almost necessary adjunct of worship.

Bell towers in Southern Europe, especially in Italy, are often built separate from the body of a church, whereas in Northern Europe they form part of the building.

CONSECRATION OF BELLS

Canon Law orders that "the bells of churches must be consecrated or

Belfries.

blessed according to the traditional rites found in liturgical books."[2] The consecrating prelate must normally be the bishop of the diocese.[3] The rite is one of the most elaborate in the Roman Pontifical, and has much in common with Baptism. There are exorcisms, together with intricate ceremonial involving the use of the holy oils, water, salt, and incense. Each bell is given a name, and at one time a godparent was customary. It should be noted that bells have to be consecrated *before* they are fixed into the belfry.

BLESSING OF BELLS

In churches which have not been consecrated the bells may be blessed with a short form found in the Roman Ritual. The Ordinary or an exempt religious superior can delegate a priest to bless bells.

USE OF BELLS

Church bells can be used for other purposes than for announcing that a service is to take place. In many places, especially in Italy, a bell is rung every evening to remind the faithful to pray for the departed. Even to-day there are towns and villages in England and Scotland where the pre-Reformation "curfew bell" is rung every night between eight and ten o'clock. The ringing of the Angelus, three times a day, may have developed from the curfew bell. From about the thirteenth century it has been the custom in many Catholic countries to ring one or more bells at the Elevation of the Host at High Mass on Sundays and feast days.

It is forbidden by Canon Law to use church bells for purely secular purposes, but with the permission of the bishop they may be rung on special occasions of public rejoicing.

PRACTICAL SUGGESTIONS

Installations of bells may be classified as follows: carillons, chimes, ringing bells, and single bells.[4]

A carillon is a group of bells comprising at least two chromatic octaves (twenty-five bells), and may extend to a range of five octaves (sixty-one bells), or even more. The bells hang stationary and are played either by the "carillonneur" (bell player) or automatically.

Ringing peals form a scale of five, six, eight, ten, or twelve bells, rung in full swing by means of wheels and ropes, one ringer being required to each bell: thus a peal of ten bells requires ten bell-ringers to ring them in "change ringing." This method of ringing a peal of bells is common in Britain, Germany, and Eastern Europe, where nearly every village has or had its team of bell-ringers whose art has been handed down from generation to generation.

Chimes may be divided into two groups, i.e.: (a) bells used for clock chimes, (b) chimes used for tune playing, changes, etc. Clock chimes comprise five or more bells, according to the tune played, the largest bell being used for the hour strike. Chimes for tune playing are similar in some respects to a carillon,

the chief difference being that a chime consists of a limited number of bells, for the playing of single-note melodies, whereas upon a carillon music in two or more parts may be played. The minimum number of bells needed is eight, i.e., a diatonic octave. But in order to extend the range of tunes it is usual to add some extra bells and to extend the scale beyond the octave.

Combination of eleven, thirteen, fifteen, or eighteen bells are often used for this type of chimes, and in some places the number of bells has been increased so that it forms a carillon.

A chime is played by one person from a "hand clavier," the keys of the clavier being connected to the bell clappers by a system of wires, rollers, and levers. A hand clavier is best placed in the chamber immediately underneath the bell-chamber; too great a length of wire connections between the clavier and the bells means lost motion which tends to reduce the power of blow of the clapper and to prevent the player from bringing out the best tone of the bells. In the case of large chimes with heavy bells, the clavier is often provided with pedals — like those of an organ, the heavier bells being operated either by the hand lever or by the foot pedals. Some large chimes have keyboards fitted to the clavier, and even automatic music-roll players can be installed with electro-pneumatic mechanism.

Single bells are installed in gable turrets, or in towers, when lack of funds or other circumstances do not permit the installation of a number of bells. A separate tolling hammer operated from the ground floor by a bell-rope is useful for tolling for funerals or for weekday services when a bell-ringer is not available.

If a church tower is designed to accommodate a swinging peal of bells, as distinct from a peal hung stationary, the walls should, of course, be of strong and massive construction and the bellchamber must be of larger area in the case of a swinging peal. A bellchamber whose internal dimensions are, say, 13 ft. square would accommodate a swinging peal of bells of average weight, i.e., tenor bell about 14 cwts., all the bells of the peal to be in one tier. If the peal is to be hung stationary, i.e., a "chime," this same size of peal could be put into a bellchamber of about 8 or 9 ft. square. The tower should be of such a height that the base of the window openings come not below the ridge of the church, and the sound openings, or louvers, should be in the upper part of the bellchamber, well above the level at which the bells themselves are placed. The idea of this is that instead of the sound being directed down to the ground around the church, it escapes in an upward direction and the bells are modified in the vicinity of the church, yet heard at a greater distance away.

Another point is that louvers should be avoided for use in bellchamber windows as they deflect the sound of the bells downwards instead of upwards. It is better for the bellchamber windows to be left unfilled and a waterproof floor to be provided to the bellchamber for rain to drain off. The weather will not hurt the bells.

Bells are expensive things, so, perhaps, they must be regarded as a luxury of worship and not an essential!

NOTES

1. C.J.C. 1169, § 1.
2. *Ibid.*, § 2.
3. Only the Holy See can delegate powers for another bishop to consecrate bells.
4. This data has been kindly supplied by John Taylor & Co., of Loughborough, whose famous bell foundry has an almost unbroken history since the fourteenth century, and whose bells are known all over the world.

CHAPTER XXII

LIGHTING, HEATING, AND VENTILATION

LIGHTING

Windows

The natural lighting of a church is a very important matter, if only to avoid needless waste of money on artificial illumination. But the chief thing to aim at is the concentration of light on the high altar which must be the focal point of the building. The functional purpose of a window is to admit light and sometimes air. The openings of the walls of churches have to be filled with glass, and as they are necessarily large openings, a single sheet of plate glass the size of the opening might seem to be the most logical way to keep out wind and rain. But as church windows are usually fairly high up and not generally made to look out of, there is no reason to use plate glass as in the case of a shop front. Small panes are more convenient, either set in wood or lead or steel, and, if funds permit, the glass can be decorated, i.e., stained or painted, provided that the function of the window is kept in mind — to admit light, not obscure it.

St. Charles Borromeo devoted considerable space to the natural lighting of churches in his *Instructions on Ecclesiastical Building*. What he says applies just as well to modern churches as those of the sixteenth century. He recommends that there should be windows on both sides of the nave, as high up as possible, and also in the side walls of the aisles. "In order that the church and its Sanctuary may receive the best light a circular window proportioned to the size of the church, and, as it were, regarded as an eye, should be constructed in the western façade above the great doorway . . . in other parts of the building and in the façade the windows should be of oblong form in accordance with the judgement of the architect. Moreover, light may also be admitted for the illumination of the Sanctuary and the rest of the church through the cupola at the intersection of the nave and transepts by means of a lantern. . . . In the Sanctuary and other chapels windows should be placed upon both sides that light may be admitted both ways." St. Charles drew up his instructions for a country where light is much stronger than in Great Britain, and so it is not surprising that he discouraged placing a window low down immediately above any altar. He states that windows "should be constructed as high up as possible." He was doubtless familiar with some of the very crude pictorial stained glass of the Renaissance period and so it might be expected that he would favour plain glazing, "so that a better light may be admitted for the benefit of the nave, sanctuary, and chapels."[1]

Stained Glass[2]

Historical Notes. Stained glass, which appeared so complete and fully developed, as it were suddenly, in the eleventh or twelfth century, was the North-European's response to the stimulus of Mediterranean mosaic. In countries where for about half the year the light is not over brilliant, it is obvious that that light transmitted through glass is a method of conveying colour on a far higher scale than by light reflected from coloured walls and paintings. Coloured glass, stained but unpainted, had been used by the Egyptians three thousand years ago. It was used in the Church of the Hagia Sophia at Constantinople and in other Byzantine churches of the same period. It was also used by the Romans and was employed by the Persians. But the coloured glass was merely embedded in cement or alabaster, rather like a lantern.

When stained-glass windows appeared in the Middle Ages, the same technique was employed as for mosaic work, but the glass was used translucently instead of by reflection. Translucent glass was put into the same position as mosaics in Mediterranean countries, chiefly as a rainbow setting for the high altar. If one compares the twelfth- and thirteenth-century Norman glass in the apse of Canterbury Cathedral it will be realized that it has just the same effect as mosaics in the apse of Byzantine or Basilican churches and uses the same subjects. So, it may be stated quite definitely that the purpose of stained and painted glass in North-European churches, and in other countries where there is no violent

sunlight, was to produce intense colour decoration, which would be impossible with painting, mosaic, or embroidery owing to the absence of sufficient light to show them up. Colour was needed to emphasize whatever in architecture needed emphasis, and stained glass was employed just as mosaic had been done, that is to intensify traditional lines.

Now stained glass was needed above all to create a coloured lantern setting for the high altar. This point cannot be emphasized too strongly; it is the key to the subsequent development, not only of all northern glass, especially English, but even of the planning of the whole church building. Many late mediaeval church builders, especially in East Anglia, sought to place their high altar in a lantern, with coloured light playing round it, as in the midst of a rainbow, making north and south windows together take up more wall space than the single east window.

As Geoffrey Webb reminds us: "even without the stained glass which originally made the Altar's setting a rainbow rather than a lantern, the result is to flood the Altar with daylight of a clarity and softness that no artificial flood-lighting can match for beauty, and yet with the same absence of glare which the artificial method provides. And while all that original jewelled and silver glass still remained in place, the Altar's setting must have mirrored the glow of the fields and flowered hedgerows outside, which could be seen through the glass as if through the mist of sunrise."

Stained glass was regarded by mediaeval builders as the ideal background of colour for the suspended pyx above the high altar. It was used in close relationship with painted stone or wood-work on the walls, ceilings, and columns — a point often ignored in modern churches where the glass clashes with the rest of the colour decoration instead of being part of them.

Practical Consideration. As the purpose of a window, that is a hole in a wall, is to *admit* light, stained glass should not stultify this purpose. Stained glass is always the highest key of colour in any building. No reflected colour can ever compete with it, and it sets the tone for the interior of the whole building. It is disastrous to start, as do so many modern glass firms, on a foundation of a dull greenish white which immediately sets a standard of smug respectability and sentimental piety. The bright silvery white of English mediaeval glass at once sets a standard of adventure, gaiety, courage, and even humour. It has the quality of spring meadows and hedge flowers. Much of the nineteenth-century glass produced by commercial firms has the smell of the nineteenth-century conservatory, gas brackets, and sham antiques. Even worse is a certain type of modern stained glass, which is so blatant and noisy in colour that it kills everything else in the church. But glass must always be considered in relation to the quality of the normal sunlight; for instance, in a city church, surrounded by tall buildings and where fogs are prevalent in winter, it would be stupid to insert dark glass, whereas in another place the ideal would be to create a dim, dark, cool interior as a contrast to the blinding glare of the sunlight outside.

The East Window

In the earlier editions of the *Directions for the use of Altar Societies and Architects,* we are told that "in the diocese of Salford the Bishop does not approve of windows being placed at the back of High Altars in new churches. They are apt to distract the eye, to interfere with Exposition, etc."[3] A similar opinion was expressed more recently by the editor of *Art Notes,*[4] who informed her readers that she is "convinced that an East Window over the high altar can rarely be used with success. It puts the altar in the dark and prevents one assisting at Mass with comfort."

It is difficult to understand this objection to east windows in churches, considering that "the stained glass of the east window was the English parochial reredos" for several hundred years.[5] The late mediaeval builders,[*] especially in

---

[*] It should not be forgotten that the late medieval architects did not create what might be called ideally liturgical churches, i.e., churches *primarily* for the central mystery of the Holy Eucharist as action. In cathedrals like Notre Dame de Paris, Cologne, Milan, and, to a lesser degree, Canterbury, the main altar is hardly visible. The building became more of long, narrow, and tall "tunnel" with the altar in the dim, faraway distance. Proportionately the sanctuary was generally too low. The whole tendency of the late Gothic period discarded the basilical idea — still very much alive in early Gothic churches — and, instead of gently guiding the eye to the focal point, the altar, it drew it upward from every point of the floor with irresistible vehemence. It was, if we may overstate our problem a little, the church of the lone mystic, best expressed in the *Imitation of Christ.* This does not detract from the greatness of this architectural period, but warns us that not always the virtuoso and genius in the arts is also the right man to shape the vessel for our liturgy. — *H. A. R.*

Northern Europe, felt that there should be more light round the high altar than anywhere in the church. Their aesthetic sense would have revolted against setting back the altar in a windowless recess when the main body of the church was well lit. Granted that St. Charles Borromeo discouraged the erection of low windows above altars, yet he was all for good lighting in the sanctuary. More than sufficient proof that a "coloured-lantern" sanctuary can be treated in the most ultra-modern manner can be found in Cachmaille Day's highly original star-shaped church at Wythenshawe, near Manchester, England; in Notre-Dame de Raincy, near Paris; and in the famous "glass and steel" church in the Ruhr . . . the mediaeval ideal of the glass-lantern sanctuary treated in twentieth-century forms.

The corrective to glare is not to treat the east window by itself, but as one of a set surrounding the high altar which needs a strong light north and south. Should a church be orientated, the east window certainly needs to be filled with coloured glass. But there is no necessity to treat the side windows in the same way. They often look better and admit more light if they are filled with clear white glass, not tinted "cathedral" glass of a green or pink tone.

It should never be forgotten that stained glass is essentially a form of decoration. Owing to the limitations of technique a stained-glass window should not try to compete with an oil painting or frescoe. The tracery of a window is not a frame to enclose a picture visualized as a pictorial composition on canvas or other non-transparent material. It

may be a mistake to fill the entire window with a design. At times, small painted glass panels, set in clear glass, always look well, and once again, do not take away from the light in the building.

Stained-glass windows must be considered in relation to each other, not as separate entities. For instance, the windows in the sanctuary must not clash with those in other parts of the building. They should harmonize, to a certain extent, not only in colour and texture, but in scale, handling, and the distribution of parts — at least in a new church. Here the selection of painted glass should always be entrusted to an expert, not to the donors of the particular windows. Every window should be designed for its individual setting and definite surroundings. It need not be elaborate to be good. But only an experienced craftsman is capable of dealing with the subtle problems of how colours react in light, the effect of light from surfaces and other windows, and much else besides which may completely neutralize the effect of what was a good window until it was set in the particular opening in the window.

Artificial Lighting

Historical Notes. We are so accustomed to artifical lighting in places of worship, that few of us realize that it is only since the invention of gas that churches were provided with any adequate system of artificial illumination. In the Middle Ages, a few lanterns would have been hung about on the choir-stalls for the use of the clergy or monks who had to take part in the

Divine Office. The candles on or round the altar helped the priest to read the missal. As for the laity, most of them sat in darkness, except on the greater festivals when candles were lit on brackets on the walls or suspended from the roof on large candelabra. What a mediaeval church must have looked like at night can be realized when assisting at the office of Matins and Lauds in a Carthusian church, where the only source of illumination still consists of small, shaded oil lanterns hung above the choir-stalls, with the light thrown down onto the books. Oil lamps remained the only means of lighting at night if candles were not used, until the invention of gas. There are some of us who can still recall the almost universal smell of a church in the days of our youth — for there always seemed to be a leak in the gas burners somewhere or other in the building. Naked gas jets blazed away from elaborate Gothic standards of correct ecclesiastical design, except where incandescent mantels were used, spoiling and soiling everything within range of the flame. When electricity superseded gas, the ease with which it could be put anywhere and everywhere resulted in most churches being over-illuminated. This danger still exists.

Practical Consideration. Oil lamps, gas, and electric lighting may be used in churches for purposes of illumination, but never in connection with or as a substitute for the prescribed candles on or round the altar at Mass or other ceremonies. The instructions issued by the cardinal vicar for the churches of Rome in 1932 state that "by preference, the ordinary internal lighting of the church should be effected by means of electric light from hidden sources; and the same method may be used with due caution to light up pictures or images with a soft and sufficient light. On occasions of greater solemnity an 'extraordinary' illumination may be prepared with standards, brackets, or chandeliers lit with electric candles, provided that their direction and position be determined in a manner perfectly corresponding to the artistic requirements, the nobility of sacred edifices, and the dignity of sacred worship, with scrupulous care not to inflict damage on the walls, painting, or marble; and provided that the power of the light be as low as possible. . . . We condemn and prohibit all illumination with a series of exposed lamps, fixed to rods of wood or iron, tracing architectural lines and motives in the interior of a church or an Altar; as well as stars or other devices in place of electroliers."[6] It may be objected that these instructions tend to encourage the worst type of flood-lighting, but *concealed* flood-lighting, such as the cardinal vicar recommends, may be all right when it is carried out by experts, but it is so easy to abuse it, that as a general rule a church is better illuminated by direct lights. In any case flood-lighting should only be inserted with great reserve, and the power of such be kept low.

For a small church bronze or wrought-iron lanterns, hanging from brackets on the walls, or suspended from the ceiling, look well, provided the design is simple and unobtrusive. What should be remembered above all is that half the beauty of a church is lost if there are no shadows. The ceiling itself is much better left in darkness. It is often forgotten that in all natural lighting the sun cannot be on two sides at the same time. Remembering this fact, it is better that an electric light should not shine directly from the front and from two sides at the same time, but only from one side. Try this experiment in a sanctuary of a church that is flood-lit and notice the difference to switching on all the lights at once.

When there are electric lights primarily for the object of enabling the congregation to read, it is better that they should be hung fairly low down, not high up in the ceiling. The bulbs can be concealed in electroliers, specially designed to suit the building. In a small chapel or oratory electric lights look very effective if set on wooden staves in the middle of the pews or chairs; one stave to every two rows of seats. There can be a switch to each light so that they can be used as required.[7]

Brass chandeliers, such as are so common in churches in Holland, add greatly to the interior of a church if hung in the nave and aisles, fitted with a corona of low-powered pendent electric lights, not sham candles.* As to the sanctuary,

anything like a "theatrical" effect should be avoided at all costs. At Benediction, especially, there is no need to flood-light the altar, for by so doing, the effect of the candlelight on the altar is entirely lost.

On the other hand, it is very important that the priest should be able to read the Missal, therefore there should be two lights on each side of the altar, about 9 or 10 ft. above the *mensa*, arranged in such a way that they will give a direct light onto the book without casting shadows. If these lights are placed too low half the book will be in darkness and the light will be on the same level as the priest's eyes.

The function of artificial lighting in a church is to enable people to read prayer-books, not to create a picturesque effect. A church is not like a ballroom or a theatre — both of which are designed for artificial illumination. Nothing is gained by trying to turn night into day so far as a church is concerned.

Lastly, all electric light fittings should be arranged so that bulbs can be changed if possible without the need of steps or ladders.

HEATING

It is hard to realize that no attempt was ever made to warm churches during cold weather until less than a century ago, except when a fireplace was inserted into the squire's pew in some of the country churches, examples of which can still be seen, not only in Britain,

---

* By sham candles we mean a small "flame-shaped" light bulb on top of a "candle" made of tin, painted or lacquered, with artificial wax drippings and dust streaks to make them look more natural — a dozen of such candles with about two versions of drippings! With or without this added feature such silly and dishonest light fixtures should disappear by now. I know of a church with a beautiful French crystal luster which has been completely spoiled by these tin stalks, in candle shape. As if the masters who made the wonderful crystal lusters

made them for the wax and not rather for the light to be reflected in the delicate facets! Small, clear light bulbs set right down into the sockets would have made the chandelier perfect. — *H. A. R.*

but in other countries of Northern Europe. In Italy and Mediterranean countries, where heating is seldom provided and where the churches can be far colder than ever is the case in England, owing to the marble or stone pavements, it is the custom to take a small charcoal brazier to church, and if one is a woman, place it beneath one's dress! It is not uncommon to find charcoal braziers on the altar so that the priest can warm his hands during Mass.

From about the middle of the eighteenth century, churches in Northern Europe began to be warmed by stoves, fitted with chimneys that did not improve the looks of the building, no matter how effective they were in getting rid of the smoke. Very often the smoke and fumes blew back into the church, and the stove did nothing more than set in motion a mass of air that added to the cold draughts that filled the church. The ugliness of these stoves led to their being hidden away in pits with gratings in the floor above them, or with flues to distribute the warmed air throughout the building.

Then came hot-water pipes, either laid in trenches under the floor or placed along the walls. Both arrangements had the disadvantage of collecting dust, especially when the pipes were under gratings, with the result that the heating power was lessened and the lungs of the congregation filled with poisonous gases from the accumulated filth of years. In recent years many other heating systems have been devised.

It is not always realized, at least by the clergy, that no matter how perfect a heating installation may be installed in a church, it will always be difficult to keep the building warm if the roof is thin. Mediaeval churches are generally much warmer than modern ones — at least cheap churches — just because they have a covering of lead, whereas in many churches erected in the Gothic Revival style during the past century, only thin boards covered with slates separate the worshippers from the weather. When a building like a church has a thick roof it takes longer to get cold, for it retains the warmth inside. But when a church is artificially heated, the warm air rises up, where it meets the cold air and drives it down again, thus making draughts on the heads of the congregation. Open timber roofs, no matter how picturesque they may look, are not nearly so warm as ceilings, whether concave or flat. Roofs should always have double covering with an air space within. A well-built ceiling should be insisted on in a church even before heating is installed. It can be of any material — wood, plaster, or vaulted in brick, stone, or concrete. But let it be solid. "It is as reasonable to ask for the warming of the open street, as for that of a church with a roof which gives no protection."[8]

VENTILATION

Until churches began to be artificially heated there was no need to consider means of ventilation. It was much more necessary to keep out draughts and cold air, so it was not often that even windows were made to open. But in these days the problem of how to ventilate a church is just as important as how to heat it, and the two cannot be dissociated.

Even a small church should not depend entirely on its windows for ventilation. When windows are filled with painted glass the casements are removed, and in any case open windows often result in draughts.

The most simple plan is to insert air inlets into the window-sills and outlets in the roof, both of which should be made so that they can be opened or closed easily. In a large town church electric fans help to draw off the stale air.*

CHAPEL FOR ENCLOSED
COMMUNITIES OF NUNS

For architects who have to design chapels for communities of strictly enclosed nuns, it may be useful to give the directions supplied by St. Charles Borromeo.[9]

The church should consist of one nave only, without aisles. There should not be any sanctuary at the east end, but a wall should be erected across the church, so as to divide it into two parts: an inner one for the nuns, and an outer one in which Mass is celebrated. The altar should stand against this wall, and of the usual dimensions. "At the level of sight from the altar, a window should be made in the cross wall, so that the nuns may be able to see and hear the Holy Sacrifice of the Mass. The width of this window should be equal to the length of the altar and it should be made about 2 ft. 9 in. in height. Its sill should stand in the wall about 2 ft. above the surface

of the altar. It should be provided with an iron grating, which should be double and similar throughout, the two parts thereof standing about 8 in. from each other. But the bars of each railing should be so close together as to leave an interval of only 2 in. between each other; and they should be so well put together that it may be no easy matter to pull them asunder or disjoin them. Inside, it should have door panels secured by means of a latch and lock; and these panels should be made to open either by the sliding at the sides, or else by sliding upwards by means of a pulley and a counterpoised rope.

"The altar may be covered over with an arch, either by making the wall thicker at that point (so as to allow of a recess), or else by erecting two small columns or piers at a short distance from the wall itself, so as to support the vaulting or arch. [This allows the requisite 'canopy' above the altar on which the Blessed Sacrament is reserved.] The two columns should stand at a distance of 2 ft. 9 in. from both corners of the altar. . . . If no vaulting of the kind is made, the altar may be covered with a wooden canopy, or such a one as may be made of silk or of cloth suitably ornamented, and which is called a *capocielo*.

"In the transversal wall intervening between the outer and the inner church, on the side which is nearest to the nuns' sacristy, an opening should be made suitably provided with a turning box; and by means of which may be set forth the vestments used for Mass. This turning box should be constructed at the height of about 4 ft. 1½ in. above the

_____

* For our American conditions with its excessive extremes in temperatures the answer is, of course, air-conditioning. From here on the answers will be found in the classified advertisement department of the Catholic Directory or the clerical magazines. — H. A. R.

floor; and it should be made so that it may stand nearly altogether placed in the thickness of the wall, which may be made thicker, on that account, by means of additional plastering at that point. It should be secured on both sides with folding doors, and on each side these doors should be provided with locks.

"On the other side of the altar, in the same transversal wall, another opening should be constructed in a recess adorned with carving and gilding and pious emblems; and through which the nuns can receive Holy Communion. The sill of the recess should be on the same level as the opening, and placed at a height of 3 ft. 8 in. above the floor. Towards the outer church, this recess should be 2 ft. wide; 2 ft. 4 in. high; and from this size on its outer face, it should go on diminishing to about 1 ft. 4 in. square towards the inner side. The recess should be made within the entire thickness of the wall, which should be about 1 ft. 4 in., so that inside, towards the nuns' part, the remaining thickness of the wall be not more than 2 in. The sunk space, so produced within the recess, should be about 1 ft. 4 in. square, and in this space should be made a small opening 5½ in. in height, by 4¼ in. in width, through which Communion can be given to the nuns.

"Within this opening should be placed, inside, small panels of iron or brass, so as to be closed by means of a lock and key. On the outer side there should be panels of a larger size to close the holes of the recess, and they should also have lock, key, and latch. Immediately under this recess should be placed on the church floor a small platform, about

5½ in. high, on which the priest may stand when administering Communion to the nuns. On the inner side of the church in the nuns' choir, may be erected another small platform, about 2 ft. 9 in. square; so arranged that when the nuns kneel down their faces may easily reach the small opening through which they receive Holy Communion."

St. Charles also gives directions for the construction of two more openings: one for the passing through of relics belonging to the convent and which would be used for the adornment of the altar; and another for passing through the holy oils. But such extra openings are not essential in these times.

With regard to the details and sizes of the sanctuary and other parts of the secular church, i.e., where Mass is said, they would be the same as in any other building. Only a small sacristy is required, for vestments are not kept there, being passed through the "turn" before Mass. In some convents of enclosed nuns it is more convenient to have the turning box for vestments, etc., fitted into the wall of the sacristy, although it is strictly forbidden by St. Charles, on the ground that it may afford a communication with the nuns' convent, either by sight or hearing. He also forbids the construction of any apartment above the sacristy, to which the nuns may have access. One or more chapels may be erected in the outer part of the church should it be necessary to have several Masses celebrated at the same hour.

Further details are given about the altar window, which must be placed that there is no possibility of looking out through it from the nuns' side, above all, not into the public highway, should there be a door directly in front of the altar. St. Charles recommends that the door should be made at the side of the outer church.

As to the inner church or nuns' choir, it should consist of an oblong hall, without chapels. Its floor should be on the same level throughout, and not raised in any part by means of steps. The pavement should be on the level with the predella of the altar outside the intervening wall. Windows should not be built overlooking a public highway.

On the other hand, the windows of the part of the church open to seculars should not look towards the convent. If there is a belfry, it should not in any way communicate with the outer church. There should be no windows in the upper floors; only narrow gratings. But there can be openings of the usual kind in the bellchamber, provided that it is kept locked.

Full details of the planning of a convent for enclosed nuns are also given by St. Charles in Chapter XXXIII of his *Instructions.*

NOTES

1. *Instructions,* Chap. VIII.
2. I must acknowledge my indebtedness to Geoffrey Webb, who supplied me with most of the historical and technical data in these brief notes on stained glass.
3. *Directions for the use of Altar Societies and Architects,* p. 9.
4. *Art Notes,* winter, 1944.
5. Bond, Francis, *The Chancel of English Churches,* p. 53.

6. *Osservatore Romano,* March 19, 1932.
7. Powys, A. R., *"The Care of Churches"* (Truman), p. 77.
8. Micklethwaite, J. T., *Occasional Notes on Church Furniture and Arrangement,* p. 15 (article in *The Church Builder,* reprinted by the Incorporated Church Building Society, 1908).
9. *Op. cit.,* Chap. XXXII.

INDEX